BUILDINGS FOR THE ARTS

BUILDINGS FOR THE ARTS

BY THE EDITORS OF ARCHITECTURAL RECORD

AN ARCHITECTURAL RECORD BOOK

McGraw-Hill Book Company
New York   St. Louis   San Francisco   Düsseldorf
Johannesburg   Kuala Lumpur   London   Mexico
Montreal   New Delhi   Panama   Paris
São Paulo   Singapore   Sydney   Tokyo   Toronto

Library of Congress Cataloging in Publication Data
Main entry under title:

Buildings for the arts.

    "An Architectural record book."
    Includes index.
      1. Art centers. 2. Art museums. 3. Libraries.
I. Architectural record.
NA6812.B84   720   77-8006
ISBN 0-07-002325-5

The editors for this book were Jeremy Robinson and Martin
Filler.

The production supervisors were Patricia Mintz and
Teresa Leaden.

The designer was Elaine Golt Gongora.

It was set by University Graphics, Inc.

Printed by Halliday Lithograph.

1234567890   HDHD   7654321098

ARCHITECTURAL RECORD BOOKS

Apartments, Townhouses and Condominiums, 2/e

The Architectural Record Book of Vacation Houses, 2/e

Campus Planning and Design

Great Houses for View Sites, Beach Sites, Sites in the
Woods, Meadow Sites, Small Sites, Sloping Sites, Steep
Sites, and Flat Sites

Hospitals and Health Care Facilities, 2/e

Houses Architects Design for Themselves

Interior Spaces Designed by Architects

Office Building Design, 2/e

Places for People: Hotels, Motels, Restaurants, Bars,
Clubs, Community Recreation Facilities, Camps, Parks,
Plazas, Playgrounds

Recycling Buildings: Renovations, Remodelings,
Restorations, and Reuses

Techniques of Successful Practice, 2/e

ARCHITECTURAL RECORD SERIES BOOKS

Ayers: Specifications for Architecture, Engineering and
Construction

Feldman: Building Design for Maintainability

Heery: Time, Cost, and Architecture

Heimsath: Behavioral Architecture

Hopf: Designer's Guide to OSHA

Portman and Barnett: The Architect as Developer

Redstone: The New Downtowns

CONTENTS

PREFACE   vi

CHAPTER ONE:
LIBRARIES   2

BROWN SCIENCES LIBRARY   5
FARMINGTON PUBLIC LIBRARY   8
PORTSMOUTH PUBLIC LIBRARY   10
BRIGHTON BRANCH LIBRARY   11
SKIDMORE COLLEGE LIBRARY   17
SCOTTSDALE CIVIC CENTER LIBRARY   18
CORAM LIBRARY, BATES COLLEGE   21
BRYDGES PUBLIC LIBRARY   26
JAMES BARKER LIBRARY, MIT   31
CHIBA DISTRICT CENTRAL LIBRARY   37
SHERBORN LIBRARY   40
DULUTH PUBLIC LIBRARY   42
ROBARTS RESEARCH LIBRARY   44
CENTRAL LIBRARY, NEGEV
  UNIVERSITY   48
TOUGALOO COLLEGE LIBRARY   50
NORTHWESTERN UNIVERSITY
  LIBRARY   52
MOUNT ANGEL ABBEY LIBRARY   59
CENTRAL LIBRARY, NIAGARA FALLS   64
GREENBURGH PUBLIC LIBRARY   66
TRENT UNIVERSITY LIBRARY   68
LIBRARY RESOURCE CENTER, WRIGHT
  STATE UNIVERSITY   70

CHAPTER TWO:
ART MUSEUMS   72

VILLA MUSEUM   74
DENVER MUSEUM   77
MUSEUM WEST   83
KASELOWSKY MUSEUM   84
MAEGHT FOUNDATION ADDITION   86
RENWICK GALLERY   88
GARVAN GALLERIES, YALE
  UNIVERSITY   91
SCAIFE MUSEUM   94
TOCHIGI MUSEUM   100
TEL AVIV MUSEUM   103
BROOKS MEMORIAL GALLERY   107

WINCHESTER/NORWICH CATHEDRAL   114
HUNTINGTON GALLERY ADDITION   116
UNIVERSITY ART MUSEUM, BERKELEY   118

CHAPTER THREE:
**HISTORIC AND
CULTURAL MUSEUMS**   122

FLINT RIDGE MUSEUM   124
HUNTER MUSEUM   128
NATIONAL MUSEUMS, MEXICO CITY   130
OHIO CENTER   134
FLORIDA MUSEUM   139
PEABODY MUSEUM   145
OAKLAND MUSEUM   147
ONTARIO MUSEUM   154
OREGON HISTORICAL SOCIETY   160

CHAPTER FOUR:
**PERFORMING ARTS
CENTERS**   162

WESLEYAN   164
AMHERST   169
CASA THOMAS JEFFERSON   174
HAMILTON PLACE   176
JUILLIARD SCHOOL   183
OPERA FACTORY   193
MILWAUKEE KRANNERT CENTER   199
UIHLEIN HALL   203
WEHR THEATER   204
VOGEL HALL   206
MARX THEATER   208
HEINZ HALL   214
PAUL MELLON CENTER   218
IOWA PRAIRIE AUDITORIUM   225
PHOENIX CIVIC PLAZA   231
COMMUNITY CENTER, NEWARK, N.J.   234

CHAPTER FIVE:
**ARCHITECTURAL
ENGINEERING**   236

BLOSSOM MUSIC CENTER   238

INDEX   244

PREFACE

The resurgence (or, some would say, the birth) of interest in the arts in America that became openly fashionable in the early 1960's had been growing for a good hundred years before that. The increased wealth that propelled a new class toward new interests in the years following the Civil War brought about the first general awareness in America of music, painting, sculpture, architecture and the performing arts. But, because of the insecurity of those who were uneasy about their new-found wealth, the standards for these art forms were always set by Europe, with America's own outstanding contributions distrusted or ignored except by a small intellectual elite.

But the development of a strong and innovative tradition in each of the traditional art forms, along with the birth of several new ones strictly American in origin, gave an increasing sense of assurance to those who felt that there was something vaguely un-American about an interest in pursuits whose origins had heretofore been decidedly foreign. By the 1920's, Americans were on the cutting edge of cultural innovation, with such figures as Gershwin in music, Duncan in dance, Wright in architecture, O'Neill in drama, and Hemingway in literature able to stand among the most influential creators of their times.

The great hiatuses of the 1930's and '40's did not mean an end to artistic development because of the Depression and World War II—in fact, both decades were as rich as the Twenties in many ways—but they did represent an understandable reordering of national priorities in which the availability of culture to the masses was given a decidedly socially-responsible edge when it emerged at all. It took the years of post-World War II prosperity, and the realization that more was needed in our life as a nation than a house in the suburbs and another car in the garage, to bring the arts into their proper place as an essential component of the American experience.

The example of a leader whose interest in the arts made such interests at least fashionable gave the arts in America of the early 1960's an undeniable lift. But it was the Federal legislation of the mid-1960's which created the two National Endowments, and the concurrent support of the large corporate interests and their foundations, that gave the real backing to the projects whose built expressions are illustrated in the pages which follow. What the buildings in this book prove is the diversity and permanence of those cultural interests, which are now ensconced permanently as part of our American landscape.

The civic impulse that predated the purely cultural building types discussed in this book was nevertheless dovetailed in the prevalent form these structures took in cities in the early 1960's: the cultural center, arts complexes that gave cultural packagedeals in neat agglomerations of opera houses, concert halls, libraries, dance rehearsal halls, theatres, theatre workshops and schools for every performing art, began to spring up from coast to coast. But this early phase of development—which might be called "Too Much Too Soon" in the frantic attempt to make up instantaneously for decades of cultural neglect—was soon supplanted by a more intelligent and well-reasoned approach to housing these newly esteemed institutions. How these buildings related to their functions and the needs of the communities they served began to become more important than erecting another travertine extravaganza to mark the fact that We Too Have Culture.

The works discussed in *Buildings for the Arts,* then, are by and large from the second wave of building activity in the culture boom which has continued more or less unabated for the past twenty years. The gamut of building types is covered, from libraries to art galleries, from schools and conservatories to theatres and concert halls, with stops along the way at an inner-city settlement house for the arts, an "opera factory," a renovated 1920's movie palace-turned-concert hall, an ethnographic museum, a cathedral treasure room and an outdoor summer festival theatre. All suggest the possibilities inherent in building for the arts, and all show the innovative solutions that

the art of architecture can provide for all its sister arts. The one characteristic that unites all these structures, regardless of their location, their cost, their users, or their ultimate success or failure as works of art in and of themselves, is that they function alike as repositories of those special things—whether objects, ideas or physical expressions—which can make all our lives more enjoyable and more meaningful.

Among all building types, then, buildings designed to house the arts perform a function quite unlike any other building type. They are most effective when they serve to set off their functions in as clear and unobtrusive a manner as possible, realizing, as did Yeats, that it is hard to tell the dancer from the dance. Libraries that encourage reading and research, galleries that make great art the true focus of our attentions, concert halls that provide a serene and acoustically responsive setting for music, are all performing programs that are by definition the charge of the architect beyond any other requirement. Frank Lloyd Wright's controversial Guggenheim Museum, completed just at the time that Culture became the new American by-word, is a worthwhile case in point. Hailed by some as a daring breakaway from the alleged "tyranny" of rectilinear interior spaces in which art had been displayed for the most part until then, the Guggenheim twenty years later has succeeded in overshadowing the works it houses to the extent that the building presents a much more vivid tyranny than the one it promised to overcome.

The basic functions of display and viewing in that building are subordinated to the imposition of an architectural statement that competes all too successfully for our attention, and not too satisfyingly at that. The lesson is, of course, that housing the arts must take its cues from those art forms themselves, and from the people that create and enjoy them. The buildings that follow do that to a high degree of excellence, and show that the arts have finally come of age in America, and, quite aside from being well housed in buildings, are likewise being well housed in the lives of countless Americans across our country.

BUILDINGS FOR THE ARTS

CHAPTER ONE

LIBRARIES

BROWN SCIENCES LIBRARY

Brown is one of the first universities in the nation to combine all its science departmental collections into a single library. In the interest of aiding interdisciplinary research in chemistry, biology, mathematics, physics, engineering, geology, psychology and medicine, the science collection is concentrated in a tower of 14 stories, at the pivot of the science complex.

The tower form, which until recently has been an anathema to librarians, was accepted in principle by Dr. David A. Jonah, librarian of the University, with the stipulation to the architects, Warner Burns Toan Lunde, that the typical floors of the tower would have sufficient area to house the largest separate collections (medicine) on not more than two floors of 45,000 volumes per floor. There was to be room for the appropriate number of carrels, open and locked, faculty study areas, conference rooms and other necessary facilities. The movement of readers and books is accomplished by means of elevators, book conveyors and a pneumatic tube system. The stack functions as an efficient information storage system with ease of access.

BROWN SCIENCES LIBRARY, Brown University, Providence, Rhode Island. Architects: *Warner Burns Toan Lunde—partner-in-charge: Danforth Toan; project architect: Michael Willis; interior design: Gertrude Gray.* Engineers: *Severud Perrone Sturm Conlin Bandel* (structural); *Joseph Ward & Associates* (foundation); *Syska & Hennessy* (mechanical and electrical). Landscape architects: *Sasaki Dawson DeMay.* General contractor: *Dimeo Construction Company.*

Louis Reens photos

The main library floor on the lower level of 25,000 square feet contains the reference and current periodicals collections, and a technical services area. This floor is dropped below a podium which is skylit at both ends. On the main lobby floor (photo, page 5) is a generous space for exhibitions and lounging with a circular control desk and shelving which houses and regulates the reserve book section. The undergraduate reading room is on the mezzanine just above with access by means of the free-standing stair located on the north side of the building. Sunken patios, attractively planted, are located at the four corners of the tower. The architects designed the interiors, and the carrels, tables, card catalog enclosures, bookshelves, circulation desk and the reserve and rare book displays were all custom designed by them. Wherever possible, the furniture has flexible vinyl nosings to reduce wear and scratching.

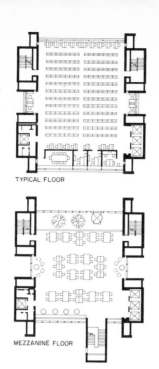

TYPICAL FLOOR

MEZZANINE FLOOR

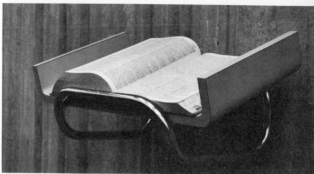

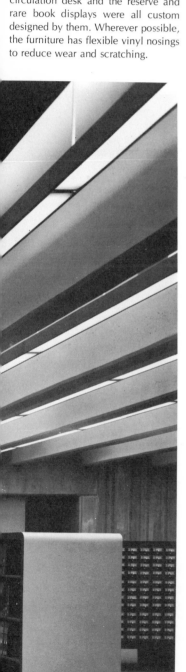

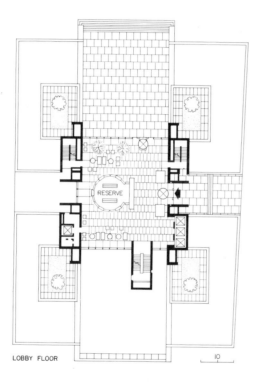

LOBBY FLOOR

RESERVE

10

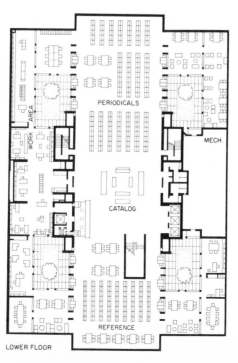

PERIODICALS

WORK AREA

MECH.

CATALOG

REFERENCE

LOWER FLOOR

FARMINGTON PUBLIC LIBRARY

The design concept of this small suburban public library evolved mainly from the desire of the library board, the librarians and their architects, to devise a system of control and operation which would be housed within large open spaces. The reading rooms are organized into a large reading and reference area, functionally separated only by furniture arrangement, and a separate children's reading room. A small room houses the rare book collection and offers an area of relative seclusion and quiet for dues-paying members of the library. As the plan (right) indicates, the administrative offices, meeting areas and the circulation workroom are conveniently related to both the main entrance and the service and receiving area. Smaller satellite workrooms are provided off the main reading room and at the lower level adjacent to these areas. The circulation desk, elevator, toilet and locker facilities are located in the central spine for ease of access and for control.

At the lower level (not shown) is a large meeting room with a stage and audio-visual facilities which serves the community at large, during and after library hours.

FARMINGTON PUBLIC LIBRARY, Farmington, Michigan. Architects and engineers: *Tarapata MacMahon Paulsen Corporation—principal-in-charge: Richard K. Albyn; design: Peter Tarapata and John Kinsella; job captain: C. E. Bentley; chief structural engineer: Samuel V. Tavernit.* Consultants: *Mohrhardt & Ulveling* (library); *20th Century Design Inc.* (landscape) Contractor: *Freeman-Darling Inc.*

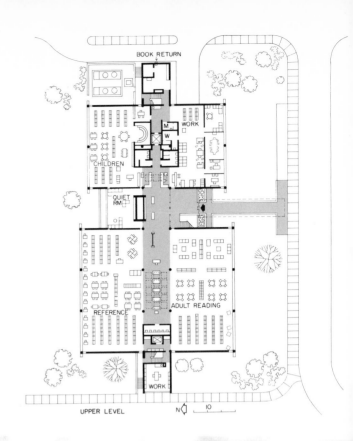

UPPER LEVEL

The long, low form of the library is well suited to its rolling site. From the main road (below), it appears to be a single-story building. Service to the upper and lower levels is located at the rear of the sloping site. The central spine, as it bisects the adult reading and reference area (right), serves as the location for the card catalogs. It is differentiated from the reading and research areas by means of its brick paving and higher ceiling. All reading rooms and work stations are carpeted for acoustic control and ease of maintenance. In the children's room is a tiny amphitheater which users call a "story hill" (bottom) where story hours are held. The construction cost of this 31,700 square foot fully air-conditioned building was $903,770, or approximately $28.52 per square foot.

Balthazar Korab photos

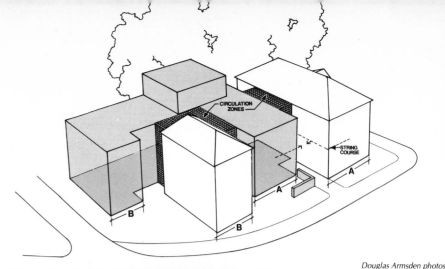

PORTSMOUTH PUBLIC LIBRARY

The public library in Portsmouth, New Hampshire unites, by infill construction, two unused landmark buildings—which were a potential drain of maintenance costs on the municipal budget—to produce a needed civic amenity. And the financial advantages of utilizing "found" space have been increased by a sound knowledge of currently available funding.

The two joined early 19th century buildings, the Benedict House and the Academy, are an invaluable contribution to the aspect of Portsmouth and are listed on the National Registry. However, what the landmark-rich city needed was not two more museums; it needed a libaray which neither building could accommodate on its own. The program called for 10,000 square feet of space beyond that available in both. Accordingly, Stahl/Bennett's design has incorporated the two existing buildings for a special collections department, in the undisturbed rooms of the house, and for the major reading room in the large space of the public hall. Offices, a children's library and stacks (because of the heavy loading on floors) are placed in the new connector. As in the Peabody Museum (page 145), the disparate elements are separated by glass links that reveal the original walls of the older buildings. An added advantage to the links is the elimination of the juncture of the new brick facing and the old. Concrete plank floors were attached between the flanges of the steel beams to produce maximum ceiling heights and still align with existing floor levels—while accommodating mechanical services.

By drawing on funds to be spent by the Federal government, Portsmouth was able to reduce local cash commitment to 50 per cent of the construction cost of $700,000. About one-fifth of this cost was obtained through the State Library and over one-tenth through the State Historic Society. Most interestingly, 25 per cent of all municipal costs came from HUD in the form of a forgiven loan, because the project qualified as an ancillary support facility within an urban-renewal area.

PORTSMOUTH PUBLIC LIBRARY, Portsmouth, New Hampshire. Owner: *City of Portsmouth. Architects: Stahl/Bennett, Inc.—F. A. Stahl, partner-in-charge; Roger Lang, director of restoration and renovation; Frank Adams, project architect.* Engineers: *Weidemann, Brown, Inc.* (structural); *AMC Engineers* (mechanical); *Metcalf Engineering* (electrical); *Conmatan, Inc.* (specifications). General contractor; *Picci Construction Co.*

Douglas Armsden photos

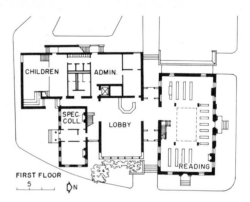

FIRST FLOOR

The new part is placed between and around a landmark house and a public hall (respectively left and right in the photo above). The new wing, to the far left, replaces a latter-day addition to the house. Competition between the different architectural styles is avoided by the lack of individual windows in the new building, which appears as a floating band of bricks (matching the original building's) that floats above a visually recessive band of dark glass. The glazed links can be seen, in the diagram at top.

BRIGHTON BRANCH LIBRARY

The Brighton Branch Library, designed by The Architects Collaborative Inc., is the first to be completed in a group of regional libraries planned for the Boston Public Library system. As such it offers more substantial services to a greater number of patrons with more demanding reading and reference interests than the typical neighborhood branch library can provide. New in its concepts of library function, it is appropriately original in plan and fresh and attractive in its architectural expression.

Phokion Karas

The building is composed of three wings—adult, children and community service—on three levels conforming to the natural contours of the sloping site. The three areas are connected by a ramp system which eliminates the need for stairs and opens onto a central entrance lobby and control point. The adults' and children's areas as well as the stacks are daylighted through clerestory vaults of unequal size, both of which appear in the photos (above and right). As can be seen in the plot plan, the three separate wings define three corresponding outdoor courtyards. One serves as an entrance court, another is an extension of the children's wing and the third located just beyond the lobby adds to the pleasantness and openness of that space.

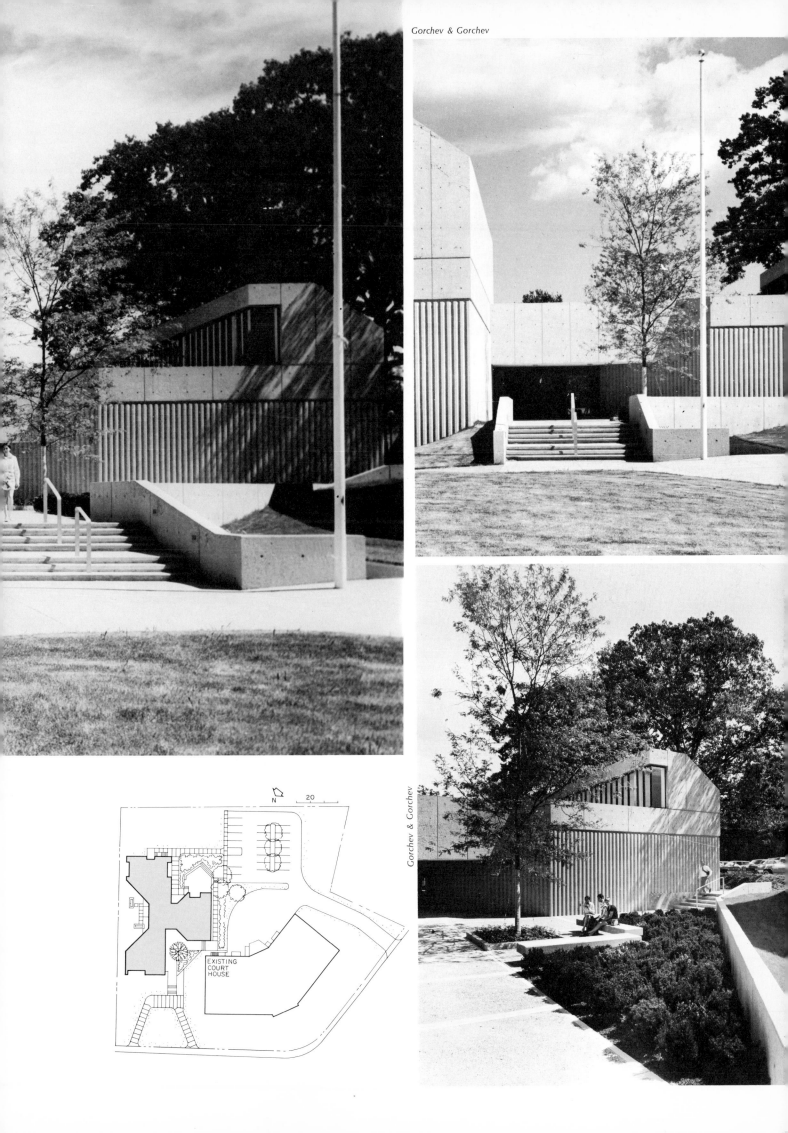

Gorchev & Gorchev

Gorchev & Gorchev

EXISTING
COURT
HOUSE

N   20

Gorchev & Gorchev

The new library shares its site with a neo-classical courthouse and special attention was given to the problem of coordinating scale, color and materials with the older structure. It was considered of particular importance that the library not only relate to the residential character of the neighborhood, but that it not appear too large in relation to the courthouse and crowd it. The architects also hoped to conserve as much of the site as possible for lawns and courtyards. To conserve space and reduce the apparent size of the building the wing designed to house facilities for young adults, adults and stacks has been organized in three tiers at the portion of the site which slopes downward, as shown in the plans and section (right).

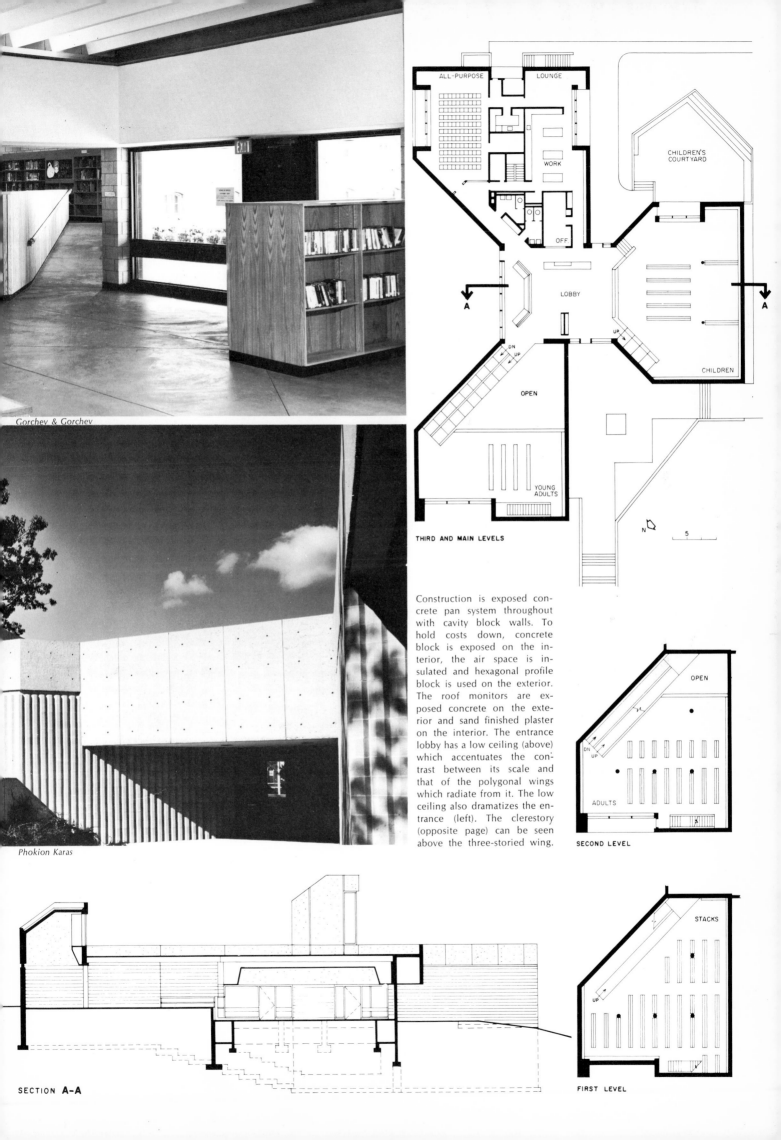

Gorchev & Gorchev

Phokion Karas

THIRD AND MAIN LEVELS

LOBBY

ALL-PURPOSE   LOUNGE

WORK

OFF

OPEN

YOUNG
ADULTS

CHILDREN'S
COURTYARD

CHILDREN

N   5

Construction is exposed concrete pan system throughout with cavity block walls. To hold costs down, concrete block is exposed on the interior, the air space is insulated and hexagonal profile block is used on the exterior. The roof monitors are exposed concrete on the exterior and sand finished plaster on the interior. The entrance lobby has a low ceiling (above) which accentuates the contrast between its scale and that of the polygonal wings which radiate from it. The low ceiling also dramatizes the entrance (left). The clerestory (opposite page) can be seen above the three-storied wing.

SECOND LEVEL

OPEN

DN
UP

ADULTS

FIRST LEVEL

STACKS

UP

SECTION A-A

Phokion Karas

Shown above is the ramp system in the three-tiered wing. The children's wing (below) overlooks the lobby-control area. Well-scaled, it occupies an entire polygonal wing, and has its own reading or story-telling court. The entire library, including the adult and young adult section and the stacks has a 79,000-volume capacity. The total building cost was $596,000.

BRIGHTON BRANCH LIBRARY, Brighton, Massachusetts. Owner: *Boston Public Library.* Architects: *The Architects Collaborative Inc.* —principal-in-charge: *Norman Fletcher;* associate-in-charge: *Michael Prodanou;* structural engineers: *Souza & True;* mechanical engineers: *Reardon & Turner;* electrical engineers: *Verne Norman & Assocs.;* contractor: *Michael Racioppi Inc.*

SKIDMORE COLLEGE LIBRARY

The library, designed to house three times the number of volumes in the college's current collection, also provides seating for 600 students, including 216 individual study carrels. Essentially the second and third floors are open plans with a maximum of flexible space surrounding the more permanent facilities. Here, as in other buildings, precast, pre- stressed double T-beams are the key element in the structural system, permitting large unobstructed spaces with the maximum potential for various and changing uses. Since the opening of the building, a computer classroom, linked to similar facilities on other campuses, has been installed on the fourth floor located within the mansard roof.

SKIDMORE COLLEGE, Saratoga Springs, New York. Architects: *Ford, Powell & Carson— L. D. Cloud, project architect;* planning consultant: *S. B. Zisman;* engineers: *Feigenspan & Pinnell (structural), D. W. Torry & Associates (mechanical & electrical).*

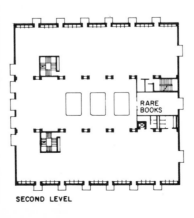

RARE BOOKS

SECOND LEVEL

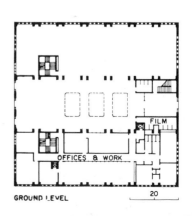

FILM

OFFICES & WORK

GROUND LEVEL

20

SCOTTSDALE CIVIC CENTER LIBRARY

This library is open and inviting, reflecting the informal Southwestern way of life which the Council, in its brief charge to the architects, indicated was one of its criteria for the buildings' design. The central sunken space is used as a periodical lounge, with reading rooms and book shelves in the various reading rooms on the level above. The great central area has the dignity of monumental space but because of the angled direction of the massive columns, is also quite informal. All public services, as well as cataloging and processing, are located on the entrance level. Here, too, is a 100-seat auditorium, accessible from outside the building and from the lobby. On the mezzanine are administrative offices, staff lounge and board room, and a gallery currently used for art exhibitions but ready for expansion. The building was designed for a projected capacity of 125,000 volumes. The furnishings were selected by the architects and are not typical library furniture; some equipment was specially designed.

SCOTTSDALE CIVIC CENTER, Scottsdale, Arizona. Architects: *Gonzales Associates*. Engineers: *Foltz, Hamlyn & Adam, Inc.* (structural); *Richard E. Joachim & Associates* (mechanical); *William E. Meier & Associates* (electrical). Landscape architects: *Gonzales Associates*. General contractor: *Arnold Construction Company*.

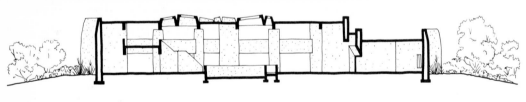

LIBRARY SECTION   10

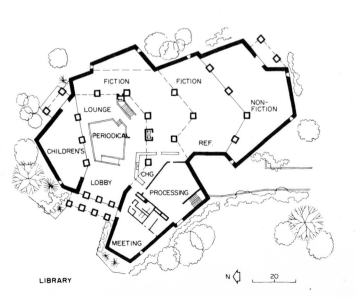

LIBRARY   N   20

Earth colors are used in the interiors of both city hall and library. Brown carpet contrasts with white textured walls and ceilings; wood furniture and colorful upholstery fabrics are lively accents. The total effect is of hand-crafted, non-commercial quality. Faceted colored glass skylights, are placed in the ceilings of both buildings to admit more warm colors in winter than in summer. The architects designed all interiors.

CORAM LIBRARY, BATES COLLEGE

Bates is a small co-educational liberal arts college with an enrollment of about 1,200 students. The library program, which was prepared by the chief librarian Iva Foster and library consultant Keyes Metcalf, called for a building which will serve library needs for the next 20 years. Presently programmed for 700 readers, 420,000 volumes, a 26-member staff and 10 student assistants, it can be expanded in the future without interfering with its present operation and appearance.

The librarian, consultant and planning committee called for a square 22½-foot center-to-center column module to accept multiples of the standard three foot shelf sections in either direction between 14"-16" square columns. They wished the building's main entrance to be readily accessible from four directions and level with the approach. They considered it essential that there be open access to all library materials except for storage and the special collections, but as a corollary to this, they demanded only one public entrance-exit as essential to security.

The program stated that approximately 15,000 square feet was to be provided on the main floor in order to accommodate the major services of the library. Exhibit areas were to be limited and of modest dimensions.

In commenting on the building program and her design solution, architect Sarah Harkness points out that the library should provide easy access to the collection as part of an inviting reading and research environment which encourages an independent exploratory approach to the library materials. The facilities of a campus library, she believes, should be conceived in terms of their primary educational potential, rather than as an adjunct to classroom activity. At the same time if the library is to be more than merely functional, it must, according to Mrs. Harkness, have "poetry in its spatial sequences, reflecting the active or quiet functions that take place."

In the Bates Library readers are led from the entrance to the control desk to the catalog, reference and bibliography areas in an obvious manner. Periodicals and newspapers are on the main floor along with a reserve collection open for night reading. Reading areas on all floors are conveniently adjacent to the stacks.

The shape of the building was determined by the fact that the largest volume of space was required to be on the first floor. The upper floors which house stacks and reading areas with faculty offices on the top floor need progressively less space. The long sloping roof follows the floors as they step back, making the sense of height and volume most evident at the entrance. The stacks, which require much more square foot area than the reading spaces, occupy the central parts of the building where the floor to ceiling height is uniformly only nine feet, while reading areas are placed on the periphery by windows or on the edges of balconies under the slope of the roof.

In addition to the programmatic considerations just enumerated, the site itself played a large part in the final solution. In their master plan for the college, the firm of Sasaki, Dawson & DeMay recommended a site directly behind the old Coram Library, an elegant little building built in 1900. This site was complicated by the fact that the old building had an ugly but

still useful rear addition constructed in 1948. Sarah Harkness and her team made extensive studies of this proposed site and alternate sites before electing to tear down all but the basement of the 1948 addition, roof it with a plaza and interconnect it with the basement level of the new structure. The original Coram Library will become an art museum. Its rear elevation, minus the unfortunate addition has been restored so that the building is once again intact and beautiful.

The new plaza has become the heart of the campus connecting the main level of the old Coram building to the main level and entrance of the new library. As an important advantage of this site, access from the student union, athletic building and dormitory areas is easily accomplished by means of a passage and stairway under the building from the lower level arcade to the plaza level entrance. The low side of the sloping roof respects Coram's small scale while the four-story height of the opposite elevation, with large windows overlooking the quadrangle, relates to the scale of neighboring buildings. The quadrangle itself has not been encroached upon and remains a recreational space and playfield linking the library to the athletic complex.

The total cost of the 101,676-square-foot library was $3 million. Completed in the fall of 1973, it has received a citation from the Maine State Commission of the Arts and Humanities.

THE CORAM LIBRARY, Bates College, Lewiston, Maine. Architects: *The Architects Collaborative; principals-in-charge: Sarah P. Harkness and John C. Harkness; associate-in-charge: James E. Burlage; job captain: Richard F. Puffer; landscape architect: Robert Thompson; interior design: Katrinka Ebbe; graphics: Pamela Webster; construction supervision: Wendell F. Jacques.* Consultants: *Alonzo J. Harriman Associates, Inc.* (structural, mechanical, electrical, estimating); *Keyes Metcalf* (library programming). General contractor: *Stewart & Williams, Inc.*

The section and plot plan show the relationship of the new library and its plaza to the old Coram Library. The new building although it is quite large (101,676 square feet on four levels including a separate science library) is very compact; and due to the skillful arrangement of its interior spaces as expressed on the exterior and the inclusion of a large stack capacity below the plaza level, it appears to be in good scale with the buildings which surround it. The smaller scaled elements face the rather intimate plaza (preceding page) while the larger and more imposing facades (bottom photo right) face broad campus open spaces and large neighboring buildings. Fine old trees are conserved.

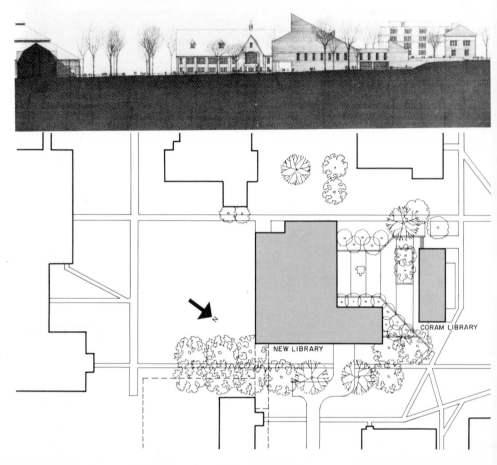

NEW LIBRARY

CORAM LIBRARY

Phokion Karas photos

SECTION A-A

SECOND FLOOR

THIRD FLOOR

MAIN FLOOR

GROUND FLOOR

10

The passageway (above) leads under the library from the plaza to the arcade facing the quadrangular playing field. The library entrance-exit is from the plaza. Diagonally placed study carrels (below and overleaf) occupy perimeter spaces. These areas achieve spaciousness without additional cubage.

Left: High-intensity quartz lamps wash the sloping ceilings with light. *Right:* Open board ceilings conceal the mechanical equipment and carry lights and acoustic material.

BRYDGES PUBLIC LIBRARY

The Earl W. Brydges Public Library is located on the main street of the city of Niagara Falls, in a depressed section. It is hoped that Rudolph's distinguished design for the library will help serve as a catalyst for the general upgrading of the area. A nearby convention center by Philip Johnson has been invested with the same hope, and so has a recently completed office building by Gordon Bunshaft of SOM.

The $5.1-million library is a highly visible focal point at the conjunction of several secondary streets which converge into the main traffic artery. It was originally designed as part of a superblock which would contain a school, its playground and a small park. Unfortunately the school (designed by others) was allowed to expand into the area reserved for the park, so Rudolph's original site concept has been considerably compromised. He has succeeded, however, in achieving his fundamental idea which was that the building should be open and welcoming to the citizens of the city.

The broad plaza (above and right) has splayed walls which draw the public in. These sloping walls reduce the apparent scale at the plaza level and in combination with the pitched roof give the building a friendly, almost domestic look. Within the building there is soft, glareless light, attributable in part to these splayed and sloping walls which extend beyond the glass infilling walls, screen the glare and increase the feeling of being enclosed and protected inside.

The lively and exciting exterior silhouette suggests a man-made hill actively carved and penetrated in an effort to improve upon nature. The line in which the building meets the sky is animated by the clerestories which are angled in several directions to catch the natural light.

The library as constructed is similar to Rudolph's initial concept (compare the rendering and the photograph taken at the same angle). Rudolph later gave the entrance a better scale. The sculpture, added by the client, was not part of the original plaza design.

Joseph W. Molitor photos

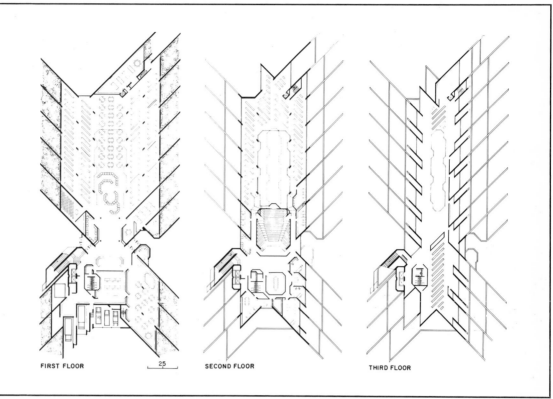

FIRST FLOOR   25   SECOND FLOOR   THIRD FLOOR

Upon entering, one has immediate access to the directory, the main circulation desk, the general circulation space, display cases, lockers, stairs, elevators, copying machines and toilets. This central space leads directly to the main reading room (right) or to the children's library (next page). As the section and photographs suggest, the three-story-high main reading room is a handsome and dramatic space, which has been only slightly marred by the oversized suspended lighting fixtures which the client insisted were needed. Rudolph believes that the daylight from the clerestories combined with the fluorescent strips under the projecting mezzanine would have provided adequate light for the central space. The book stacks are placed at angles to the main axis of the room exposing books rather than stack ends. While the library may appear to be an all masonry structure, the columns are of steel, clad with a striated concrete block. Steel tie rods resolve the outward thrust of the roof. The rest of the structure is of concrete block with poured-in-place beams and slabs.

Shelving has been housed in cases designed by Rudolph and edged with copper-finish mylar. Copper sheathing is used on the table tops in the reading room. Shown are work areas (top), the children's library (middle) and the desk in the main circulation area.

EARL W. BRYDGES PUBLIC LIBRARY, Niagara Falls, New York. Owner: *City of Niagara Falls*. Architect: *Paul Rudolph—project manager: Terrance Mullen*. Engineers: *Lev Zetlin* (structural); *Walter Sherry* (mechanical/electrical). Consultants: *Bolt, Beranek and Newman* (acoustical); *Mohrhardt and Ulveling* (library planning). General contractor: *Albert Elia Building Co.*

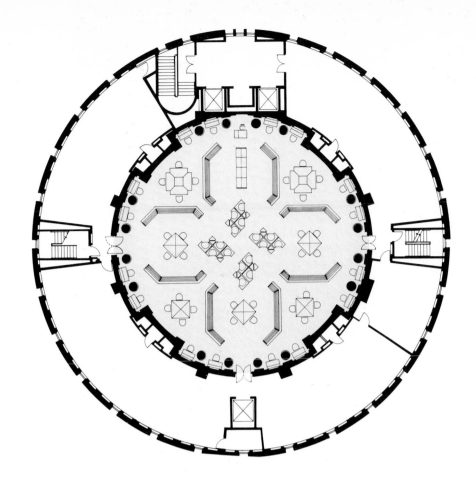

JAMES BARKER LIBRARY, MIT

MIT's long-range campus plan calls for concentration of instructional, research and administrative facilities. One result of this program has been extensive remodeling for greater intensity of use. SOM's reconstruction of MIT's engineering library to accommodate this policy was a unique challenge because of the beauty and symbolic importance of the dome in which it is housed.

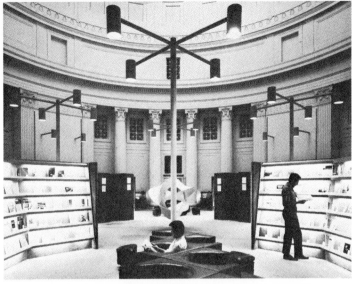

The Massachusetts Institute of Technology dome is an imposing landmark, as seen from the principal entrance facade (below). Designed by Welles Bosworth in 1916 as part of his scheme for the neo-classic East Campus, it has long been the crown of the reading room of MIT's engineering library.

The library interior has recently been remodeled by Walter Netsch of SOM. Netsch has successfully juxtaposed his own geometry, based upon an intricate system of intersecting diagonals, with the classic form of the dome's interior. By this means, he has produced eight clearly articulated reading areas plus an additional study space at the center. The outer ring of the dome has been remodeled to more efficiently continue its

original function of housing stacks, research areas and administrative spaces, and to accommodate the new computer hardware developed as part of MIT's so-called Project Intrex. The latter is a new form of information transfer designed to handle the growing collection.

The library as a whole has been conceived as a flexible unit. The division between its traditional library functions—browsing, study and research—and its sophisticated, computerized information retrieval system has deliberately been made imperceptible.

For many years the interior of the MIT dome was hidden by a suspended luminous ceiling of corrugated translucent plastic lit by fluorescents. A product of an era noted for destructive remodeling in the name of function, this ceiling was hung just below the column capitals. In addition to ruining the room as a space (opposite page far left), it created a harsh and unpleasant glare. Netsch's first decision was to remove the suspended ceiling and expose the dome once more. This called for extensive restoration of the dome and its moldings. The oculus, formerly translucent, was made opaque and powerful lights were placed around its perimeter as part of a cross-lighting system designed to emphasize the shape of the dome. The pole-supported lighting fixtures also illuminate the dome transforming it into a reflecting surface. These light trees illuminate the working surfaces as well. The carrel lighting, highlighting of the publication racks and supplementary local lighting was carefully studied. Walls, columns and the dome ceiling were painted white to further brighten the room.

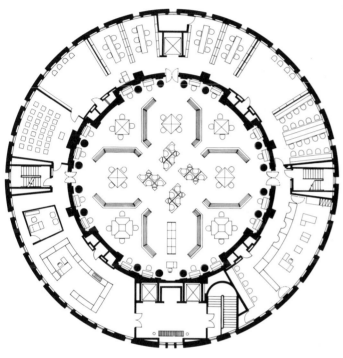

FIFTH FLOOR

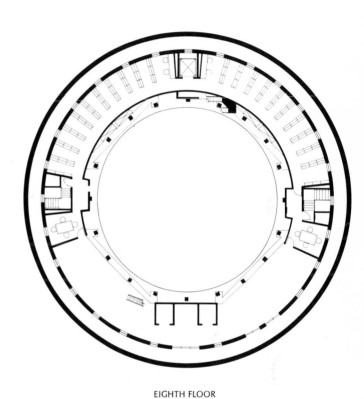

EIGHTH FLOOR

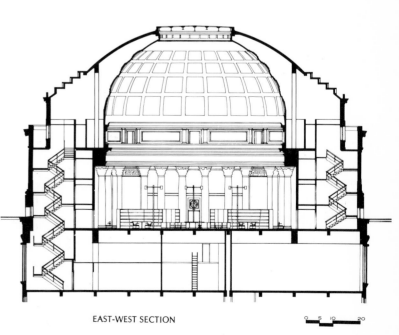

EAST-WEST SECTION

0 5 10 20

MIT photo by Robert Lyon

33

The unyielding and un-wieldy total geometry of the dome gave Netsch more repitious concentric circles and truncated pie-shapes to work with than he would have chosen, and there were other problems. The library had to be open and in operation during the entire reconstruction project; the dome though beautiful, possesses construction oddities that could not be ignored, altered or circumvented; and the remodeling budget was limited. Netsch had to achieve his effects by essentially non-structural means—furniture design and placement, redesigned lighting and acoustics, selection of sculpture, plants and color. The plan concentrates two major working areas for greater user efficiency. Nearly all requirements for searching or browsing are on the fifth floor at the entrance level. Here, in addition to circulation and reference services, are facilities for literature search, computer controlled literature search, current journals, and individual study spaces at carrels, tables or in lounge chairs. Staff members' offices and work areas are chiefly on the fourth floor—out of the sight and sound of users.

THE JAMES MADISON BARKER ENGINEERING LIBRARY, Massachusetts Institute of Technology, Cambridge, Massachusetts. Architects for the interiors: *Skidmore, Owings & Merrill —Walter Netsch, partner-in-charge;* Project Intrex staff: *Dr. Carl Overage and Charles Stevens;* hardware development: *MIT Electronic Systems Laboratory;* acoustics: *Bolt, Beranek and Newman;* lighting: *William Lam;* general contractor: *Fuller Construction Company.*

From the beginning, the library was a hard, reverberant space. Originally the dome itself was blamed for the poor acoustics and this belief helped justify the installation of the suspended luminous ceiling which Netsch removed. At the time of the current remodeling, however, Bolt, Beranek and Newman, the acoustical consultants, persuaded MIT that the hard plaster walls and terrazzo floor were the cause of the difficulty. Excessive noise and echo have now been absorbed by the use of carpet on the backs of the free-standing periodical racks (opposite page top) as well as on the floor. Although the acousticians did not think it necessary, sound absorbent panels were placed within the smallest rectangle of each of the dome coffers. The chairs (below) were designed by Vasarely. The suspended, mobile, cast-aluminum sculpture (below and opposite page) is by Robert Engman. It was donated to MIT by art collector Netsch. Both chairs and mobile are combinations of circles and are thus appropriate forms for a domed room.

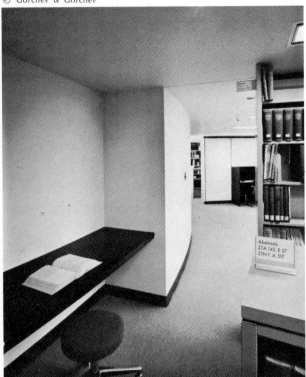

The library equipment shown below was designed by SOM to serve the traditional library functions. The Intrex system has been developed experimentally and the necessary technology is available. So far, however, due to insufficient funding, there has been only a minimal installation of computerized hardware in the library and this is not always operable or available. Eventually the contents of large numbers of books in given fields will be transferred to film and stored in a central time-shared computer. Research will begin at computer terminals which consist of teletypewriters with cathode-ray tubes. At these terminal points which will be located throughout the library, elsewhere on the campus and within the region, scholars will type out their initial inquiries, receive replies on the cathode-ray tube and eventually narrow their search to the point of requesting to read specific books, pages or quotations therefrom, all of which will be flashed on the tube. Computer printouts will be available almost at once. The inclusion of a special duct network within the library will facilitate the future location of computer terminals.

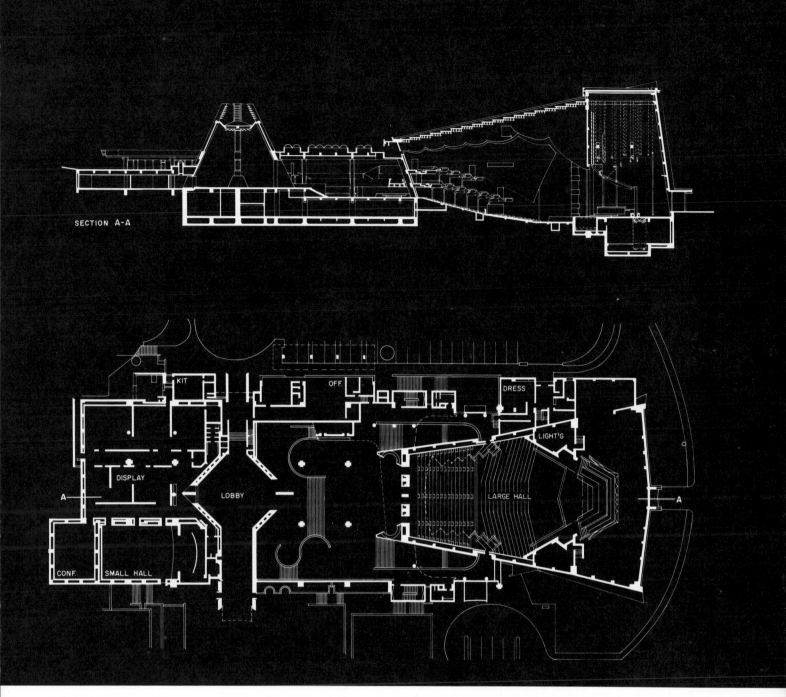

SECTION A-A

KIT OFF. DRESS

DISPLAY LIGHT'G

LOBBY

A LARGE HALL A

CONF. SMALL HALL

The large hall must serve many purposes—lecture, drama, concert, dance and film projection, it can be volumetrically adjusted and its degree of sound absorption can be adapted to the type of performance taking place. It seats 1,800 people. The building also includes a smaller lecture room for 250 people, an exhibition room, and offices.

CHIBA DISTRICT CENTRAL LIBRARY

Masato Otaka, one of the older Metabolists, founded his own office in 1961, after a twelve-year apprenticeship in the office of Kunio Mayekawa. He participated in Metabolism's first manifesto of 1960, "The Proposals for New Urbanism," but like his fellow visionaries he has yet to see any significant part of his broad solutions to urban problems implemented.

Like them he has been eminently successful in the design of large building complexes of which the Chiba District Culture Center's Hall of Culture is a distinguished example. This structure will eventually be one of four buildings.

In this building Otaka creates space which serves and expresses the fact that it is part of a concentrated cultural center with functional and spatial links to the other buildings. The entrance lobby, which joins the huge library plaza to the southwest and the ceremonial building to the northeast, culminates at its center in a great octagonal ceiling which becomes a dominant pyramidal form on the exterior (left).

The Chiba Library, like all of the best current Japanese architecture, is a vigorous and handsome as well as technologically interesting building. A genuine esthetic has been derived from its structural rigor, which proves Otaka's contention that modular planning need not be insipid if one can "develop a higher level modular system that will link parts and the whole in a fluid fashion."

For this library Otaka has developed a new structural module of precast concrete which he has also used for the main gate at Expo '70 and which has broad applications for use at an urban scale. This system permits a high degree of freedom of assembly including multi-level combinations and almost infinite expansibility by direct coupling of parts. The basic floor and ceiling unit is a precast concrete cross with a V-shaped section. The required number of sections for any given part of the building is assembled in rows at the factory and submitted to prestress before being hauled to the site. They are then joined to the required width and submitted to post tension.

The columns, cross-shaped in section, consist of two identical units which connect by rigid joints at mid-height. The flared end of the upper unit joins the ceiling, and the flared end of the lower unit joins the floor. For greater heights straight units are inserted between the flared units. The cross-shaped column capitals are joined to the grid openings by post tensioning and rigid joints.

SECTION A-A

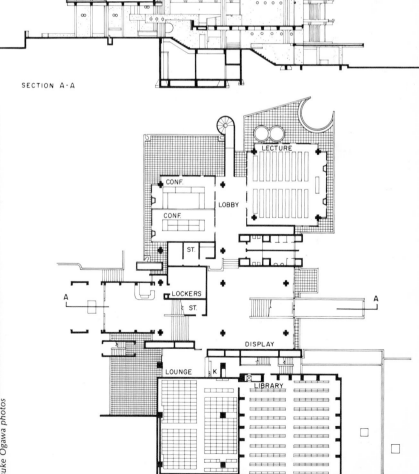

FIRST FLOOR

Taisuke Ogawa photos

SHERBORN LIBRARY

The welcoming, sheltering, almost domestic quality of this new public library in an old New England town makes it an unusually attractive environment for books. Located on a tree-lined main street with many good examples of colonial architecture, it is adjacent to the town hall, a Greek Revival church, and a nearby school; and plays a key role as part of the town center. Sherborn, Massachusetts has a population of approximately 3,000 people and is a bedroom community for the city of Boston. Since the library serves such a small community and was not considered a resource for the region, it has been designed for a maximum capacity of only 36,000 volumes. The architect has successfully managed to create a building which is harmonious with its neighbors in scale and materials. Traditionally handled brick walls, wood floor and roof decking, rough plaster partitions, and bluestone entry flooring are combined in a contemporary fashion with a laminated timber structural frame, a ridge skylight and carpeted floors. The furniture and bookstack ends are wood. The furniture is upholstered in bright shades of orange and yellow and is of an informal character.

SHERBORN LIBRARY, Sherborn, Massachusetts. Architects: *James A. S. Walker—associate: John Gerald Horne.* Engineers: *Abraham Woolf and Associates, Inc.* (structural and foundation); *John J. McEvoy* (mechanical); *Thompson Engineering Company, Inc.* (electrical). Landscaping: *Harriette W. Long.* General contractor: *Henry E. Wile Corporation.*

MAIN FLOOR

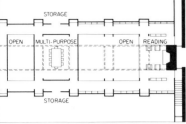

MEZZANINE FLOOR

The library consists of a main floor, a mezzanine and a basement. The principal north-south corridor separates the librarian's office and the service areas from the library proper. The latter is separated into three major areas—reference, general reading and a children's section. A large fireplace at the western end of the library functions as the building's focal point (bottom right). In addition, the library furniture is comfortable, generous, and inviting.

Phokion Karas photos

Because of the steep roof pitch, the mezzanine is narrow along the side—but this design affords a considerable bonus in shelving footage and is a quiet browsing area. In the bay which parallels the main hall and control desk, the mezzanine spans the width of the building adding a multi-purpose room. On the main floor, the stacks are arranged to create small-scaled reading and study spaces which are yet open enough to give the individual a sense of inhabiting a larger room. The double brick piers and the deep overhangs help shade the windows and thus reduce glare in the perimeter bays, while the skylight brings needed brightness to the center.

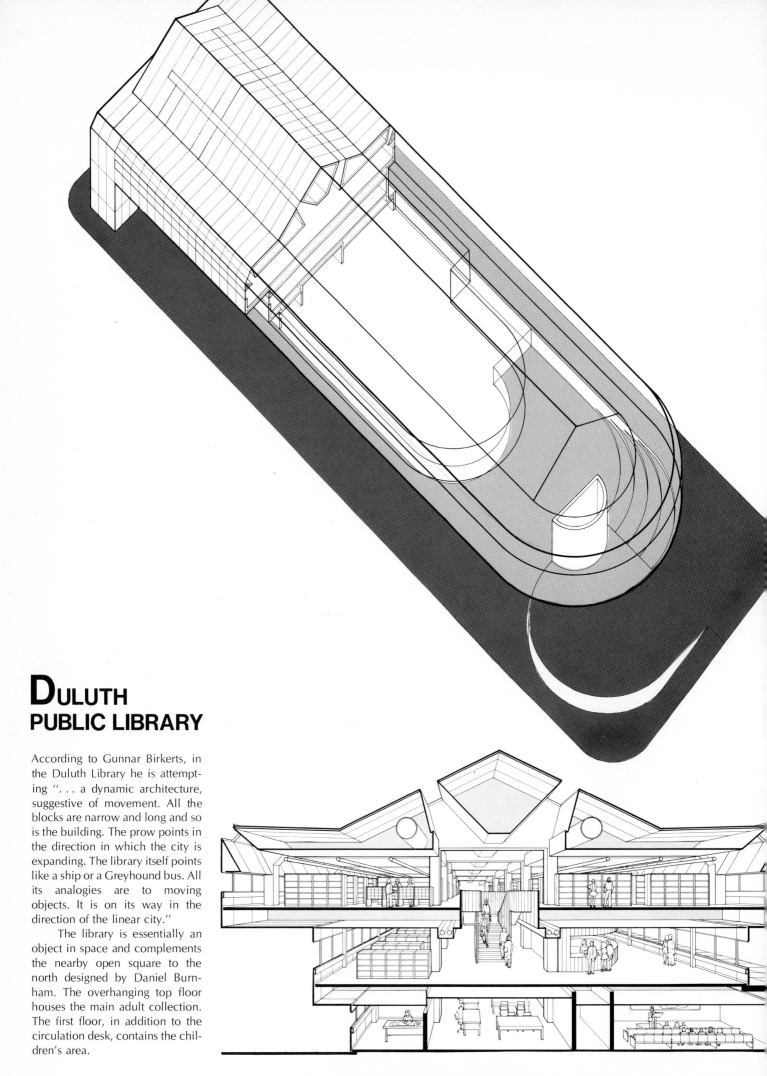

DULUTH PUBLIC LIBRARY

According to Gunnar Birkerts, in the Duluth Library he is attempting ". . . a dynamic architecture, suggestive of movement. All the blocks are narrow and long and so is the building. The prow points in the direction in which the city is expanding. The library itself points like a ship or a Greyhound bus. All its analogies are to moving objects. It is on its way in the direction of the linear city."

The library is essentially an object in space and complements the nearby open square to the north designed by Daniel Burnham. The overhanging top floor houses the main adult collection. The first floor, in addition to the circulation desk, contains the children's area.

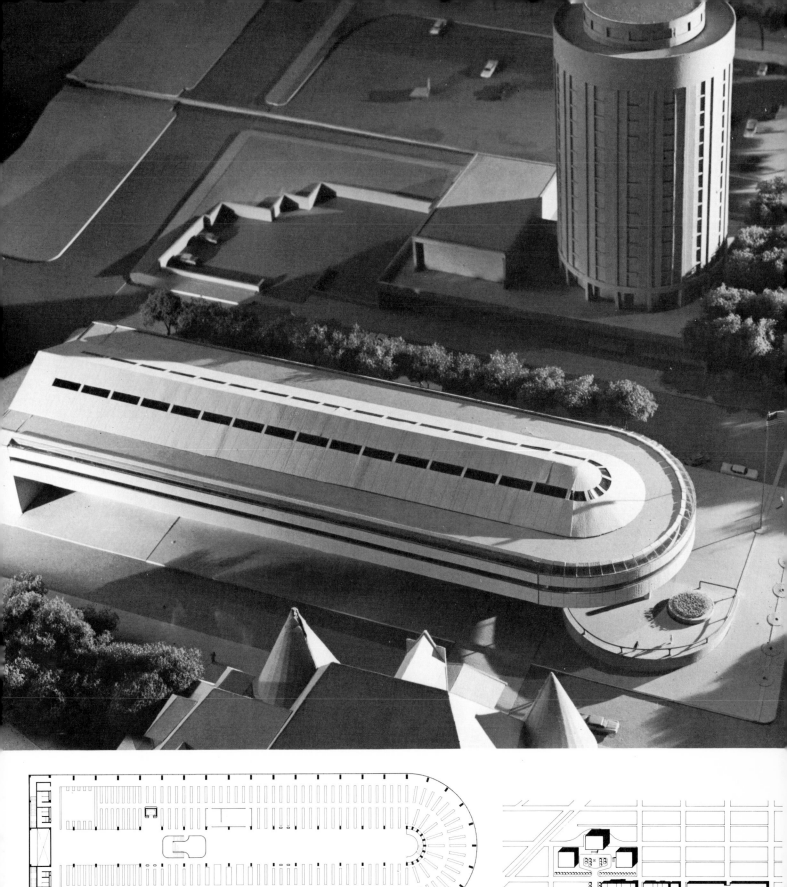

Robarts Research Library

In the 14-year interval between the beginning of the programming and designing process for the John P. Robarts Research Library for the Humanities and Social Sciences and its official dedication last spring, there were profound changes in the social and political attitudes toward higher education in Ontario. Back in 1960 the provincial government wanted the University of Toronto to have a graduate school in the humanities which would be commensurate with those of Harvard, Cornell, Princeton and the like. It was hoped that more young Canadian scholars would do their graduate work in Canada rather than in the United States.

A library is, of course, the central learning resource for the humanities, and since this library was to serve the entire province of Ontario, a four- to five-million volume facility was decided upon. The provincial government provided the money—and the budget of $41.7 million was generous.

By the time the University got around to actually building the library, however, the great waves of student rebellion had broken upon Berkeley and Columbia, and Toronto felt the backwash. The idea of education as a positive value lost favor in the province, and voters began to resent being taxed for it. Many were demanding the increased Canadianization of

the construction business and opposing the outflow of cash to the United States. Because other provincial institutions of higher learning were expanding their library facilities, others questioned the need for a central facility of the size of Toronto's. University officials had begun to say: "We better build it quietly—with rubber hammers."

According to architect Toan: "It is a lesson of educational expansion, as well as of urban renewal, that it is difficult to establish goals over a long period of time when there is so much rethinking going on." The architects were working within a master plan prepared by John Andrews, which called for the con-

The building consists of a central triangle containing the main library with its reading rooms, technical services, stacks and carrels, a rare book wing and a library school. A fourth element, the auditorium, has not been built. The entire scheme is based upon a triangular module. The architects developed five basic schemes including the final triangulated *parti.* The latter was selected because it gave distinction as a special space to each of the principal elements—library, rare book wing, and school—and because the triangular shape as used in the main library generates a lot of interior space and exterior surface. Each stack floor (see section) has a perimeter of study cubicles—three stories of cubicles for each two floors of stacks. The rows of stacks are slanted in plan in such a way as to reveal their contents as one moves through the building. The stacks, therefore, have more of the appearance of accessibility, than is offered by right-angled placement.

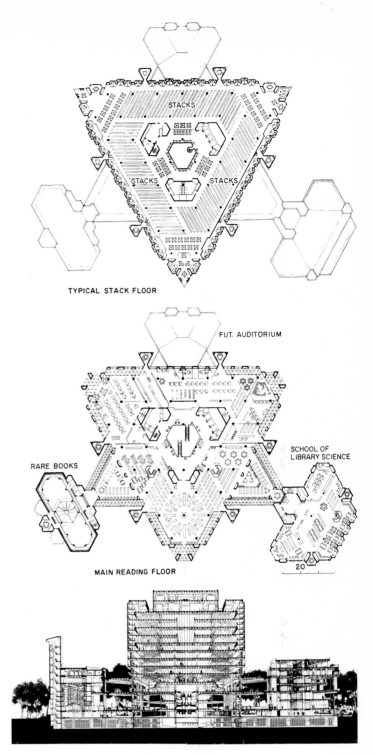

TYPICAL STACK FLOOR

FUT. AUDITORIUM

RARE BOOKS

SCHOOL OF LIBRARY SCIENCE

MAIN READING FLOOR

struction of a large number of buildings around the new library that were to be similarly massive in scale. A huge linear parking garage was to serve as a new campus wall to the west, and dormitories and two additional colleges were to have been built between the garage and the library. The architects envisioned a lot of movement toward and through the library from this direction. None of this development can now be expected to occur, and the library will appear stranded and out of scale with its 19th century surroundings for some time to come.

Unfortunately also, the entire project was bid approximately $½ million over the budget and the money was taken out of the site work.

As the rendering above indicates, the site had been contoured to provide a series of levels gently leading up and through the ground level of the building and on to the rest of the campus. Instead, an abbreviated stair was put in its place. The building now meets the ground in an awkward way and the idea of its becoming part of a larger circulation system has been abandoned for the present.

"If we had known the building was going to stand alone, we would have simplified it," said architect Toan. "But after all, we designed it in the sixties when surface treatments were less restrained." Actually the exterior expression of the library complex is more straightfor-

ward than not. Defined on the facades of the main library are the tiers of study carrels, the fire stairs and the multi-storied spaces.

Critics of the library assert that it is too large, too concentrated, that it should have been more open and accessible and that the books should be more readily available like paperbacks in a drugstore. To this Danforth Toan replies: "I am too old-fashioned to accept this. It is worth collecting human knowledge. It cannot be conveniently collected in a lot of small places. Smaller collections require the duplication of material because a single book may cut across a number of classifications. The scholar must not be asked to exam-

The library was constructed of poured-in-place concrete and precast concrete. It has been beautifully built for approximately $34 per square foot as bid in 1967. The ceilings throughout the structure are triangulated waffle slabs. The main floor (below) is completely open and can be entered from two sides. It contains reading rooms, a cafeteria and displays. This level interconnects with the rare book wing and the library school. The main reading room (left) is one of a series of multi-storied spaces of a scale and quality rarely to be found in a contemporary university facility. The rare book library has a magnificent central space (opposite page). Because of the nature of this collection, the books in this building are arranged in open galleries surrounding a high central space so that most of the collection is visible from the main floor.

JOHN P. ROBARTS RESEARCH LIBRARY FOR THE HUMANITIES AND SOCIAL SCIENCES, University of Toronto, Toronto, Ontario. Design consultants: *Warner, Burns, Toan, Lunde.* Architects: *Mathers and Haldenby.* Engineers: *C.D. Carruthers & Wallace* (structural); *H.H. Angus & Associates* (mechanical/electrical). General contractor: *Cape-Ryco.*

ine books which are widely dispersed. His whole process is one of filtering, sorting and accumulating. Do we provide for the scholarly mind? Is this too elitist? This is a decision society must make. At the University of Toronto, the decision was made on behalf of the scholar."

In response to the criticism that the library is too monumental Toan argues: "Well, it had to be monumental. It holds more than 50 million pounds of books and documents. I am glad they call it Fort Book. A library must be a stronghold of its own content. Books can't stand a lot of light or humidity. There is the problem of theft. Books are gold. The cost of that collection is three times the cost of the library complex itself."

CENTRAL LIBRARY, NEGEV UNIVERSITY

A strong sense that a building's form should be developed as sculpture is particularly appropriate in this project. The Library is the focal point of the large new Negev University which is currently under construction on the dry, flat plains near Beersheba (the site plan is below). The building is designed to both symbolize its function as a learning center and to provide a focus of visual interest on the monotonous terrain. Exposed concrete walls have been shaped to suggest a vessel for the storage of knowledge. The numerous skylights of the roof admit a diffused north light to the research and reading areas at the building's top. These cupola elements are built on a reinforced-concrete-shell principle, and are sheathed in white mosaic tile in contrast to the rougher texture below. They rest on steel beams whose minimal bulk allows a clear expression of their shape in the spaces below (photo opposite page, bottom).

When the University is complete, the library is intended to house a half million volumes and accommodate up to a thousand readers at one time (the spaces are presently divided by partitions to provide temporary classrooms). Users enter on the second level which is immediately below the reading room lit by the skylights. On this level are small-scale spaces required for administrative offices, card catalogues and lending services. Natural light and views are provided by horizontal slit-windows which—viewed from the exterior—emphasize the angled soffits of the projecting "vessel" above. At the same elevation as the entrance, a raised plaza for pedestrians is intended to connect all of the buildings and cover the vehicular-service circulation at grade. The first floor includes a cafeteria opening to a subgrade court, the mechanical rooms, truck dock and a bomb shelter. Circulation from the entrance to the various levels is gained by means of the stairs in one of the two towers on the south side of the building. Viewed from the exterior, these vertical elements form a strong contrast to the horizontal arrangement of the building's mass (extreme left of photo, opposite).

The reading room contains about half of the building's approximate 100,000 square feet, and is arranged in three main tiers like stairs whose slope follows that of the roof (see the section, top of the opposite page). The concept allows a separation of the various activities of research and reading on the individual levels, and—at the same time—maintains a sense of one large space. The books are stored in open stacks at the back of each tier, and are placed to allow the pursuit of the various sciences—each one to its own level, but visually related to those around it. The building is estimated to have cost $33 per square foot. The walls are structural concrete which was poured in place, and the foundations utilize spread footings.

THE CENTRAL LIBRARY OF THE NEGEV UNIVERSITY, Beersheba, Israel. Architects: *Nadler Nadler Bixon Gil.* Associated architect: *S. Amitai.* Engineers: *M. Lavie* (structural); *A. Zur* (soils); *Yani-Brau* (electrical & lighting). Landscape architect: *Yaron.* Library consultant: *N. Bargad.* General contractor: *Solel-Boneh Ltd.*

48

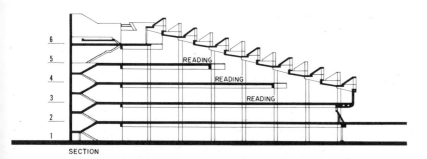

SECTION

6
5 READING
4 READING
3 READING
2
1

Bernheim-Schwerin

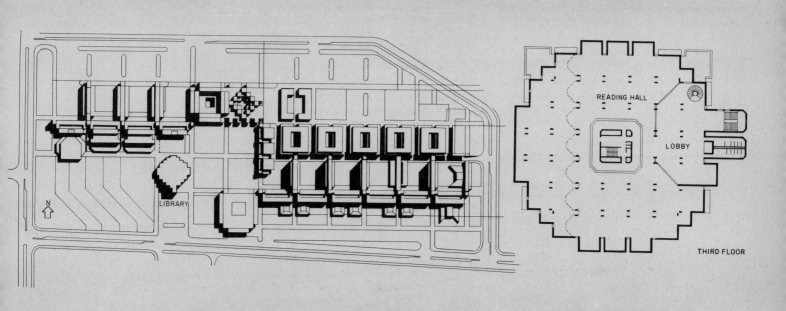

N

LIBRARY

READING HALL

LOBBY

THIRD FLOOR

Tougaloo College Library

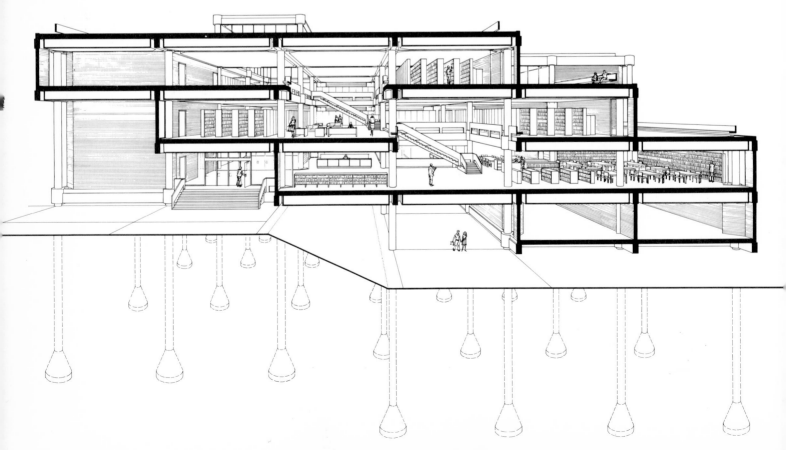

After several unsuccessful attempts to negotiate contracts for mass-produced precast components fabricated near Tougaloo and delivered to the site, the architects were put in contact with the Winston A. Burnett Construction Company, a firm which was then negotiating with a German building equipment supplier, Waldschmidt Systems of Hamburg, for a franchise for an industrialized construction plant. The Waldschmidt system, like many European mass production systems, is able to produce one-piece exterior and interior wall and floor elements, cast with all door, window and mechanical openings included. The Burnett Company needed an actual construction project to secure the franchise, and so an agreement was reached between it and Tougaloo College for a portable plant to be set up on the campus.

Thus in the spring of 1969 Gunnar Birkerts and Associates began final revisions on the dormitories and library, implementing the Waldschmidt techniques. Construction was to begin in the spring of 1970, but was delayed because of late shipping of equipment, difficulties in adapting it to local electrical supplies, and a longer setup time than had been expected (some of the equipment was involved in a dock strike).

The library embodies certain features that were not in the system used for the dormitories, because it required longer spans and much heavier floor loads. Here the system has a square bay, 30 feet by 30 feet. It is adaptable to a number of varying architectural requirements (section perspective, opposite), and it allows a free flow of mechanical systems through the entire structure. The system uses prestressed beams on all four sides of each bay; these rest in recessed seats in cylindrical precast column capitals. The capitals are doughnut-shaped, with hollow cores slightly smaller than the diameter of the columns. This design made it possible to tie together the reinforcing in the columns and beams, to fill the cores with grout, and thus to make the structure continuous.

The precast prestressed hollow-core floor planks are placed in checkerboard fashion; that is, they span in different directions in alternate bays. The result of this arrangement is that the beams on all four sides of most bays receive more or less equal loading. The beams themselves have an 8-foot by 15-inch opening mid-depth at mid-span; these openings allow mechanical equipment to pass from one bay to the next, and some of them can be seen in the interior photograph above, where they are used as registers.

The structural system allows interesting juxtapositions of one- and two-story bays, both inside and out. Inside on the main floor one ascends a stair through one two-story space and arrives at another on the second floor. From there one progresses to the third floor by means of another stair; here there is still another two-story space with a double-height window, which can be seen on the opposite page.

The library is the prototype building for the academic matrix in the over-all master plan for Tougaloo, just as the dormitory buildings are the prototypical residential facilities. All were finally dedicated in May, 1973. Eventually the library will be exclusively for study and research; for the time being it also doubles as a place for public assembly.

TOUGALOO COLLEGE LIBRARY, Tougaloo, Mississippi. Architects: *Gunnar Birkerts and Associates*—project director: *Charles Fleckenstein;* director of production: *Vytautas Usas;* director of field supervision: *Gunars Ejups.* Engineers: *Robert M. Darvas & Associates* (structural); *Hoyem Associates, Inc.* (mechanical/electrical). General contractor: *Frazier-Morton Construction Company.*

Balthazar Korab photos

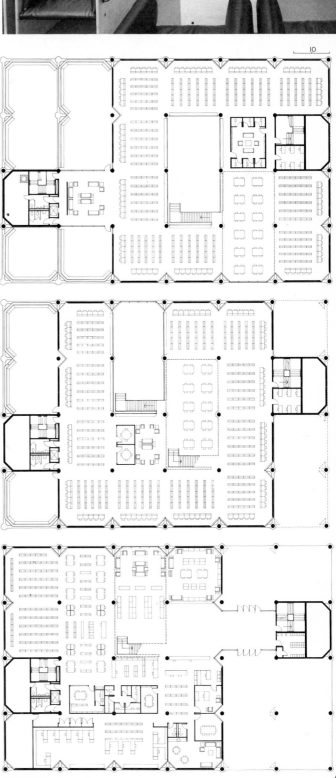

NORTHWESTERN UNIVERSITY LIBRARY

The site of the Core and Research Laboratory Library on the Evanston campus of Northwestern University is near the shore of Lake Michigan overlooking a large man-made lagoon, as shown in the photographs this page. Programmed to accommodate a so-called core-library (a collection of 50,000 basic books which are indispensible to each of the disciplines taught at the University) and a research collection of 1.2 million volumes, the new structure has a total interior net space of 329,941 square feet. Walter A. Netsch, SOM partner in charge of the library, sought a design solution which would minimize the apparent bulk of this huge structure to bring it into scale with the older Deering Library to which it is attached, and other adjacent campus buildings.

Netsch has described his basic solution as follows: "Sheltering and enclosing a broad plaza are three levels of three research towers (photos, plot plan and elevation this page), the octagonal entrance 'lantern' and Deering Library (photo opposite page). Beneath the plaza a single area exceeding 90,000 square feet has been devoted to cataloguing, reference, bibliography, periodicals, technical services, data processing, receiving new materials and administration. This space forms the main level and acts as a transitional base—physically as it connects to the Deering Library, and esthetically as a nodal interchange on the main north-south campus walk. This level functions as a walk interchange to the passive meadows of the lagoon and lakefront campus, and will eventually connect to a new complex which will include student services, art and music and the performing arts.

"The first level above the plaza contains those special group reader environments that logically participate on the plaza—the core library, the reserve collection, an assembly room, the poetry and audio-visual spaces and the student and coffee lounges. Reached by a separate stair from the entry lantern, each of these spaces can function independently of other library activities."

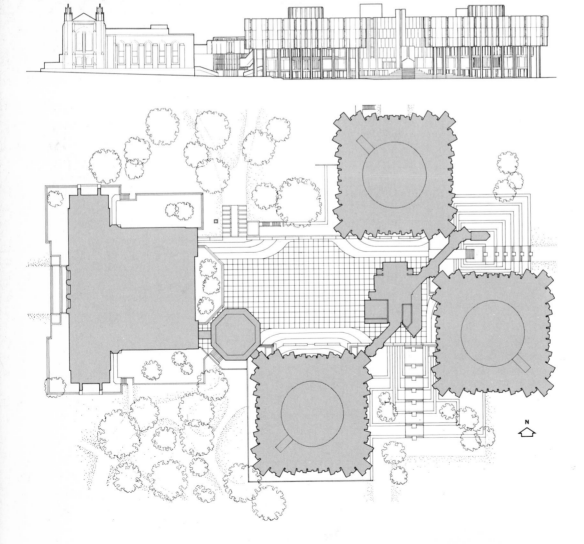

According to Netsch: "The programmatic forms (the seminar, study and carrel alcoves in the research collection); the combined orthogonal-radial column spacing; the relatedness of textured concrete and limestone to the older Deering Library all contribute discrete design elements to the exterior structure. The primary contribution, however, came from the combined common purpose of maximizing edge to give light to as many individual readers as possible and to give this immense library an over-all reader scale as a collection and as an object in the environment." The geometric variety and size of the columns and overhangs provide a sheltered foreground which emphasizes the lake and campus vistas. Netsch has designed the building, both inside and out, "to become at times an object, at other times a place, and at other times a continuous event. For all of this to happen, a building must be both used and perceived—fortunately a common set of goals for a library."

Netsch's plans for this building have a crystalline geometric beauty rarely found in the work of his contemporaries. Since the library was designed before Netsch had fully developed his now famous Field Theory, it is not a two- and three-dimensional lattice of interlocked rotated squares as his subsequent designs have been. The strong radial patterns formed by stack and study areas converging toward informal reading centers do prefigure the Field Theory, however, and represent an important step in its development. As in the Field Theory the geometries of this structure disallow the arbitrary and capricious. They appear to function superbly, as careful study of these plans will prove.

In each of the research towers the major collection is shelved in an environment of radial book stacks, which make search easier, and enclose readers in small private libraries, leaving the periphery of each collection to windowed carrels, conference seminars, faculty studies and future electronic recess centers. In the center of each floor is an informal seating area related to the search cycle.

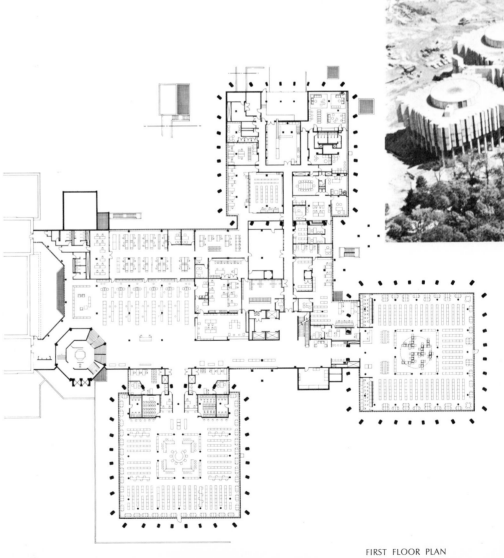

FIRST FLOOR PLAN

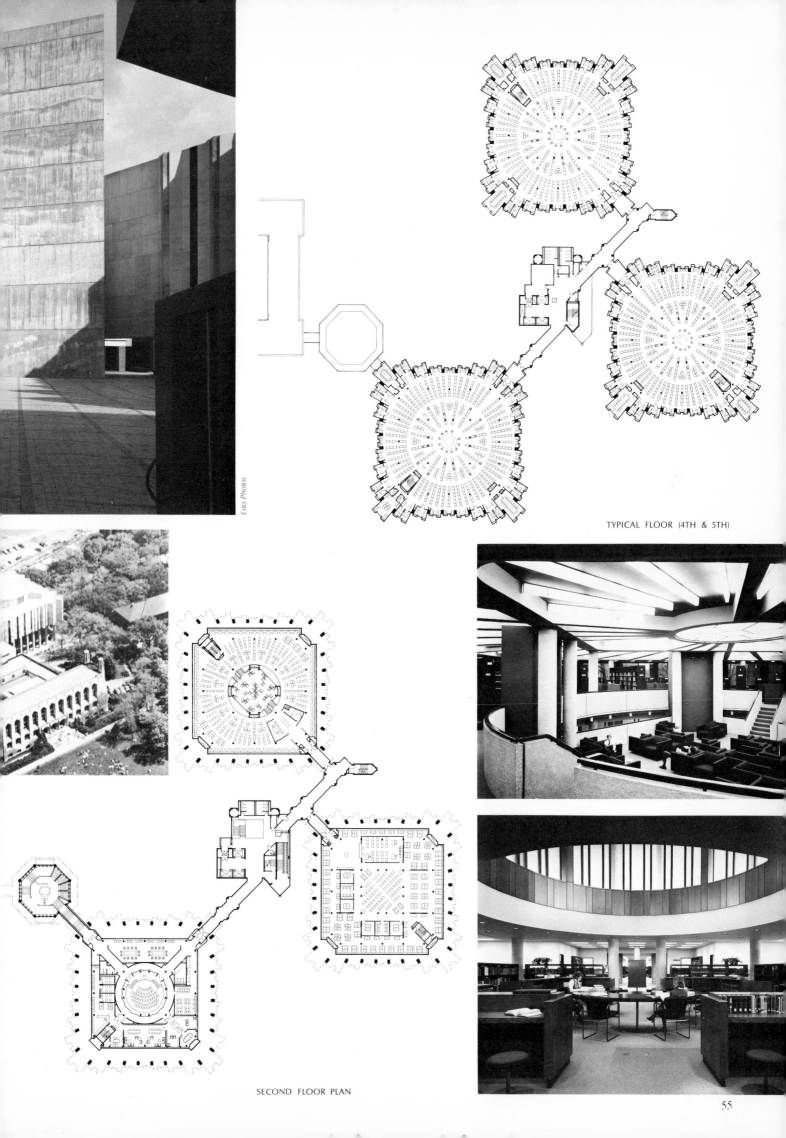

Esto Photos

TYPICAL FLOOR (4TH & 5TH)

SECOND FLOOR PLAN

55

Clarence L. Ver Steeg, chairman of the faculty planning and building committee, points out that the library is strongly user directed. Entering freshmen and distinguished scholars alike enjoy the same freedom of access to the collections and all library services and facilities in a setting conducive to the maximum integration of people and books. Private study and research space for undergraduate as well as graduate students is made possible by the individual seating at any given moment of 40 per cent of the undergraduates, 80 per cent of the graduate students in the sciences and the humanities, and more than 30 per cent of the social science and humanities faculty—an achievement unequaled in any other university library.

Because of the internal arrangement of carrels, group study rooms, faculty studies and typing and seminar rooms, each person can find the particular study environment he or she wishes. Each level of each tower not only provides for a close relationship between the user and the resources, but between different types of users—the undergraduate, graduate and faculty—thus fulfilling one of the principal academic goals of the library and university, the preservation of the sense of human scale in an intellectual environment which makes a community of scholars possible. The radial pattern of book stacks integrates the three types of users at the perimeter of each level of each tower by a planned sequence of seminar rooms, faculty studies and graduate and undergraduate carrels. This pattern is repeated 12 times in each research tower. Each level of each tower contains 120,000 volumes, and the three towers combined have more than 1,600 carrels. The three research towers include a total of 18 seminar rooms, 136 faculty studies, 50 faculty carrels and 18 typing rooms.

Corridors (right top) link the three towers. Here the inevitable change in noise level provides an aural break. Located in the corridors are exhibit spaces, book charge-out stations, elevators internal telephones and toilets. Staff work centers border the corridors.

Netsch's design team, including Robert D. Kleinschmidt, project designer for the interiors, developed a new type of library seating which consists of a complete line of chairs and stools of bronzed steel tubing enclosing a structural plastic seat shell supporting the special upholstery module. Two of these seating types appear in the photos (right and above right). Special carpets, tables and bentwood study carrels (above right) were also designed by SOM.

CORE AND RESEARCH LABORATORY LIBRARY, Northwestern University, Miller Campus, Evanston, Illinois. Architects and engineers: *Skidmore, Owings & Merrill, Chicago—Walter A. Netsch, partner-in-charge of design; Fred W. Kraft, partner-in-charge; Albert J. De Long, project manager; John Hartmann, project designer; Robert D. Kleinschmidt, project designer for interiors; Silvio J. Belmonte, project engineer; Contractor: Pepper Construction Company.*

MOUNT ANGEL ABBEY LIBRARY

Alvar Aalto's second American building is a library for a Benedictine monastery on a knoll in a quiet Oregon valley—far from his Finnish home and office, and from his other American building, Baker House at M.I.T., completed in 1947. The library at Mount Angel Abbey is, nevertheless, unmistakably Aalto. In the Aalto manner, there are recognizable trademarks: the visually simple handling of complex relationships; forms, like the fan-shaped plan of the library's reading rooms and stacks, and the curved skylight that floods this three-story space by day; details, like the parabolic roof wells which are light sources by day and by night; the use of natural wood in small-sectioned strips; and the white interior surfaces.

But most characteristic of all is the complete individuality of the solution based on the uniqueness of the building's requirements and of its site.

The site is remarkable and beautiful, an epitome of the ideal monastic situation. It is a wooded knoll (not unlike some of Finland's low wooded hills) rising several hundred feet above the farming fields of a peaceful valley, looking over the Willamette River valley to Mounts Hood, Adams, St. Helens and Rainier and, on the horizon, to the Coast Range on one side and the Cascade Range on the other. The monastery is, in effect, removed from the world but with and in full view of it. The site fits the Benedictine program of teaching and study (the

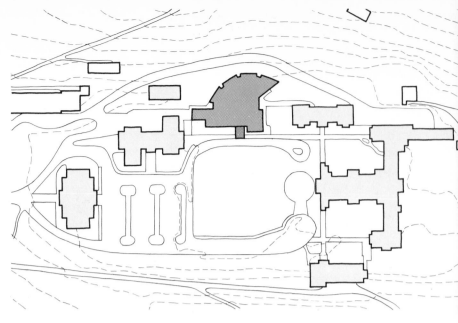

Abbey includes a college and a seminary) but its location within a few miles of Oregon's capital city, Salem, and within 50 miles of Portland, makes it accessible to a variety of cultural interests for which the Abbey hopes to become a focus. The new library building makes available for the first time its full collection of rare books, unique in the Northwest region, and through its planned audio-visual tape system brings discourses taped at distant places to scholars sitting in Mount Angel's carrels. It was the site, and the monks' appreciation of their responsibility for its sensitive development, along with the Benedictines' emphasis on a contemporary approach to the world, that led the monks to Aalto. His understanding of nature and his emphasis on man, exemplified in his statement of some years ago that "true architecture—the real thing—is only to be found when man stands at the center," was the basis on which they wrote to him in 1963, and in 1964 approved his appointment as architect for the library. At the time it seemed a rash act—or an act of faith—by both parties: neither knew where the money to build the building could come from. But in 1967 an anonymous donor gave a million dollars for its construction. With the Abbey's own funds, this made the $1,272,000 building a reality.

The important Abbey buildings are located on the crest of the knoll, and the library is entered from this level. Unlike the other buildings (designed in pseudo-romanesque) only the library's top floor is visible from the campus; the other two floors descend the hill into which the building fits. Approached from the campus, the library seems unpretentious and small scaled. Its calm and simple facade conflicts in no way with its neighbor buildings, recognizing only the color of their stone in its buff-colored brick. The tempered restraint of the exterior, however, gives no hint of the drama of the building's interior. The great three-story reading and stack area, flooded with daylight from a curving skylight at the

Edmund Y. Lee

roof, opens directly from the entry area. The carefully controlled light (from Aalto's familiar parabolic roof wells) in the lobby and entry emphasize the white walls and the quality of light in the multi-story space. From the control area there is visual surveillance of every part of this space. The line of the exterior wall is repeated in softened form by the curved balconies, and below the control area, on which reading and stack areas are located. Study carrels line the wall; reading desks, each with an Aalto-designed stool and lamp, range along the curve of the balcony. Stacks radiate like spokes from the center toward the outside wall. All furnishings are Aalto-designed.

The process of executing Aalto's design was considerably simplified by the appointment of DeMars and Wells of Berkeley, California, as executive architects, responsible for carrying out Aalto's concept and developing working drawings, and of American designer Erik Vartiainen who had worked for Aalto in Finland while schematics were being developed. Vartiainen represented Aalto in Berkeley during preparation of final drawings, and DeMars and Wells in Mount Angel during construction. In charge for the Abbey was Father Barnabas Reasoner, the Abbey librarian.

MOUNT ANGEL ABBEY LIBRARY, Saint Benedict, Oregon. Architects: *Alvar Aalto*, Helsinki, Finland; *Erik T. Vartiainen*, designer in charge for Alvar Aalto; *DeMars and Wells*, executive architects. Engineers: *S. J. Medwadowski*, structural; *Cooper-Clark & Associates*, foundation; *O'Kelly & Schoenlank*, electrical; *Walter Soroka*, acoustical consultant. Contractor: *Reimers & Jolivette*.

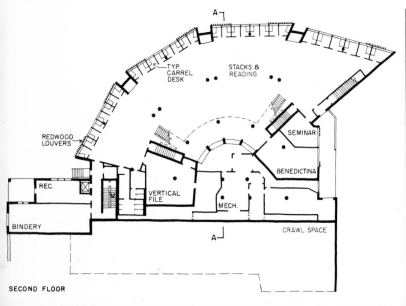

SECOND FLOOR

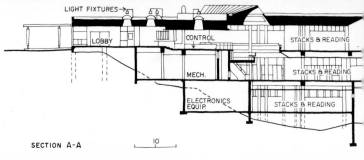

SECTION A-A

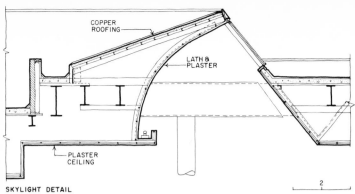

COPPER ROOFING

LATH & PLASTER

PLASTER CEILING

SKYLIGHT DETAIL

2

A free and natural use of wood was an early Aalto trademark, and at Mount Angel Library the tradition is continued. The furnishings, from study desks (right) and stack ends to radiant ceilings, make use of fir, birch, hemlock and oak. Wood window guard strips on the exterior, however, are of redwood. The door handles (left) of brass, like the desks and chairs, are Aalto-designed. Above the two story stacks and reading room area light from the curving skylight bounces off the deep cove to fill the area with daylight (detail above). Off the lobby, easily accessible to the public, is the rare book and meeting room, the Abbey's special means of inviting the world to its cultural events. Its undulating wall and ceiling of radiating fir strips recall such details in other Aalto buildings (below).

It has been said before that Rudolph's superb drawings so enchant the eye that one is diverted from the designs themselves into contemplation of the wonders of his draftsmanship. To counteract this tendency, it may be useful to set forth those attributes of his work which form its essential design content and which Rudolph himself considers most characteristic.

For him the site is a key consideration. His design is a response to the site and its environment. Where a strong environmental ambiance exists, he reinforces it. Where it does not, he creates it.

His concern with the environmental aspects of design leads him to freshly restate the design problem each time, and causes him to utilize a great variety of forms, scales and materials. His buildings are designed to be read from varying distances and from the air. Buildings are often dramatically articulated from story to story.

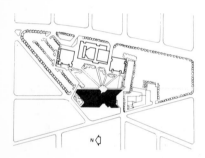

Clearly expressed and essentially simple structural systems are juxtaposed to specific elements such as stairs, elevators and mechanical and toilet shafts which have been elaborated as forms. In general, fixed elements are juxtaposed to more flexible generalized uses. The fixed elements often play a dual role acting as "hinges" and "joints" as his buildings sinuously move to follow a street pattern, turn a corner or form a plaza. Frequently these elements are used to lead the eye around the building. Such elements are essential means by which Rudolph manipulates scale. They take many shapes, thus a small conference room might be circular, elliptical, square, a rectangle or a triangle. Often the choice of shape becomes a highly personal one.

CENTRAL LIBRARY, NIAGARA FALLS

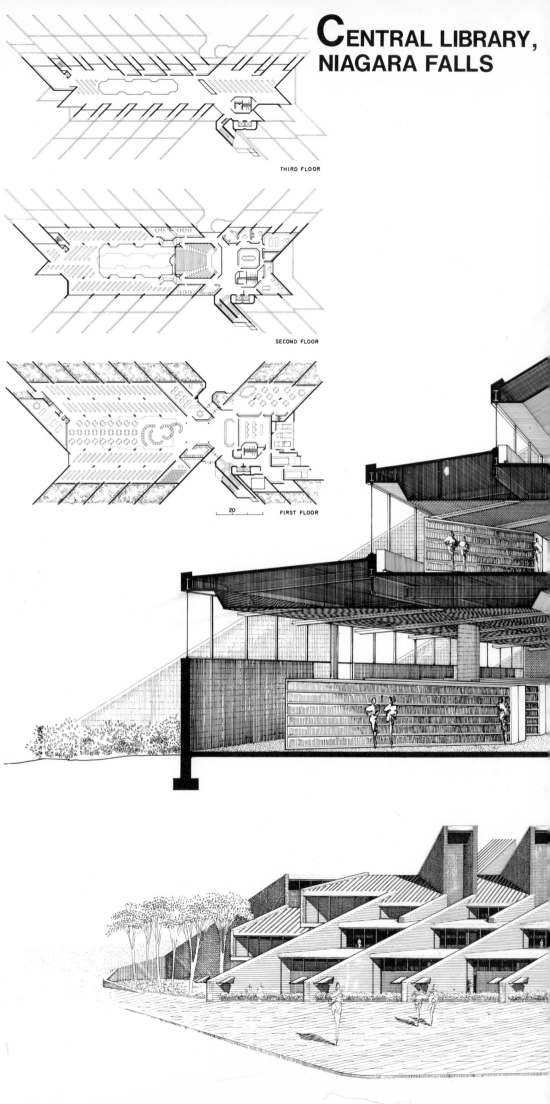

The lively exterior silhouette is created by clerestories which are angled in several directions to catch the natural light. Once inside the visitor is drawn to this higher and more brightly lit space. The book stacks are placed at angles to the main axis of the room, thereby exposing more books to the visitor. There are few columns in this space and no fixed walls, so that furniture, bookstacks and other equipment form the divisions of space. Terraces adjoin the building on its two long sides and are directly accessible from the main reading room.

The children's library is much more intimate, filled with small scaled spaces appropriate to children. A teaching and story hour room is included as a separate space. Access from the children's portion of the library to the main reading room has been clearly articulated, as an invitation to growing children to investigate the adult space and its books. The children's library includes a fireplace, separate areas for various children's activities and a flexible arrangement of interior space. The principal floor also contains shipping, loading, bookmobile, workroom and garage facilities.

The second and third floors have meeting rooms, offices, an auditorium seating 250 people, technical processing areas and closed stacks with carrels. This floor overlooks the main reading room space so that the sense of continuity of the library interior as a whole is maintained and the second floor also receives the shafts of light.

The building has a regular structural system with few partitions which cannot be relocated thus assuring maximum flexibility. Precast concrete is used inside and out.

CENTRAL LIBRARY, Niagara Falls N.Y. Owner: *The City of Niagara Falls, N.Y.* Architect: *Paul Rudolph;* structural engineer: *Lev Zetlin & Associates;* mechanical and electrical engineers: *Sherry Associates;* library consultants: *Charles M. Mohrhardt and Ralph A. Ulveling.*

GREENBURGH PUBLIC LIBRARY

A two-level public library can allow an effective separation of both the child and adult collections by putting each on its own floor, as in this suburban library in the New York City region. Designed to serve the needs of the town of Greenburgh for the next 20 years, it has a capacity of 125,000 volumes. The upper floor of the library, accessible directly from the upper level parking area by a "flying bridge," serves the needs of the adults and young adults; and the lower floor, the children. The adult collection of 85,000 volumes includes the reference library, magazine and new book selection, bibliography, science, history, fiction, business and industry collection and periodicals. The seating and browsing areas are separated by bookshelves. The audio-visual section, also located on the upper floor, contains microfilm files, records and tapes. An area next to the main entrance is reserved for art exhibits. The lower level, houses the children's collection of 50,000 volumes.

GREENBURGH PUBLIC LIBRARY, Greenburgh, New York. Owner: *Town of Greenburgh—Nicholas Russo, supervisor.* Client: *Greenburgh Public Library Board of Trustees—Leon B. Siwek, chairman.* Architects for building design, interior design, furnishings and equipment, graphics and landscape: *Max O. Urbahn Associates, Inc.—Max O. Urbahn, president and chief executive officer; Philip F. Moyer, executive vice president; Martin D. Stein, vice-president and director of design; Ronald Gower, designer.* Consultants: *Wenning Associates* (engineering); *Francis St. John* (library). Contractor: *Romani & Picco, Inc.*

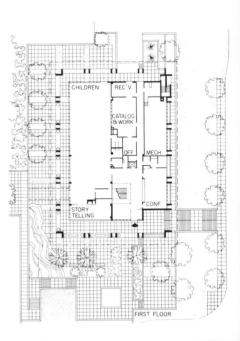

FIRST FLOOR

SECOND FLOOR

The second floor adult level (above) is a well-scaled space subdivided by shelving into small, comfortably sized reading areas. The children's level (right) has chairs, tables, bookshelves and book cradles scaled to the height and size of young readers. The remainder of the lower level consists of a staff room, receiving area, the cataloguing and work area, toilets, elevator, mechanical equipment room, shops and other ancillary facilities. Not shown is the history room which houses various books and objects depicting the history of the town. It also serves as a meeting room for the community.

The construction cost of this 23,000 square foot library was $811,000 or a little over $35 per square foot. The total cost including furniture and landscaping was $1.2 million.

TRENT UNIVERSITY LIBRARY

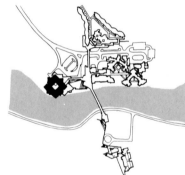

B

The Library and the University Court in front of it (A) are central to the campus as now completed, and will continue to be the main focus as new colleges are built. University Court (C) is considered the major outdoor space of the campus; it is tiered and shaped with its system of steps to provide various directional views and focuses, and may be used for large gatherings. A walkway at the third level (B) leads into a part of the library and serves as a gallery to University Court below. The library sits almost in the water (E), and there is access to the river from the ground level of the library. The principal material of the library is the large-aggregate concrete used on Champlain College, with smooth concrete used for the louvers, horizontal spandrels, and sun shades. The main stair (D) begins at the second level and leads up to the stack areas at levels three and four.

The library plan (right) has been generated by taking two squares equal in size and rotating one 45 degrees to the other, so that eight "corners" are exposed equally on the exterior. One of the implied squares within the library plan has its four corners shattered into many interlocking turns, forming the stairwells, air shafts, and louvered windows. On the exterior, these corners appear as solid masses in the composition, their primary characteristics being permanence—solid, muscular walls of giant aggregate reinforced concrete—and verticality—the concrete walls continuing uninterrupted from one floor to the next, with rhythmic vertical louvers running from ground to roof. The exposed corners of the other implied square are strongly stated in plan as simple 90-degree turns, and its walls are primarily glass, not concrete. In elevation this plan element is expressed in sweeping horizontal lines, thin and delicate, with wafer-like overhanging sun shades. Both squares, in plan, have been rotated about a central stairwell, itself a square, and this stairwell focus is expressed on the exterior by a large glass and concrete skylight. The main entrance to the library is on the second level directly off University Court. On the first level are listening rooms, rare books, duplication machinery and storage, and the first level spaces run underneath the full extent of University Court above.

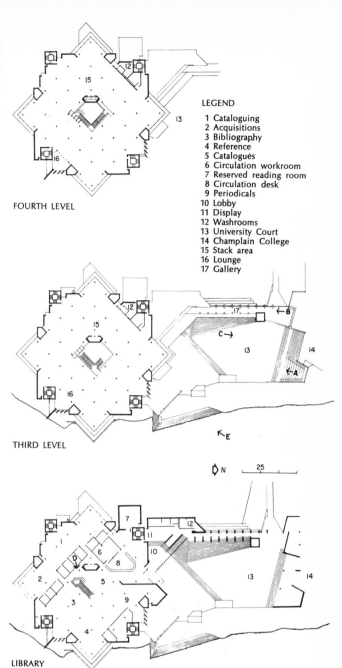

FOURTH LEVEL

LEGEND

1 Cataloguing
2 Acquisitions
3 Bibliography
4 Reference
5 Catalogues
6 Circulation workroom
7 Reserved reading room
8 Circulation desk
9 Periodicals
10 Lobby
11 Display
12 Washrooms
13 University Court
14 Champlain College
15 Stack area
16 Lounge
17 Gallery

THIRD LEVEL

LIBRARY
SECOND LEVEL

TRENT UNIVERSITY, Peterborough, Ontario. Architects: *Thompson Berwick Pratt & Partners—Ron Thom, partner-in-charge of design; Paul Merrick, design architect; Peter Smith and Alastair Grant, project architects; Dick Sai-Chew, supervising architect; Caroline Souter, interiors.* Structural: *M. S. Yolles and Assoc. Ltd.;* Mechanical and electrical ,for Chemistry, Library, & Champlain: *R. E. Crossey & Assoc. Ltd.;* Mechanical, Lady Eaton: *G. Granek & Assoc.;* Electrical, Lady Eaton: *Jack Chisvin & Assoc.;* Site services: *James MacLaren Ltd.*

LIBRARY RESOURCE CENTER, WRIGHT STATE UNIVERSITY

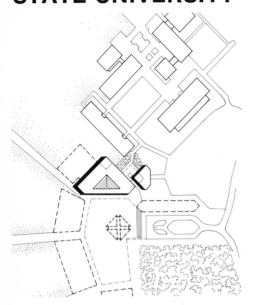

Wright State University is an emerging campus outside Dayton and Hisaka's commission was for a Library-Resource Building to serve as the first increment of a multi-building University Center. The triangular plan he developed is an architectural resolution of axes laid down in the master plan which foresees a radial growth pattern around the future University Center (see site plan).

The program required housing a substantial collection of books as well as audio-visual equipment, language courses, and several radio and television studios. These media elements are housed separately in a small structure to the north and connected to the library underground—part of a below-grade circulation system that will link the whole campus.

The main structure is kept relatively open at grade. Students flow through the building to other campus destinations or enter the library through two control points. The main reading room (see cover) is on the second level. Three stories high and sheathed in glass, it faces the University Center site and provides the large volume against which all the smaller volumes can effectively play. These small volumes, tucked under balconies, contain catalog and reference areas as well as stacks. These stack areas respond to the program by placing six subject divisions on three levels.

As in the case of the buildings that follow, the Library-Resource Building at Wright State is poured-in-place, reinforced concrete with a handsome level of interior finish. And like the others, its massing and siting make a clear assertion of its importance in the university community. Budgeted at $4.5 million, construction was completed for about $3.9 million—or just over $34 per square foot.

LIBRARY-RESOURCE CENTER, Wright State University, Dayton, Ohio. Architects: *Don M. Hisaka & Associates with Lorenz, Williams, Lively & Likens.* Engineers: *Lorenz, Williams, Lively & Likens* (structural); *Heapy & Associates* (mechanical and electrical). Contractor: *Frank Messer & Sons Construction Company.*

George Cserna photos

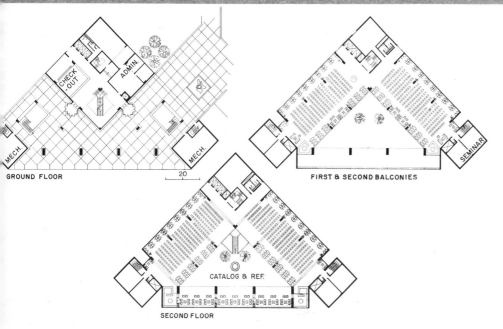

GROUND FLOOR

CHECK OUT

ADMIN.

MECH.

MECH.

20

FIRST & SECOND BALCONIES

SEMINAR

CATALOG & REF.

SECOND FLOOR

CHAPTER TWO

ART
MUSEUMS

Villa Museum

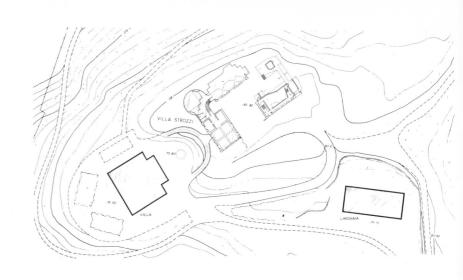

One of the more unusual projects in Richard Meier's (or anyone's) office is this Museum of Modern Art for the City of Florence, Italy. It is planned in a way that may make strict preservationists shudder—but it is completely within the new spirit of building modern facilities that respect the visual richness provided by older buildings. There is to be a whole new architectural entity here, incorporating two existing walls of the stables of the 19th century Villa Strozzi. The old walls will visually tie the new building to a nearby structure, which is being restored by architect Hans Hollein, and will respect the existing relationship of the stable to the courtyard and courtyard-approach views (see site plan left).

Tradition is respected without fakery—illustrating that the best of the old and new can be integral, when there is something of value left with which to start. As can be seen in the photo of the existing building (overleaf, top), the walls to be saved were regarded by Meier as they were by the original Villa architect, Guiseppe Poggi, as an independently important part of the original structure—for Poggi, a screen to hide the lesser building behind. Meier has taken great care to match his new materials to those of the original building, which was constructed of a dark gray stone (and later covered with stucco, which will be removed in the new work).

The Museum is to be a carefully articulated frame for the older walls, which are presented as sculpture. At the same time, the walls provide an anchoring solid mass, against which Meier has always generated his freely flowing public spaces. The heavy wall itself takes the place in the composition of strongly defined spaces. The visitor passes through (or in this case, around) a confining introduction to the spatial drama beyond. The main room of the museum is to be a multilevel space, connected by ramps (between the second and third levels) to a remote exhibition space (lower level in the photo left). Visitors will be confronted with far more visual interest than the paintings on the walls: alternating solid and transparent wall-planes will provide surprise views of Florence in the distance, as well as of the exhibition hall, all from various elevations and angles. The two separate building volumes will provide additional views toward and into each other.

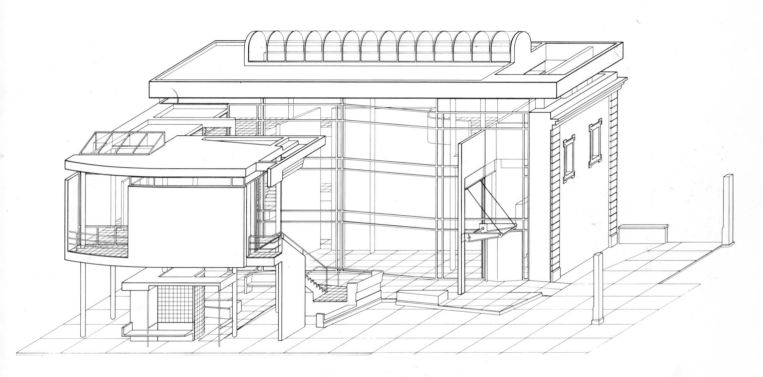

Contained within two existing walls of a stable, this new exhibition gallery will have spiraling-loop circulation between the balcony levels in the main hall and the floor of the secondary gallery. The latter is projected from the large building to form an enclosure for the adjacent courtyard (see site plan, opposite page, top). It is reached by a ramp, in a connecting neck, from the second level of the main room. Another sloped ramp, located alongside, leads visitors to the top balcony in the main room and the end of the circuit. Much of the light will be natural, introduced by skylights and the glass walls, most of which face north. The structure is steel with a rectangular grid of round columns that belies the planned visual complexity, and gives a lightweight appearance, in contrast to the visual weight of the existing walls.

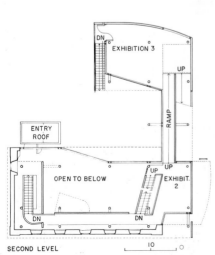

SECOND LEVEL

Existing building and models for new structure showing relationship of walls and courtyard.

VILLA STROZZI, for Florence, Italy. Architect: *Richard Meier.*

DENVER MUSEUM

Unusual and provocative in design and plan, exceptional in its functional clarity, the lively new Denver Art Museum Building by James Sudler Associates of Denver and Gio Ponti of Milan, Italy, breaks with tradition in both museology and architectural expression to provide a 79-year-old institution—the only major museum in the mountain region—with the first real means of displaying its extensive collections of art and artifacts.

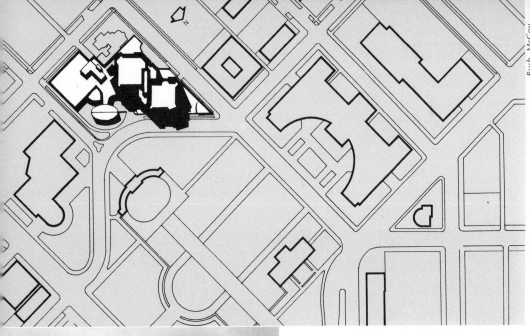

Neither James Sudler of Denver nor Gio Ponti of Milan had known each other before the opportunity developed for collaboration on the design of the new building for the Denver Art Museum. The museum board, mindful of its need to get popular support for building the museum (which had never had a proper building) and to raise funds for the project, wanted to add the prestige of an international name to that of its local architectural firm, James Sudler Associates. Sudler chose Gio Ponti, partly because he greatly admired the Pirelli Building, partly because of Ponti's wide and long architectural experience. Neither difference in language nor in generation interfered with the collaboration. In four intensive visits to the Ponti studio in Milan, Sudler and Joal Cronenwett, his partner, absorbed the Ponti philosophy and fused it with the program requirements and the museological theories of Otto Karl Bach, the museum's vital director for the last 27 years. Dr. Bach's request that only artificial light be used for displays played easily into a Ponti axiom: when there are only facades to design, make a composition of openings. Although no openings were needed, windows of varied sizes and shapes are used in a highly sophisticated pattern, cunningly and with great artistry designed to suggest, but not to describe, the interior spaces. In plan, the building seems to be two cubes joined by a core element. In elevation, however, it is a multiplanar structure of inexplicit geometry, tantalizingly

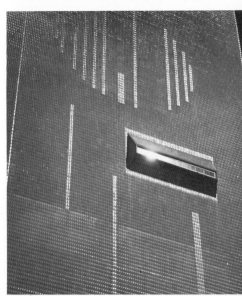

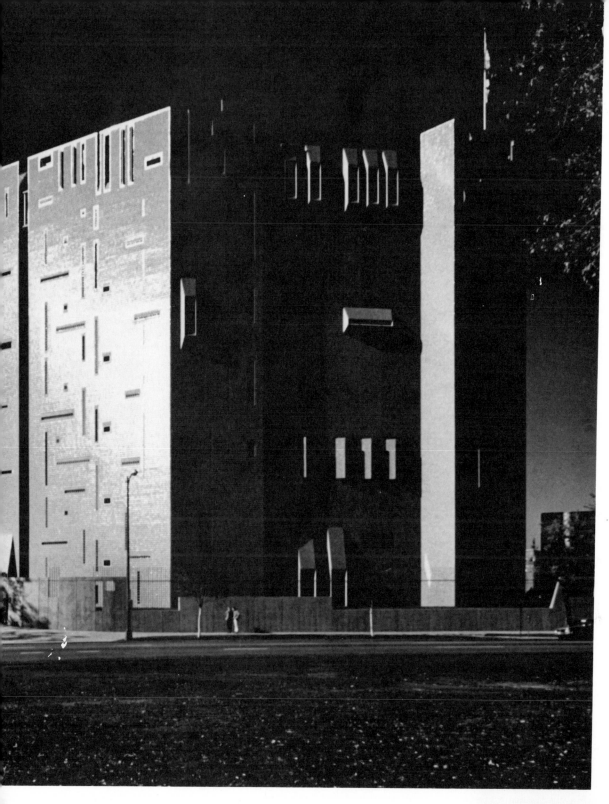

The new museum is part of Denver's civic center complex, and its entrance—an open-ended stainless steel tube with glass doors—faces the park around which the buildings are located. Exterior wall surfaces are faced with special glass tile, used instead of Ponti's more usual ceramic tile which proved unsuited to Denver's extremes of heat and cold. The gray tile are in two shapes: pyramidal for general use, and flat to define edges of planes and to create patterns in large unbroken wall areas. They are handset, an undercut on each side holding each securely in the mortar bed. (See drawing.)

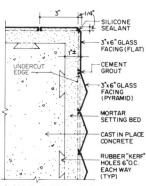

GLASS TILE INSTALLATION DETAIL

Wayne Thom

Rush McCoy

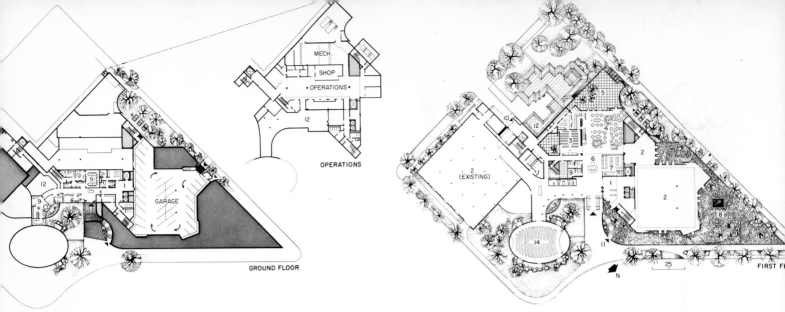

GROUND FLOOR

OPERATIONS

FIRST FI

N   25

Technical provisions are important: the environment is kept at a constant 40 per cent relative humidity; an ionization detector system is sensitive even to match smoke; all windows are double-glazed, dark reflective glass inside, clear glass outside. Inch-thick plastic foam, glued on the

OPEN GALLERY		
GALLERY	6	ROOF, FUT. RESTAURANT
GALLERY	5	GALLERY
GALLERY	4	GALLERY
GALLERY	3	GALLERY
GALLERY	2	GALLERY
GALLERY	M	
LOBBY	I	CHANGING EXH.
ADMIN.	A	GARAGE
OPER.	O	
EXIST. GALLERY		

20

concrete walls, provides both vapor barrier and thermal insulation. Ponti's desire for "nocturnal architecture" is acknowledged in concealed neon strips which light some of the vertical panels at night, augmenting the patterns formed by the lighted windows. The building has the height over-all of a 10-story structure but since its floor-to-floor height is 17.6 feet, it actually contains seven floors.

Wayne Thom

Wayne Thom

Rush McCoy

Wayne Thom

but indefinably, reminiscent of something medieval and most particularly provocative in its utter unrelatedness to anything in Denver's past or present.

Eleven galleries were needed for the museum's extensive collections of American Indian, medieval and Oriental art. The small site would not have permitted the typical horizontal solution, but since Dr. Bach wanted no skylights, stacking the galleries presented no problem; in fact, it offered an almost unique opportunity to design as directly for the viewer as for the viewed. The galleries, two to a floor, are each 10,-000 square feet in area, exhibit space that can be seen by the average viewer in 45 minutes (the average attention span for museum-goers). Each gallery is directly accessible from the elevator lobby, and with only two galleries per floor, the visitor always knows where he or she is, and can easily and quickly go from entrance to gallery. Elevator lobbies, light and airy, contrast with the galleries, where a low level of illumination is used. Lighting equipment is exceptionally flexible.

THE DENVER ART MUSEUM, Denver, Colorado. Architects: *James Sudler Associates—James S. Sudler, Joal Cronenwett;* and *Gio Ponti—John M. Prosser,* project drawings; *Douglas I. Johansen,* administration; *William D. Webb,* inspection. Consultants: *Gio Ponti (Studio Ponti, Fornaroli, Roselli, Milan, Italy),* design; *Sudler Monigle Cronenwett Inc.,* graphics; *Duane Newlin & Associates,* kitchen. Engineers: *Andersen, Koerwitz & Hawes, Inc.,* structural; *Woodward-Clyde,* foundation; *Francis Stark, Lynn Wray,* mechanical; *Swanson-Rink & Associates,* electrical. Landscape architect: *Jane Silverstein Reis.* General contractors: (Phase I) *Mead & Mount Construction Co.;* (Phase II—Interiors, floors 3-6) *Berglund-Cherne Co.*

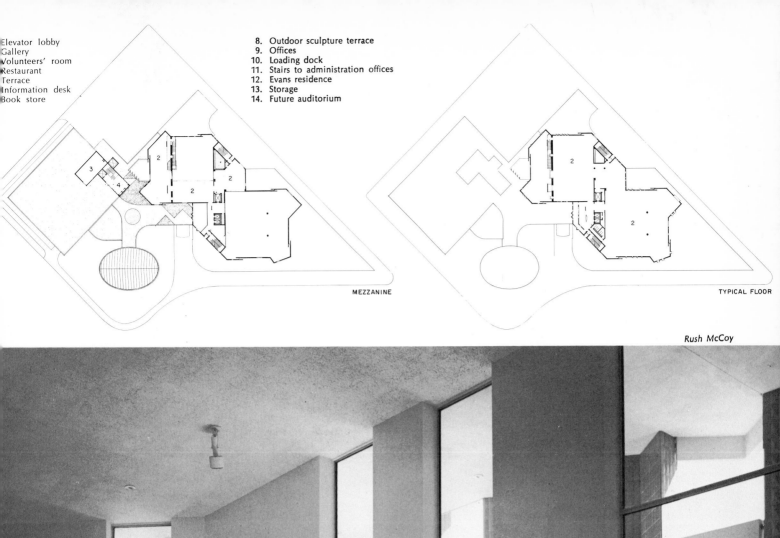

Elevator lobby
Gallery
Volunteers' room
Restaurant
Terrace
Information desk
Book store

8. Outdoor sculpture terrace
9. Offices
10. Loading dock
11. Stairs to administration offices
12. Evans residence
13. Storage
14. Future auditorium

MEZZANINE

TYPICAL FLOOR

Rush McCoy

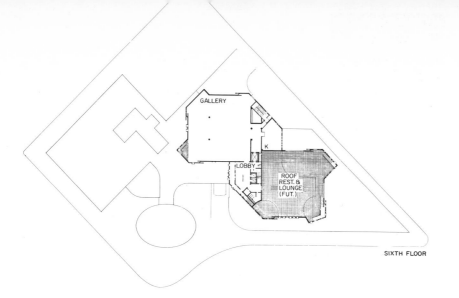

GALLERY

K

LOBBY

ROOF
REST. &
LOUNGE
(FUT.)

SIXTH FLOOR

The restaurant on the first floor (designed to double as exhibit space if needed) opens on a sheltered outdoor terrace on the sunny south side of the building. The three hooded openings are doors to the terrace; vari-shaped windows flood the interior of the restaurant with daylight. Floors two through five are typical in arrangement; the sixth contains only one gallery. The rest of its area is reserved for a rooftop viewing area and, eventually, a members' lounge and restaurant. The openings in the high parapet are unglazed, emphasizing the shell-like character of this part of the wall. In two places, great arcs are cut to provide panoramic views of the city and the Rocky Mountains.

Rush McCoy

Wayne Thom

MUSEUM WEST

This small space, a temporary West Coast annex for the American Craftsman's Council, defers gracefully to the objects it displays except in the plane overhead where a three-dimensional steel grid asserts itself vigorously. The museum's only powerful architectural element, this grid provides flexible, inexpensive support for hanging displays with minimum visual interference.

The museum's small scale and simplicity of plan combine to facilitate easy, loosely directed circulation and eliminate the "labyrinth-itis" so often experienced by visitors to larger museums. Walls are exposed brick, painted white and carpeting is a soft brown sisal.

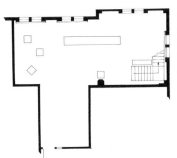

MUSEUM WEST, San Francisco, California. Architect: *James Leefe* of *Leefe & Ehrenkrantz*. Mechanical Engineer: *G. A. Gendler*. Electrical engineer: *Stanley Anderson*. Contractor: *Victor McKinnon*.

Rondal Partridge photos

KASELOWSKY MUSEUM

An impressive museum set in a small park in Bielefeld, Germany, achieves the air of a protecting, but inviting, treasure house for art. The bearing walls of the granite-clad, concrete structure are emphasized inside and out—giving pattern and modulation to the exterior, and generating basic, fixed gallery spaces on the interior. A series of carefully placed garden walls extend the building horizontally for a close link with the park. Three above-grade floors are exhibit spaces. The lower floors contain service areas, library and lecture hall. All exhibit floors are similar, but the third floor is windowless for added hanging space.

RICHARD KASELOWSKY MUSEUM, Bielefeld, Germany. Architect: *Philip Johnson*. Associate architect: *Architekt Professor Casar F. Pinnau*. Engineers: *Jaros, Baum & Bolles* (mechanical); *Severud, Perrone, Sturm, Conlin, Bandel* (structural). Acoustics: *Bolt Beranek & Newman*; graphics: *Elaine Lustig Cohen*; lighting: *Jack Kilpatrick*.

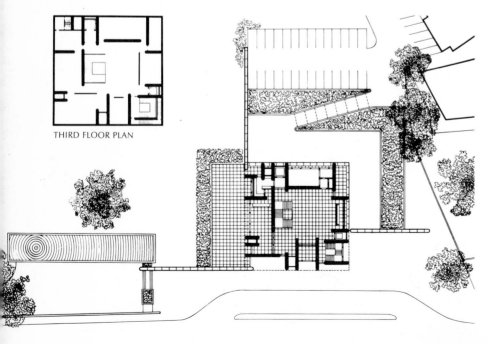

THIRD FLOOR PLAN

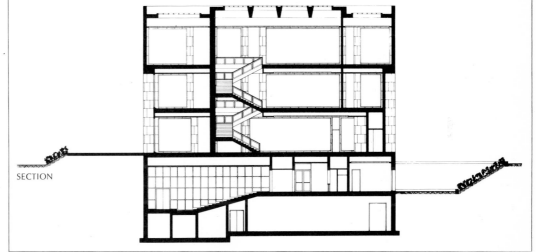

SECTION

As an extremely pleasant place for people, as well as art, the main level of the museum opens directly on a series of terraces and a long pool (right). The top floor of the building is windowless, but skylighted. A depressed area at the back of the building provides well-screened and convenient access for deliveries and service. As in many of Johnson's museums, the display walls on the interior are surfaced with carpet to permit rearrangement of the exhibits without visible damage to the walls. The three upper floors are linked by an open stairwell.

Maeght Foundation Addition

The arts destined to meet in the original Maeght Foundation in Saint Paul de Vence, completed in 1964, were, most prominently, painting, sculpture and architecture. The painters and sculptors included Braque, Miró, Chagall, Giacometti, and Calder, and their works were meant not merely to be housed in and around the museum, but actively to become a part of it. The architect was Josep Lluis Sert, and the patron was Parisian gallery owner Aimé Maeght.

All that was ten years ago. Now it has come time to construct a second phase of the *Fondation Maeght*. Anticipated from the beginning, this extension continues the original format of a series of simple brick-walled enclosures lit from above by whitewashed concrete light scoops. But the second phase is also influenced by a decade's working experience, and by a demonstrated need for facilities for festivals, conferences, musical performances, ballets, and movies—a need, as Sert puts it, for "more changeable, active and animated spaces," where not only the arts but the arts and people can meet in concert.

ADDITION TO THE MARGUERITE AND AIMÉ MAEGHT FOUNDATION, Saint Paul de Vence, France. Architects: *Sert, Jackson and Associates.* Associated Architects: *Bellini Lizero and Gozzi.*

Pierre Joly-Véra Cardot

Steve Rosenthal

Claude Gaspari

The small photograph above left shows a doorknob designed by Giacometti for the first phase of the Maeght Foundation. Immediately left is one of the galleries built in the first phase, and below is one of the informally landscaped lawns, populated by an Alexander Calder sculpture.

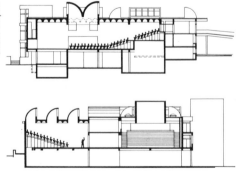

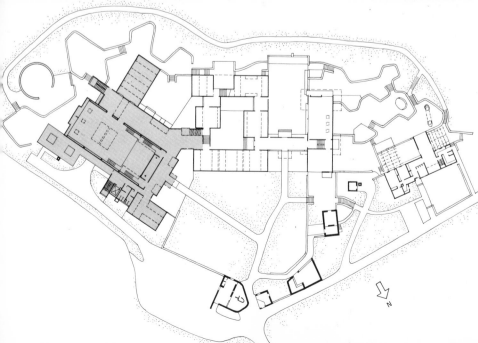

A model of the Maeght Foundation, phases I and II, is shown above and immediately below; the shaded portion of the plan on the left is phase II.
The principal room in this addition, designed for use as a multi-purpose auditorium and exhibition space, is shown in the sections on the opposite page.

Steve Rosenthal

87

RENWICK GALLERY

The Renwick Gallery was begun in 1859 as the original Corcoran Gallery of Art. Before it could open it was seized by the Union Army quartermaster corps for use as a Civil War clothing warehouse and did not open as an art gallery until 1871. Later the collection was moved to the present Corcoran Gallery and in 1899 the building became the U.S. Court of Claims.

When the Court moved out in 1964, the building stood crumbling. In the same year, John Carl Warnecke's firm had produced a feasibility study of the restoration and rehabilitation of Lafayette Square. Included in the study was the old Court of Claims, which had been retained as a stylistic complement to the Executive Office Building across the street. (Both are excellent adaptations of the French Second Empire style which architect James Renwick used for the first time in the United States in his design for this building.) Warnecke's firm urged that the old Court of Claims be returned to its original function, that of an art gallery.

In 1965 President Johnson approved the transfer of the building to the Smithsonian and restoration began shortly thereafter. Warnecke's firm made the basic interior renovations, replacing the plumbing, wiring, heating and ventilating systems, as well as strengthening the structure in critical areas and removing the various partitions installed by the Court of Claims.

More than a century of weathering had obliterated more than 90 per cent of the original exterior ornament. A joint research team staffed by Warnecke and Universal Restoration Inc. researched various archives to find illustrations of the lost ornamentation, and succeeded in uncovering in the Library of Congress photos taken by Matthew Brady, as well as Renwick's original drawings. Hand-carved models were made from blow-ups of the drawings and photos and latex molds were made from these. The new exterior ornamentation is actually a cast composite containing crushed particles of the previously removed stonework, which blends extremely well in color and texture with the older portions of the building.

Hugh Newell Jacobsen & Associates won the commission to further restore the interior in the spirit of Renwick's time. It has been refurbished with period furniture of the last third of the 19th century. Several of the rooms including the Grand Salon (opposite page) and the Octagonal Room (overleaf) are designed as permanent exhibitions. The paintings in the Grand Salon include many which were displayed there almost a century ago when the building served as the original Corcoran Gallery. The works are on loan from the new Corcoran.

The Renwick has no collections of its own. In addition to the two great rooms which are its permanent displays, it holds design exhibitions of all kinds.

Many years elapsed from the time architect James Renwick finished his design for the original Corcoran Gallery of Art to its completion as a museum, and during this period he had gone out of fashion as an architect. While he was responsible for shaping the noble interior spaces of the gallery, he subsequently had little influence on the interior finishes of the building or the selection of furnishings. Nonetheless, even without the Renwick touch, the 19th century interiors of the Corcoran represented the epitome of the taste of the time. Architect Hugh Jacobsen's task was not to reproduce these interiors but to evoke them, which he has done with great skill. In the process he came to admire Renwick's ingenious manipulation of scale. "Renwick wanted to make the person smaller, the building grander" says Jacobsen. "Although 8 inch baseboards are customary, some of Renwick's are 14 inches. His chair rails are not all at the usual 36 inches. Some are 30, 48 or even 52 inches." The main foyer and stairs (opposite page, above) have the dark brown wainscoting, light beige walls and ochre trim which was typical of the period. The stair leads directly to the Grand Salon (above). In this room, which is also used for presidential receptions for dignitaries staying at the adjacent Blair House, the paintings are hung on plum colored walls in tiers, just as they were over one hundred years ago. The gigantic urns are from the Philadelphia Centennial Exposition of 1876. Unlike the Grand Salon and the Octagonal Room (overleaf), the remaining galleries will not be restored to their past grandeur as permanent exhibitions in themselves but will be used for changing exhibits (opposite page, bottom left). Such rooms are painted in white or light tones and their moldings and other architectural details are not emphasized by color accents as they are elsewhere. These rooms are high-ceilinged, spacious, and filled with daylight.

The Octagonal Room (above) is centered on the main staircase opposite the Grand Salon which can be seen in the photo (above left) taken from the Octagonal Room. The latter space is directly above the entrance foyer and its dome is expressed on the exterior by the central, curved mansard roof. Befitting its importance in the overall spatial hierarchy of the building, including its axial relationship with the Grand Salon, it too has received full and elegant restoration to the gilded age. By deliberate contrast, the stairhall itself, like the foyer below is of a subdued beige color, its ornament accented only by a change to ochre. The bottom photograph was taken soon after the old Court of Claims moved out and just before renovation.

Garvan Galleries, Yale University

Once a work of art was thought to be an artifact which at its creation passed out of time and accident into a realm where it stood alone, independent, unique and timeless. Once the perception of a work of art was thought chiefly to involve a dialogue between the imagination of the beholder and the object hanging on a wall or standing on a pedestal. It was all very private, and a little hermetic. Now it is also passé, for our presumptions have changed, and the displaying as well as the creation of art has come actively to include art's environment—its relation to other art and to culture as well as its independence from them, its timeliness as well as its timelessness. Thus openness and accessibility have become buzz words even for museum curators, taking their place alongside traditional passions for accessions, deaccessions, provenances and bequests. The headlong rush to win the with-it prize has produced some notable catastrophies, jeered by professionals and laymen; but the impulse to understand and to experience art as an intelligible cultural activity is not silly, and in one way or another it underlies all of the successful designs for display shown on the following pages.

Norman McGrath

The permanent exhibition of American art shown on this and the opposite page has been set up in a rambling series of Beaux-Arts rooms in the old Yale Art Gallery, which was designed by Egerton Swartwout and completed in 1928 (and to which the more famous gallery of 1953 by Louis I. Kahn is an addition). These once grand and ample rooms have now been divided by more or less freestanding partitions into exhibition spaces that are smaller, brighter and cozier, and that are meant to encourage close and detailed study of the objects on display, with the aid of information from extensive labels, motion pictures and slide shows. "The goal of this exhibit," says Charles F. Montgomery, curator of this part of Yale's collection, "is to create an exciting teaching museum and to do what a good teacher does—to stimulate and excite the student (and the public); to see each thing in relation to its fellows in time and space; to see art objects individually and collectively as manifestations of the culture and creativity that is America."

THE MABEL BRADY GARVAN GALLERIES OF THE YALE UNIVERSITY ART GALLERY, New Haven, Connecticut. Architects and Designers: *Cambridge Seven Associates, Inc.*—principles-in-charge: *Ivan Chermayeff and Paul Dietrich.*

Norman McGrath photos

At the Garvan Gallery at Yale objects in different forms and different media are juxtaposed, united only by the period in which they were made. They are also seen from surprising angles, as in the wall of Chippendale chairs immediately below, or the contemporary chairs below right.

Scaife Museum

An initial mandate for Edward Larrabee Barnes' design for the Sarah Scaife Gallery at the Carnegie Institute in Pittsburgh was that there be an abundant supply of pellucid natural light to illuminate the gallery's paintings. The paintings—first-rate Impressionist, Post-Impressionist and American works, plus what director Leon Arkus calls a "spotty" collection from other periods—are a part of a museum of art, which is in turn (with a library, music hall and museum of natural history) a part of the cultural institution founded in Pittsburgh in 1890 by Andrew Carnegie.

Barnes' Scaife Gallery is an addition in several senses—physically it is an addition to an existing building, first built in 1895 and then greatly enlarged in 1907. More generally, though, the new building is an addition to a public institution of mixed use and considerable tradition. So the design task (in addition to providing good natural light for the paintings) was to make the new building well integrated with the old one—caring, for instance, for the modulation between the new galleries and the existing ones, and for the way the stark facade of the addition meets the more softly articulated (but bigger) Carnegie facade.

Scaife Gallery has two main entrances (above and left),

one of them facing the street, though set back from it, and echoing something of the formality of the older Carnegie Institute building. The second entrance, which is on the other side of the building and a full level below on the sloping site, opens onto a vehicular access road and, beyond that, to terraced parking lots that can accommodate up to 320 cars. From this entrance, the visitor moves directly into the gallery's courtyard (plans right), which steps gently back upwards to the level of the street entrance, and which is embellished with a waterfall, trees and, of course, works of sculpture from the museum's collection. On two sides the courtyard is flanked by glass-walled promenades (which also double as galleries), and from one of these a massive stone staircase leads upward still farther to the main gallery spaces.

In form the building is a rectilinear mass two stories high on the front and three on the back, with two wings that embrace the courtyard and connect to the existing Carnegie Institute building. On the lowest level (not shown in the adjacent plans, and accessible only from the back side of the building) are a small auditorium, a children's room and rooms for storage and for mechanical equipment. On the main level are the street entrance lobby, a small cafe, a museum shop, more storage and administrative offices and workrooms. Above this level are the main galleries.

Having all of the main gallery spaces on the top floor of the new building obviously provides the chance to achieve ideal natural lighting in them, and, as importantly, it puts them on the same level as the existing galleries in the Carnegie Institute. In a three-story building, however, it also results in a relatively small amount of the building's total floor area being devoted to gallery

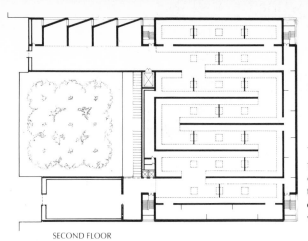

SECOND FLOOR

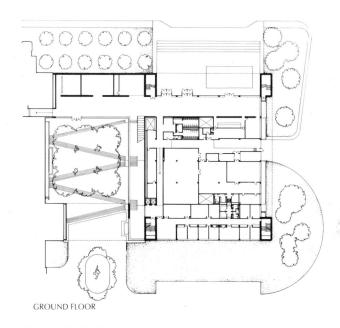

GROUND FLOOR

The photograph below shows the stairway from the street side of the building, looking back through the courtyard. Stone cladding is thermal finish Norwegian emerald pearl granite.

John L. Alexandrowicz

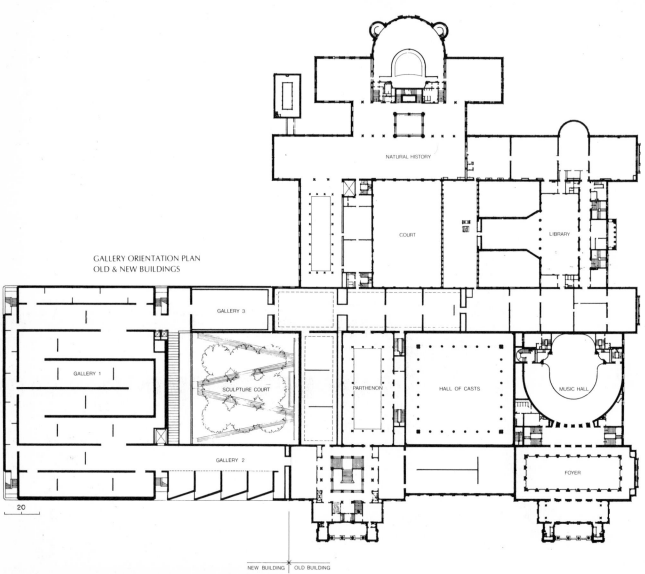

GALLERY ORIENTATION PLAN
OLD & NEW BUILDINGS

NATURAL HISTORY

COURT

LIBRARY

GALLERY 3

GALLERY 1

SCULPTURE COURT

PARTHENON

HALL OF CASTS

MUSIC HALL

GALLERY 2

FOYER

20

NEW BUILDING | OLD BUILDING

Ronald A. Layport photos

Much of the plan form of the Scaife Gallery is generated by the older Carnegie Institute to which it is joined. The two wings that surround the courtyard are extensions of protrusions on the older building, and the square plan of the courtyard itself recalls the square Hall of Casts inside the Carnegie building. The rectangular mass of the main part of the new building expansively suggests a third pavilion to complement the two Beaux Arts ones next door. The photograph on the left show the fountains just outside the street-side entrance.

The photograph on the right shows the courtyard of the Scaife Gallery seen from underneath the main stairway leading to the upper floor. The suspended glass wall system is made of ½-inch tempered glass with ¾-inch tempered glass fin to provide wind bracing in place of mullions.

The section through the Scaife Gallery on the right shows the natural lighting system in the galleries on the top floor. Daylight enters through skylights on the roof and passes first through a set of horizontal diffusing glass panels and then through a second, vertical set into the gallery space. The pyramidal skylights above the suspended panels are also diffusers above panels that can be removed to admit light straight down onto a piece of sculpture. The artificial lights seen in the photograph above provide substitute light at the same angle as daylight.

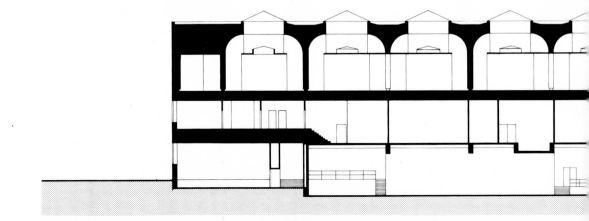

John L. Alexandrowicz

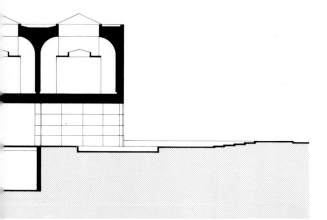

space—a phenomenon which, according to the architects, caused no rancor here because of the need for a number of non-gallery rooms in the building, including generous storage and workrooms that serve the older galleries as well as the new ones.

In plan, the new galleries are a series of interlocking U's and demi-U's on which works from the Scaife's permanent collection are displayed. Smaller, more self-contained exhibition areas flank these main gallery spaces on three sides. In connecting the new galleries to the old ones, Barnes has developed an even and unjarring choreography—albeit one that encourages (and almost demands) a linear pilgrimage by the visitor.

In the Scaife Gallery, says Leon Arkus, there are "no intrusive artifices of architecture. The art comes forward unembellished, with all the life the artist gave it." And, according to Barnes, "the second floor—white space with soft modulated daylight—turns all attention to the paintings." Thus the director and the architect of the Scaife articulate the prevailing contemporary view of how art should be displayed: with as little intrusion as possible from the surrounding environment. (This view, it is worth noting, stands in contrast to the centuries-old custom of hanging paintings on colored and textured walls in elaborate architectural spaces, and Barnes himself points out that the Modern penchant for white walls suits some paintings, like Impressionist ones, better than others, like somber Old Masters.) The Scaife Gallery follows the non-intrusive Modern persuasion, but elegantly varies and enlivens it with a soft and even shower of natural light that enters through skylights, passes through two diffusers and then bounces from vaults that spring from the walls where the paintings are hung— providing the greatest level of intensity there (in contrast to the usual skylit gallery, where the ceiling is brightest), and subtly changing in color with the hour of day and with the seasons.

SARAH SCAIFE GALLERY, Carnegie Institute, Pittsburgh, Pennsylvania. Architect: *Edward Larrabee Barnes—associate-in-charge: Percy K. Keck; project architect: Armand P. Avakian.* Engineers: *Severud Associates* (structural); *Swindell-Dressler Company* (civil); *Joseph R. Loring and Associates, Inc.* (mechanical and electrical). Consultants: *Bolt, Beranek and Newman, Inc.* (acoustical); *Donald L. Bliss* (lighting); *Mary Barnes and Paul Planert Design Associates, Inc.* (interiors); *Dan Kiley and Partners* (landscape); *Dimianos and Pedone* (graphics); *Turner Construction Company* (cost). General contractor: *Turner Construction Company.*

Ronald A. Layport

TOCHIGI MUSEUM

"Many of the world's museums of modern art concentrate primarily on the autonomous nature of the works displayed," according to Kiyoshi Kawasaki, architect of the Tochigi Museum of Art, shown on this and the following tw

level, interior-oriented, artificial spaces for the exhibition of those works." By contrast, the Tochigi Museum represents an attempt to retrieve the displayed artifact from such environments, where participation in it is, according to Kawasaki, passive and even monotonous. The gallery spaces in this museum use the now-familiar exposed structural concrete ceilings, with provisions for movable lighting, in order to provide maximum flexibility in the arrangement of shows. The galleries themseslves (see plan on page 102) are freely configured, flowing into each other and opening to the outdoors, a plaza "where artists and art lovers can make their contributions to the total environment of the museum."

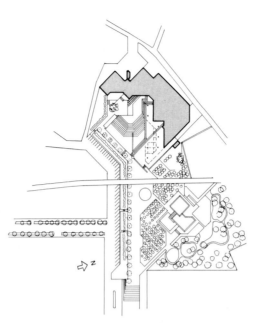

TOCHIGI MUSEUM OF ART, Utsunomiya, Japan. Architect: *Kiyoshi Kawasaki and Associates.* Engineers: *Torao Shioji* (structural); *Inuzuka Engineering Consultants* (mechanical). Consultants: *Sori Yanagi* (funiture); *Motoko Ishii* (lighting); *Reiko Ohta* (textiles); *Yoshikuni Iida* (sculpture). General Contractor: *Shimizu Construction Co. Ltd.*

Ryoo Hata

Shigeo Okamoto

Shigeo Okamoto

Above is a view of Exhibition Hall "B" from the outdoor exhibition area, whose most notable architectural feature is a large reflecting pool reached by flights of steps. Some of these steps are flooded with water flowing down into the pool, as in the photograph on the left.

Ryoo Hata

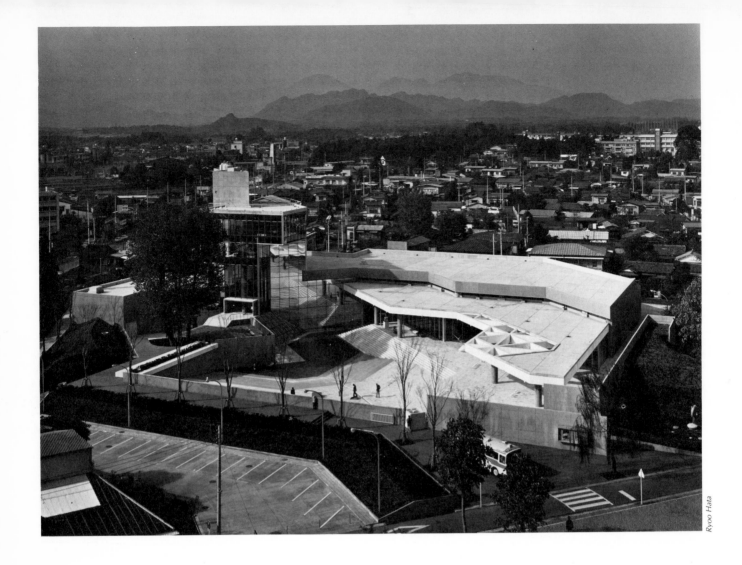

Ryoo Hata

LECTURE   ENTRY   EXHIBITION

CONF.
LIBRARY

The general view of the site shown in the top photograph above reveals the low, small-scale environment in which the museum is placed. The photograph below is an upward view of the office wing, and below left is a plan of the main floor.

EXHIBITION

EXHIB.

OUTDOOR
DISPLAY

UPPER
LECTURE

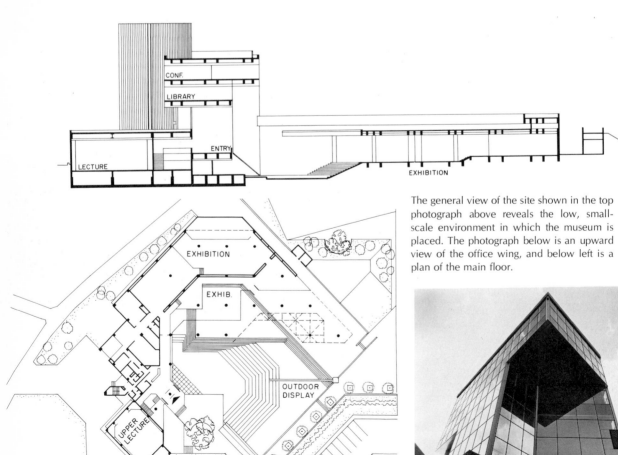

Osamu Murai

THE TEL AVIV MUSEUM מוזיאון תל אביב

TEL AVIV MUSEUM

I. Zafrin

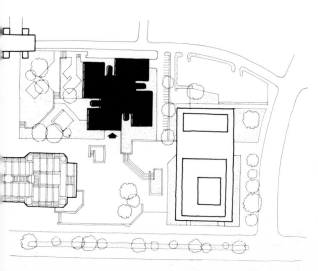

The building itself was the best exhibition at the festive opening of the new Tel Aviv Museum last April. In a city necessarily built largely for commodity, the new structure indicates a turning point towards a stronger, more dynamic and individual Israeli architecture. The design, by architects Itzhak Yashar and Dan Eitan, was awarded first place in a 1964 national competition; Italy's Bruno Zevi, who headed the international architectural jury, especially cited the building's simplicity, tranquility and the organization and circulation of the spiraling plan. And laudably it has been built, with few exceptions, in accordance with that original design to be the hub for a new cultural center for Tel Aviv.

With over 3,000 people from Israel and abroad in attendance (including Israel's President Zalman Shazar, Prime Minister Golda Meir, and Minister of Foreign Affairs Abba Eban), the gala opening of the new Tel Aviv Museum more than proved the contention of architects Yashar and Eitan that their winning design would provide easy circulation for such crowds and comfortable display of a variety of exhibitions.

The plan compactly spirals four big galleries around a huge central "festival opening hall," each gallery being a half-level above the other. These are interspersed with stair and elevator towers which, with the dramatic lacing of ramps in the big hall, offer a variety of access in addition to the progress up through the galleries themselves. Each of these elements is expressed with great simplicity and clarity both inside and out, and their almost sculptural interplay gives a vigorous silhouette to the exterior; subtle variations in color and texture of the building materials make each of the elements unmistakable and refreshingly easy to comprehend.

It is not a "grand" museum, in spite of the size of the hall and galleries. In fact, being set into a drop in grade level, it seems much smaller than it is when seen from the outside. Its appearance of having few windows is also belied inside: there is practically no space—including the links between galleries —where one cannot look across and up to the outdoors.

It is instead a strong and articulate, but, in Bruno Zevi's words, "tranquil" setting for people to see and appreciate art with ease and comfort—which is, after all, what a museum is for.

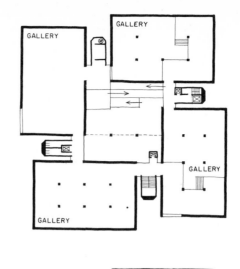

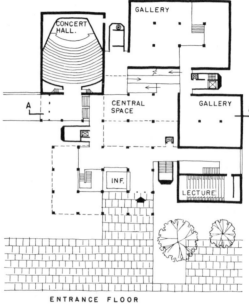

ENTRANCE FLOOR

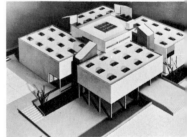

The model of the museum (above) shows the simple, clear organization of galleries and stair towers around the central block which contains the central hall (top) and library and offices above it. The library has balcony-like openings into the central hall (left). All the major spaces have skylights and toplighting, with suspended baffles to screen the glare. All materials are forthrightly handled, and the concrete frame left exposed. The stair towers are surfaced with rough, ribbed concrete which gives a distinguishing contrast to the exterior marble panels. The latter are perhaps the one finicky bit of detailing in the building, but caused, one was told, by a tardy substitution of the small donated stones for big precast panels.

The four main galleries contain 8,500 sq ft each, with the top one (left) free of columns for the display of sculpture. Skylights can be baffled (bottom) for special lighting of exhibits. The building cost about $4 million and contains a total of about 130,000 sq ft. In addition to spaces indicated on the plans and section shown, the building contains two smaller exhibition halls, a cafeteria and an outdoor sculpture garden.

The mounting of the opening exhibits was handled by the museum's director, Dr. Haim Gamzu, with appropriate restraint to let the building be the star—but the big, nicely proportioned spaces, multi-levels and unexpected openings should provide for some powerful, imaginative stagings for the future. One of them should be on what many consider to be the best of Israel's contemporary arts—the fine, dynamic architecture that is being built throughout the country.

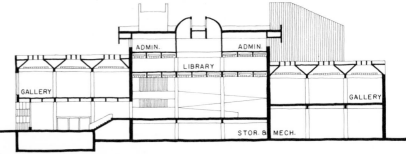

SECTION A-A

THE TEL AVIV MUSEUM, ISRAEL. Architects: *Itzhak Yashar and Dan Eitan, assisted by Dany Raz and Moshe Ashkenazi;* engineers: *Yaron and Shimoni;* supervisory engineer: *Moshe Kogan;* consultants: *David De Mayo (interiors), Arnon Adar (lighting), Yahalom and Tsur (landscaping);* contractors: *Ramir Contractors Co. Ltd., J. Udassin.*

BROOKS
MEMORIAL GALLERY

Otto Baitz photos

The Brooks Gallery has been a source of civic pride in Memphis since its dedication in 1916. Designed by James Gamble Rogers and modeled on the garden pavilion of the Villa Capriola, it has an irreplaceable grace, and a healthy scale for the surrounding area of large well-kept houses. When Mrs. Samuel Brooks donated the $100,000 construction cost in 1912, "art" was looked on as a rather elitist matter—but times change. The number of visitors and donors (including Samuel Kress) grew. In 1955 the building was expanded directly to the rear, but the addition was too small at the time of the dedication. At such a juncture, the solution has often been new construction of such overwhelming scale that preservation seems irrelevant. Architects Walk Jones and Francis Mah's housing for the new spaces, as seen at right, might well have produced that result. But . . .

Not all the planning of the new museum space involved massing problems. As the present design began, the expansion program was way behind schedule. There were the usual budget deficits that delays produce. Lacking was a set program on the nature of exhibits or the manner in which they were to be seen. Another serious problem was the fact that long-range expansion locations had never been considered despite on-going donations and steadily increasing public interest.

The shortness of schedule and budget were tackled by use of a prefabricated concrete construction system developed for low-cost housing (more on this later), but the scale of structural members had to be greatly increased. Large flexible areas were the only way to accommodate the indefinite exhibition program, and height was required for the appropriate spatial character. The operating economies of centralized facilities (versus the alternate of branch museums) produced an eventual 100,000-square-foot long-range expansion program—all on this site. This addition represents only a quarter of that area (see plan below), but plans for another increment are already under way.

The architects always intended that theirs would be a background building to both the original small scale gallery and surrounding Overton Park. Given the volume of required space and the large-scale construction system, controlling visual impact was not easy.

There were two basic massing decisions made: the new first floor level was depressed a full story below the original, and only half of the actual height is revealed from the front approach. The visual bulk is further broken into segments stepping back on a 45 degree sight-line from the older entrance facade. With such effort at sublimating its presence, it is remarkable that this background building can stand on its own design merits, as can be seen by moving around it (photo right). The architects describe their facades as an abstraction of the Rogers exterior. The new concrete wall finish resembles the older limestone facing. Still the wall panelization and opening scale are as much a direct outcome of the construction method and interior considerations as they are deference to the earlier building.

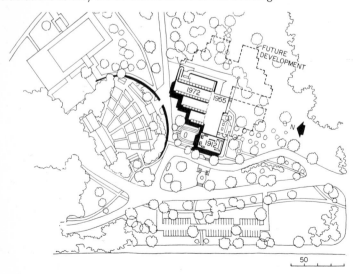

A ground slope was utilized to conceal the visible height from the front approach. The full extent of the new building is seen in stages. Passing around the original gallery the viewer first sees the most forward of three segments successively set back to reduce visual bulk (photo, near right). Farther around the new building, the slope begins to reveal the true massing (below), and finally the full height is seen from the rear (far right) where a berm conceals the sculpture court and a bridge spans between exit and stairs.

The addition is entered at a second part-floor seemingly suspended by separation from the walls (photo overleaf, top left). The other two views show the relation of the second floor to the first. A full orientation to the double height space is gained before descending the stairs. To accommodate the indefinite program, floor areas were kept as open as possible, but certain divisions were inevitable. Because of loading dock location, more temporary exhibits are housed on the first level, where direct access to trucks is available.

Francis Mah explains the firm's design concerns this way: While the space was to be open, it was not to be amorphous and the finished building shows strong visual direction. There are controlled views of the park outside, and the exterior sculpture court is related to the interior by the long horizontal glazing at the first level. A continuous circulation flow, without backtracking, and a visitor's understanding of location without signs, are successful planning results. Lighting was a primary concern, and the architects' preference was to maximize natural sources. The high skylights deflect direct sun to protect the exhibitions. In an open floor plan, an inherent lack of necessary wall space exists, and hanging plywood cubes were designed to be built locally at a third of the original display system budget. Museum director Jack Whitlock is highly pleased with the new building. He can now organize the artwork presently stored (by a weeding-out process of rotating exhibits), accept traveling shows, and bring professional as well as community-related programs to life. He now plans to carpet the first level which will weaken the visual contrast with the upper (carpeted) level, but allow a more comfortable relation between art and viewers.

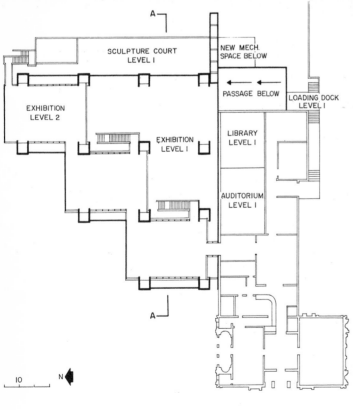

SCULPTURE COURT
LEVEL I

NEW MECH.
SPACE BELOW

PASSAGE BELOW

LOADING DOCK
LEVEL I

EXHIBITION
LEVEL 2

EXHIBITION
LEVEL I

LIBRARY
LEVEL I

AUDITORIUM
LEVEL I

10   N

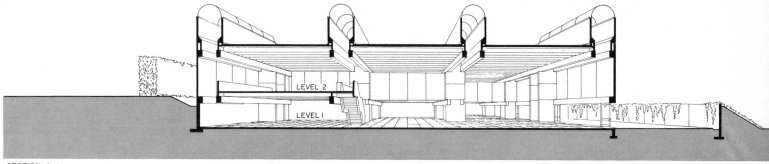

SECTION A-A

The Mah-Le Messurier Construction System used here was originally developed for the architects' local housing authority work, and possessed proven cost and time-saving advantages for taller buildings. It relies on simple pre-cast concrete members consisting of large U-shaped support cores (see plan page 112), beams, and double tees with concrete panel infill walls. The straightforward expression can be seen in the photos. The spans and, consequently, the scale of members had to be increased from previous applications. Manufacturing and handling of the new sizes (plus the lack of inherent system efficiency only gained by greater heights) produced structural costs in the neighborhood of standard poured concrete construction ($238,-000), but the erection time was only eight weeks. The over-all construction cost was held close to $30 per square foot (well under the original budget). This is particularly surprising when the special detailing is considered. The stair treads (photo left) are individually cantilevered from the adjacent wall by tension-rod supports capped with the visible special fittings. Separations between the walls and second floor have railings of laminated glass to facilitate views to the floor below. The confines of the structural system were employed to produce spaces of great visual interest within the rectangular grid of massive support cores. These carry mechanical risers, break up the otherwise open space, and provide a diagonal orientation to the course of travel.

THE BROOKS MEMORIAL ART GALLERY ADDITION, Memphis, Tennessee. Owner: *Owner: City of Memphis.* Architects: *Walk Jones + Francis Mah, Inc.—Francis Mah, principal-in-charge of design.* Engineers: *Le Messurier Associates, Inc.,* (structural): *Henry C. Donnelly,* (mechanical). General contractor: *Harmon Construction Company, Inc.*

WINCHESTER/NORWICH CATHEDRAL

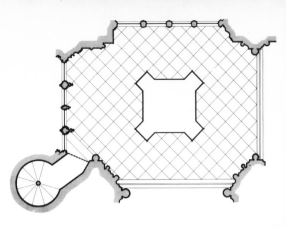

The cathedrals of England and the parish churches of their dioceses often possess beautiful and valuable collections of old silver and gold—chalices, patens, basins, ewers and other objects used in ecclesiastical ceremony. Until recently in modern times, these were almost always kept stashed away in bank vaults, available on loan for special exhibitions or brought out occasionally for major church festivals. Well over a decade ago, however, the idea of cathedral treasuries—special places where these collections could be displayed—was advocated and underwritten by the Worshipful Company of Goldsmiths, a semiofficial, benevolent band of craftsmen and enthusiasts roughly equivalent in essence if not in style to an American professional association. The first cathedral treasury, at Lincoln, was opened in 1960, and since then treasuries have been installed at Winchester, Norwich and York. Those at Winchester and Norwich were designed by London architects Stefan Buzas and Alan Irvine, and they are shown on this and the following page.

The Winchester treasury, shown on this page, is in a small 15th-century gallery above the nave of the cathedral near the west door; the entrance is by a small door and a short winding stairway. In the gallery is a single

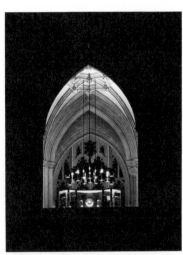

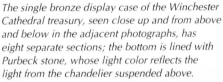

The single bronze display case of the Winchester Cathedral treasury, seen close up and from above and below in the adjacent photographs, has eight separate sections; the bottom is lined with Purbeck stone, whose light color reflects the light from the chandelier suspended above.

showcase elegantly constructed of bronze; its translucent glass top admits light from the 16-lamp chandelier suspended above. The chandelier is made of bronze-anodized aluminum to minimize its weight. The central, cruciform-plan showcase was chosen in order to give adequate circulation space around the case and to leave the balustrades clear and thus to preserve two excellent views of the cathedral.

The Norwich treasury, shown on this page, is also situated in an existing gallery—this one in the ambulatory of the cathedral, and possessed of notable 14th-century frescoes on the vaults above. There are four display cases, of which two form part of the glass walls within the semicircular arches enclosing the treasury. Above each of these showcases is a seven-light bracket made of bronze. There is also a shallow showcase in the north wall, and a central showcase, whose lighting also illuminates the frescoes on the ceiling.

WINCHESTER CATHEDRAL TREASURY, Winchester, England; NORWICH CATHEDRAL TREASURY, Norwich, England. Architects: *Stefan Buzas and Alan Irvine.* Engineers: *Ove Arups* (structural, for reinforced concrete vault at Winchester). Prime contractor: *A. Edmonds & Co.* (for fabrication of bronze showcases).

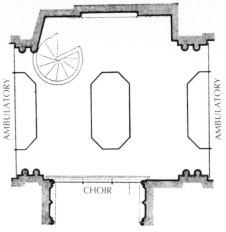

The Norwich Cathedral treasury was installed in a gallery above the north choir aisle, used in medieval times for the display of relics, and enclosed now by glass walls, making the treasury visible from below. The architects of the treasury also designed the iron gate at its entrance.

Edgar Hyman and Peter Chorley photos

HUNTINGTON GALLERY ADDITION

The new addition to the Huntington Gallery in West Virginia by TAC has all the trademarks of having been designed in Boston. It expresses once more the familiar vocabulary of form, structure and materials which has been developed and perfected by TAC and other leading New England firms during the past 15 years—a system of interrelated box-like forms characterized by the use of a carefully articulated concrete frame with brick infill and exposed concrete waffle slab ceilings. Thus the building is essentially conservative in its architectural expression, particularly if compared to Mario Ciampi's museum overleaf. In spite of (or perhaps because of) its conservatism, the new addition competently serves the purposes of the program.

It is well lit by a carefully balanced system of natural and artificial light in which, during the daytime, natural light predominates. The interiors are flexible, spacious and in good scale with the small to medium sized works of art which the museum acquires and exhibits— an effect achieved by establishing a moderate ceiling height. The interior spaces do not impose themselves on museum-goers' consciousness to forcibly distract them from the works of art, but they can distract themselves if they like, by looking through the large windows which frame good views, or by enjoying the landscaped courtyard (below) or the terrace (opposite page top).

A second courtyard (see plan) will be formed when the last two of the five workshops are constructed. These generous, well-lit studios which are used by the community—and particularly by the young—for the development of their own creativity, were considered by the late Walter Gropius, principal-in-charge of the project, to be essential to the success of the gallery as a lively, contemporary institution.

HUNTINGTON GALLERY ADDITION, Huntington, West Virginia. Architects: *The Architects Collaborative—principal: Walter Gropius; associate-in-charge: Malcolm Ticknor; associated architects: Walter S. Donat; structural engineers: Souza & True; mechanical and electrical engineers: Beyers, Urban, Klug & Pittenger; lighting consultant: William Lam; concrete consultant: Architectural Concrete Consultants; general contractor: Persun Construction Co.*

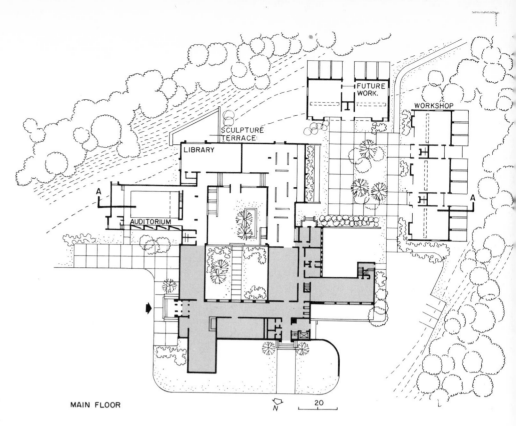

MAIN FLOOR

N   20

The only art gallery within a 75-mile radius, Huntington is located on a small plateau several miles outside of town. TAC's U-shaped addition contains gallery space, a research library and a 300-seat auditorium. A pathway underneath the addition connects the sculpture court (opposite page) and the lower sculpture terrace (top) which has been located to take advantage of the spectacular view. As the photograph (bottom left) indicates, the new addition has been carefully sited to enhance the principal entrance which had been the design focus of the older neo-classic structure. In scale, proportion and general architectural character, the new addition is sensitively related to the old museum. Natural daylight is brought in through half vaults as can be seen in the section (below) and the photo (opposite page bottom). Artificial lighting can be plugged in almost anywhere within the ceiling module. The parquet floors and fabric covered walls match the older structure.

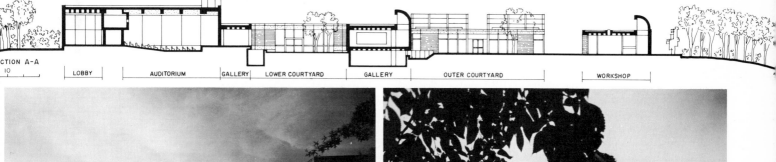

SECTION A-A
10

| LOBBY | AUDITORIUM | GALLERY | LOWER COURTYARD | GALLERY | OUTER COURTYARD | WORKSHOP |

UNIVERSITY ART MUSEUM, BERKELEY

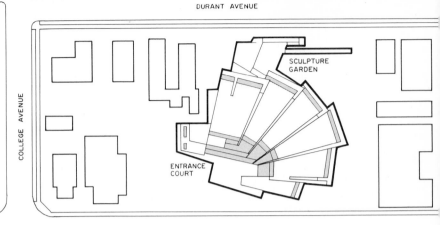

The University of California's new art museum in Berkeley is the largest university art museum in this country. This alone would make it important and interesting. But its design is of great significance in the museum field as well. Its concept is bold and innovative, although it will inevitably be compared to the Guggenheim because of its great court and its major use of ramps. Unlike the Guggenheim, however, it clearly recognizes the function of a museum building and the challenge of the works of art it must be designed to shelter. Its very special virtue is that in meeting the rigorous demands of that function it does not lose sight of its own role as an expression of the art of architecture. This unusual and exciting design for the building was selected in 1964 from 366 entries in a national competition by a jury chaired by Lawrence Anderson, then head of MIT's department of architecture. The building was financed by accumulated student fees and gifts (notably $250,000 from renowned painter Hans Hoffman). A design partnership of Mario J. Ciampi, Paul Reiter, Richard Jorasch and Ronald Wagner was the winner.

Dynamic and exciting as the building itself is, it neither detracts nor distracts from the viewing of objects on display. One of the reasons for this is that the ramps—the obvious but not the only way of reaching the galleries— lead visitors directly into the galleries: they are within an exhibit area before they can proceed further. Another reason is that the galleries, radiating from the court-like parts of a giant fan, are each 60 feet deep and, therefore, are fully adequate places for display and contemplation of paintings, sculpture and other art objects. A third and more subtle reason is the great flexibility which the building affords not only as a place in which a variety of objects in a variety of sizes and types can be displayed, but also as a place through which people move, contributing a particular dynamism to which even skeptical professionals and laymen succumb. The museum's director, Dr. Peter Selz, is especially happy with this exceptional flexibility, and with provisions for delivery storage and conservation, and special facilities like the theater, library and film archive. Of the building's gross area of 95,000 square feet—built at a total cost of $4,850,000—some 30,000 square feet are used for exhibition.

The rugged concrete exterior of the museum building is offset at the entrance by grassy mounds and a large black Calder stabile. Although the building is not on the university campus—it is across the street—it is oriented to the campus, especially to the nearby art and environmental design buildings. Even so, as the only large art gallery in Berkeley, it also has an important community role. Along the west side is a sunny sculpture garden (with a fine red Max Lieberman piece), much used by students, and overlooked by the terraces outside the main level galleries.

Morley Baer photos

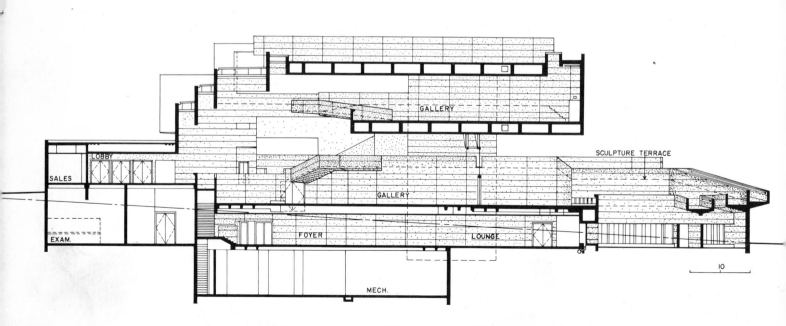

SALES

LOBBY

EXAM.

FOYER

GALLERY

GALLERY

LOUNGE

SCULPTURE TERRACE

MECH.

10

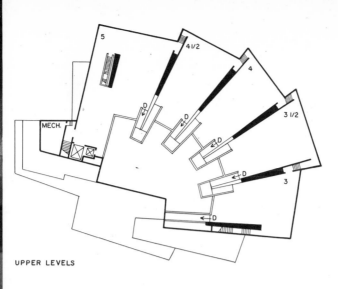

UPPER LEVELS

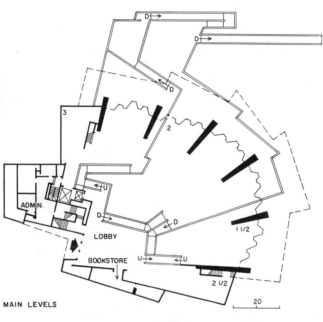

MAIN LEVELS

3   2   1 1/2   2 1/2

20

The building's plan and section are complex but the actual experience of the building is simplified by the fact that all exhibit areas are simultaneously discernible from the great court. There are 12 spaces on nine levels where exhibits can be shown (see plans at left), including the great court under whose skylight unusually tall and large sculptures can be shown. Working areas are served by separate stairs and entrance.

THE UNIVERSITY ART MUSEUM, University of California. Architects: *Mario J. Ciampi & Associates, in design partnership of Mario Ciampi, Richard L. Jorasch, and Ronald E. Wagner, design associates, John Voulkos, project architect.* Engineers: *Isadore Thompson,* structural; *K. T. Belotelkin and Associates,* mechanical; *Harold Wright,* electrical; *Dariel Fitzroy,* acoustical. Landscape architects: *Mario J. Ciampi & Associates.* For the University: *Louis A. De Monte,* campus architect; *Norma P. Willer,* associate architect; *Frederick F. Warnke,* landscape. General contractor: *Rothschild and Rafin, Inc.*

In contrast to the stark and bold exterior, the interior is dynamic, vital and exciting. The great volume of skylit space—the most striking feature of the interior—is only one contribution to this character. Ramps take off on either side of the court and lead up or down to different levels of the exhibit areas and galleries which radiate from the court. Landings cantilever over the court like tiered boxes in a theater, inviting a pause in ascent or descent to look over the court with its stationary exhibits and its human movement. Skylights over the court are set at various levels and in various planes and sizes between deep concrete beams. At the far end of each gallery is a skylight.

CHAPTER THREE

HISTORIC AND CULTURAL MUSEUMS

FLINT RIDGE MUSEUM

Commissioned jointly by the Ohio Historical Society and the Ohio Department of Public Works under a statewide program of improvement of historic sites, the three small museums shown here and on the following spread (plus two others commissioned at the same time but not yet completed) serve as focal points and orientation centers for the extensive outdoor "museums" of which they are a part.

All deal with various facets of early Indian cultures in southern Ohio, all are similar in size, and all meet essentially the same basic program requirements within essentially the same budget—a set of factors which with less imagination on the part of the architect (and client) might readily have led to all being stamped from the same mold. Yet, as architect E. A. Glendening says, "We felt very strongly that [the museums] had to be individual entities rather than duplicate structures as so many public facilities are in so many areas. Each had a different story to tell and this could only be accomplished with buildings designed to meet the detailed needs."

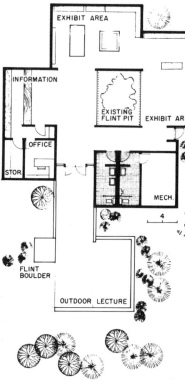

The buildings are indeed "individual entities," reflecting the particularities of their specific locations and the resulting particularities of their subject matter. At the same time, though, while no look-alikes, the museums do bear certain family resemblances, notably in their sympathetic relationship to the historic landmarks they explicate, as well as to the parking areas, picnic grounds, hiking trails, and other features incorporated to enhance public enjoyment of those landmarks. And there is consistency too in the straightforward plans (each is basically a one-room museum with minimal support facilities) enlivened by manipulation of structural forms and lighting, and in the thoughtful handling of unassuming—and inexpensive—materials.

FLINT RIDGE MUSEUM, Licking County, Ohio; FORT HILL MUSEUM, Highland County; FORT ANCIENT MUSEUM, Warren County. Architect: *E. A. Glendening, A.I.A.*

The Flint Ridge Museum, which deals with the use of flint and its importance in the development of Indian cultures in the immediate area and throughout the Midwest, is located over one of the many existing flint pits which dot the site, in order to provide an authentic illustration of the way flint was mined by long-ago Indian tribes. From a stepped, paved court used for outdoor lectures, the visitor enters a tight low-ceilinged area which expands with the upward slope of the roof into a progressively more generous space culminating in the dramatic focus of a clerestory directly above the flint pit. (As shown at right, a reflective baffle deflects light from the clerestory into the pit—and out of the eyes of viewers.) In contrast with the strong natural light thus beamed on the principal exhibit, the subsidiary displays of flint tools and weapons and unusual crystals and deposits ranged around the perimeter of the swastika-like plan are picked out by downlights which also provide low-key general illumination, and by display lighting in the wall cases. Because the setting is heavily wooded, the architect felt wood to be "the only possible choice" of materials: the building, accordingly, is of frame construction with cedar siding inside and out.

Jerry Morgenroth photos

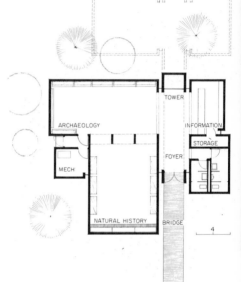

Jerry Morgenroth photos

The Fort Hill Museum, as the name suggests, is located at a site featuring a 1200-foot, steep-sided, flat-topped hill which commands a broad view in all directions, and so afforded indigenous Indian cultures an easily defended natural fortress. Because the site is significant geologically as well as archaeologically, the museum's exhibit spaces are laid out in an L shape, with separate areas devoted to the natural history of the region and to the culture of its early inhabitants. The two areas, however, are not discrete but flow into one another, demarked only by a line of brick pillars and a jump in ceiling height in the natural history section. This shift in height also adds interest to the basically simple masonry masses of the building exterior, as does the prominent treatment of a clerestory tower whose terne fascia is echoed at the entrance. On the interior, the tower becomes an alcove for special displays, highlighted from above and further emphasized by strip windows at the sides. In the passage leading from entry bridge to exhibit areas and terminating at the tower, maximum spatial and visual impact is achieved simply with a lowered, light-finished ceiling in contrast to adjacent dark wood ceilings and exposed brick walls.

The Fort Ancient Museum relates to a site distinguished by two extensive groupings of defensive and burial mounds, one tracing the culture of the very early Hopewell Indians, the other, that of the later and more advanced Fort Ancients. This duality of subject matter is reflected in the museum's plan by placing large display areas for the panoramic depiction of the respective cultures on either side of the principal exhibit space. Set off from the main room as much by their light-washed white walls as by their sunken floors and rails, these open, oversize "display cases" are supplemented by an intimate secondary exhibit area and by freestanding displays in the central space. As in the other two museums, striking effects are rendered with deceptively modest techniques of handling form, materials—and light. Here the key elements are raised domes finished in white acoustical plaster, which become in effect giant luminaires, defining as well as indirectly lighting the museum's two primary functional areas. The same in shape but different in size (the larger marking the display space; the smaller, the lobby), these squared-off, terne-faced domes also enhance the clean, low-slung lines of the exterior. The structure is loadbearing masonry, with the same golden brick repeated inside and out.

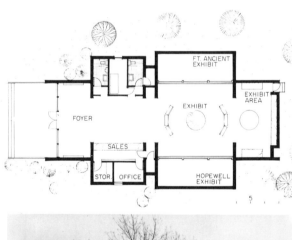

HUNTER MUSEUM

Located atop prominent limestone bluffs on the Tennessee River, Chattanooga's Hunter Museum of Art forms an appropriately romantic image in sympathy with its spectacular location. And it does this against great odds, as the mansion, which originally housed all of the institution's programs (and lends the major romance), could easily have been engulfed in a recently completed "expansion" that was several times larger—being some 50,000 square feet. The new structure, designed by architects Derthick & Henley, both continues the visual importance of the mansion and complements its natural surroundings by becoming one with them; the major part is recessed into the bluffs immediately in front of the older building and below the level of its base—a circumstance made possible because of an earth "overburden" on the rock eliminating the need for extensive blasting. Where the expansion is visible, its exposed poured-concrete walls (which form the structure) contain a limestone aggregate to match the bluff, and they are segmented and cantilevered in such a way as to appear to be growing from the rock. Curved projections echo the semi-circular colonnade on the front of the

mansion, and brick paving echoes the older cladding. The intent is a building in harmony with all of the elements of its surroundings—and one that saves its visual impact for the interior with a commendable architectural politeness. And as such, it squarely faces the increasingly important visual problem of relating new and valued older structures.

Within the new facility, budgeted at $2.3 million, are classrooms for the museum art school located below the lobby and the 180-seat auditorium. Most importantly, there is the double-height exhibition space used for temporary shows of contemporary art. This exhibition space can be expanded into a storage area on the main exhibition-level and below the holding and storage area (plan, opposite). The rooms of the mansion have been refurbished to near-original condition, and contain the museum's permanent displays of mostly older paintings.

HUNTER MUSEUM OF ART, Chattanooga, Tennessee Owner: *The Board of Trustees.* Architects: *Derthick & Henley.* Engineers: *Bennett & Pless, Inc.* (structural): *George Campbell & Associates, Inc.* (mechanical/electrical).* General contractor: *Raines Brothers, Inc.*

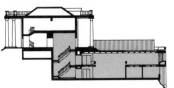

By the arrangements of the two buildings, spectacular views of the Tennessee River are obtained for both the original and new buildings (photo right). As seen in the section above, the various rooms of the new addition face the river in a poured concrete structure designed to blend with the limestone bluff into which they are recessed. The manipulation of the grades between new and old buildings can be seen in the photo, next page. The rounded structure contains the stair, which connects the upper and middle levels of the entrance pavilion.

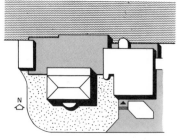

As seen in the site plan above, only the three elements consisting of the original mansion, the small loading dock and the new entrance pavilion (also top photo opposite) are visible to the arriving visitor. The bulk of the building (plan, opposite) is located below the river-front sculpture terrace which forms the "backyard" of the mansion. From the lobby the exhibition space (photo opposite) on the same level and a lower level are immediately evident.

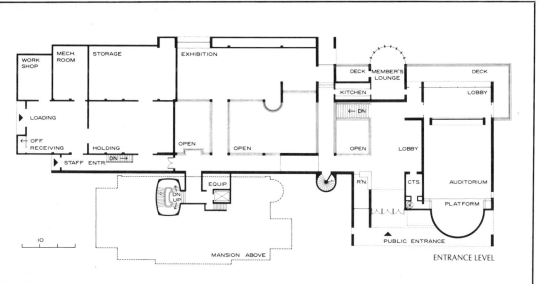

WORK SHOP	MECH. ROOM	STORAGE	EXHIBITION					
LOADING					DECK	MEMBER'S LOUNGE		DECK
					KITCHEN			LOBBY
OFF. RECEIVING		HOLDING	OPEN	OPEN	← DN	OPEN	LOBBY	
STAFF ENTR	DN							
	DN UP	EQUIP			R'N		CTS.	AUDITORIUM
								PLATFORM
10					▲ PUBLIC ENTRANCE			
		MANSION ABOVE					ENTRANCE LEVEL	

NATIONAL MUSEUMS, MEXICO CITY

Four museums recently built in Chapultepec, Mexico City's principal park, reflect concern on the part of the government-client for the betterment of the peoples' educational facilities and of Mexico's cultural institutions.

The first modern museum in Mexico was the National Museum of Anthropology in Mexico City. Architect Pedro Ramirez Vasquez, to whom the commission was given in 1960, says that the problems presented by this work were complex. Two equally difficult requirements had to be fulfilled: the building had to function as a museum, a dignified housing of a cultural legacy, and was to be contemporary yet not alien to that legacy. To achieve these aims it was necessary to search for and re-evaluate the nearly forgotten tradition of Mexican architecture in its pre-Hispanic past, evoking this tradition even though the formal solutions might be different.

In examining these unchanging values, Ramirez Vasquez found it evident that Traditional and Modern architecture in Mexico have certain underlying concepts in common, in spite of differences in technique and specific formal solutions, which he embodied in this building. For example: the influence of the geographic environment, integration into the landscape, generous use of space, preservation of materials, a plastic continuity perpetuated through the handiwork of artisans, and modes of construction that are characterized by an ambition for permanence and boldness of design.

The broad, open spaces typical of pre-Hispanic architectural ensembles in Mexico are a reflection of the profound respect landscape has inspired in man and of his communion with the natural world. Pre-Hispanic architects in Mesoamerica never created a structure that conflicted with its surroundings. The Mexican's love of his landscape, expressed in a striving for harmony between architecture and environment, began as part of an exalted conception of man that elevated the individual to a dignified place in his society. Spaces and masses were planned with a careful eye to dignifying the great multitudes that would congregate in these ritual centers. Architecture, open spaces, and landscape were all fused into a single and indivisible whole.

Volumetrically, the museum is comprised of various open and closed spaces that include its site in the Park. These spaces are assembled in a masterly fashion, in which each part achieves heightened significance in relation to the other parts. Inside, one's attitude toward the enclosed spaces is partly formed by the simultaneous experience of the definite presence of the outdoors—vegetation, sky, and the elements; conversely, open space is developed as the logical extension of the enclosures. Because the grand proportions of open spaces have been so well incorporated into the organization of relatively small architectural forms, one has the experience of an architecture of human scale but monumental proportion.

The Museum of Anthropology is not only buildings and spaces, it is also very much people and exhibits. The plaza at the museum's entrance attracts not just museum visitors, but is also a place for vendors, picnics, siestas and flirtations: It is Chapultepec Park's Piazza di Spagna.

From the plaza one enters the museum lobby, a large space that serves on occasion for ceremonies and receptions. It is also the place where one is introduced to the museum's vast collection from Mexican Mesoamerica in an Orientation Room utilizing mixed media.

The large central courtyard of the museum is reached from the lobby. The aim, says Ramirez Vasquez, was to encourage a casual and fluid circulation by the public, to give it free access to the galleries either in the consecutive manner of a tour or by individual visit according to personal preference. This aim led to the conception of a central nucleus of distribution created in the form of a courtyard or esplanade. The solution, known as the quadrangle layout, was borrowed from classical Mayan architecture. It consists of a kind of patio bounded by enclosed buildings, thus

Above left: The opening of interior spaces to the outside, a characteristically Mayan architectural solution, is enriched here by linking the courtyard level with that of the school facilities and restaurant by means of a broad stairway. Following pre-Hispanic tradition, the trees of the part were left undisturbed, and thus were made an organic part of the building. *Above:* The view from the Aztec Room shows the gigantic umbrella roof extending over half the courtyard, thus offering protected access to the adjoining exhibition rooms during the rainy season. *Below:* Gardens bordering the outer walls of the museum's pavilions are utilized as patios for large exhibits. But more importantly, they are transition zones between the man-made world of artifacts and the living world of the park and the city beyond. *Right:* The entrance plaza of the museum is only one of a succession of spaces—open and closed—in which the life of the park is exposed, a natural setting not only for museum visitors but also for vendors, picnics, siestas and flirtations.

maintaining a sense of the exterior merging with the interior.

A portion of the central courtyard is covered by a large umbrella, to enhance the feeling of spaciousness, and to permit free circulation during the rainy season. The umbrella and support form a magnificent fountain that spills onto the pavement beneath.

At the other end of the courtyard there is a pool planted with varieties of swamp plants found in the Mexican Valley. The pool is meant to be symbolic of the lake origins of the Aztecs, whose culture is most directly related to the indigenous Indian population. The principal pavilion of the museum, entered at the pool, houses the Aztec collection.

Small gardens border the pavilions. The gardens form a transition zone between the enclosed spaces of the museum and the surrounding park, and are reached directly from the courtyard when they are utilized as public spaces—the restaurant's patio—or from individual pavilions when they are utilized as a setting for large installations of sculpture and architecture. The relationship of in- and outdoors does more than provide alternative solutions for installations; it provides a place of "retreat" in a visitor's itinerary that is essential in such a vast collection.

The National Museum of Anthropology provides all the necessary adjuncts of a modern scientific and educational institution. There are about 20,000 square feet of workshops, laboratories, storerooms and research offices; a temporary exhibition hall of 60,000 square feet; an auditorium seating 350 persons; a library with a quarter of a million volumes; the National School of Anthropology, with accommodations for 500 students; provisions for school children, studios, an outdoor theater, play areas and dining facilities. These give a dynamic dimension to the museum's educational function, but within the composition of forms they are hardly in evidence. Ramirez Vasquez has given hierarchical order to these numerous functions, with stress on the prime function of the museum as a treasury of the nation's heritage.

NATIONAL MUSEUM OF ANTHRO-POLOGY, Mexico City, Mexico. Architect: *Pedro Ramirez Vasquez.*

132

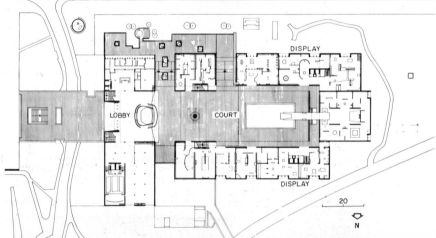

Opposite: Each major gallery opens onto a closed garden in which large objects are displayed. The plan shows the simple arrangement of pavilions around the great court. *Opposite:* The entrance lobby before entering the central courtyard. *Above:* One half of the Aztec Room as seen from an exterior gallery, one story above. *Left:* Each pavilion is divided into three parts. In the low section, ethnographical material explains the culture; in the double-storied section—which also gives way to the garden—artifacts of the culture are given a "monumental" setting. Upstairs, artifacts of the culture's indigenous society are displayed. *Right:* A large exhibit room is highlighted by a mural of Mexico's school of social realism. *Below:* A curtain of water falls from the vast umbrella roof, veiling the sculpted central support column—in fact a monumental fountain depicting in bronze relief major events of Mexican history.

Ohio CENTER

The Historical Center is, in fact, more than a children's museum. The most visible portion, which seems almost to hover above its podium, above, is the state archives and historical library. As the section, opposite page, shows clearly, the soaring library structure and the horizontal, nearly invisible, museum share a grand common space, the Hall of Fame, in which renowned Ohioans are commemorated.

Four massive columns, containing various services, support the breathtaking overhangs of the library. Forty-foot-high shear walls form a two-way, post tensioned grid that carries the weight of almost six miles of library shelving. Including the museum and reception level, the total floor area of the Historical Center is 271,762 square feet. The exterior walls have been sheathed with salt-glazed chute tile, an Ohio masonry product used principally in farm buildings.

As the busloads arrive, the children directly enter the auditorium for a briefing before being conducted through the exhibits. Then they come up onto the main level to see the changing exhibits around the Hall of Fame and return to their buses past the statue of the World War I doughboy, left. "A few stragglers always have to be pulled off the statue before the bus can leave," chuckles architect Ireland.

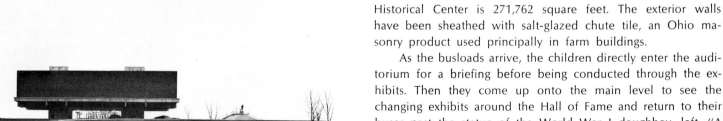

Balthazar Korab photos

134

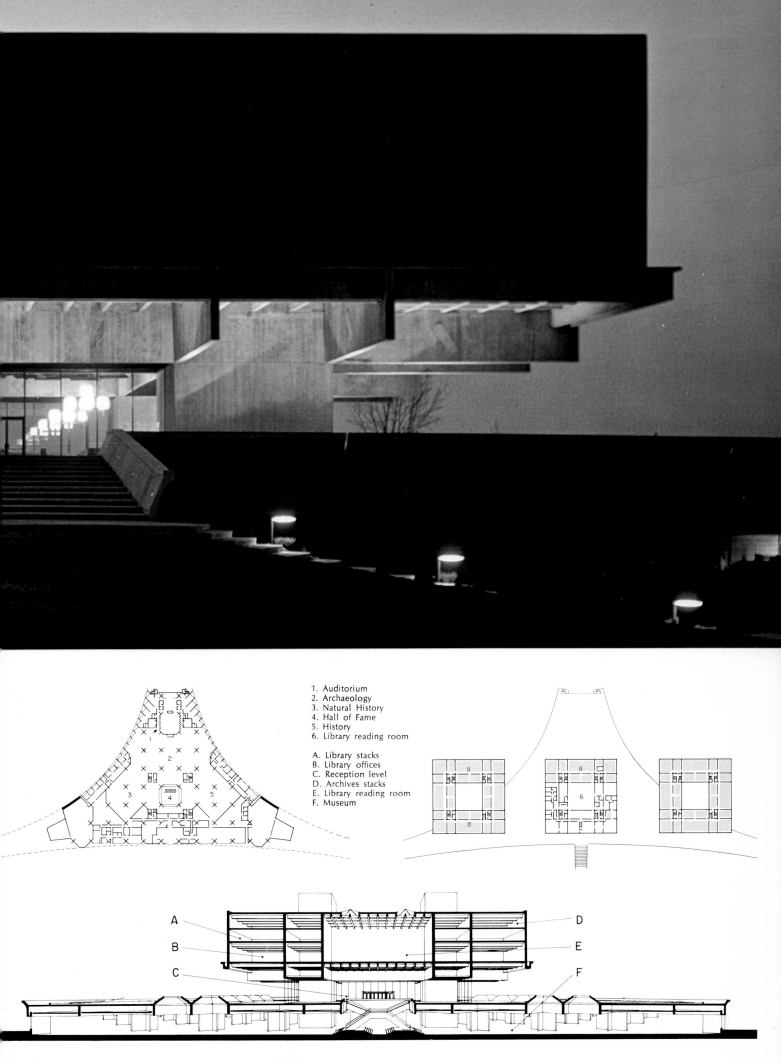

1. Auditorium
2. Archaeology
3. Natural History
4. Hall of Fame
5. History
6. Library reading room

A. Library stacks
B. Library offices
C. Reception level
D. Archives stacks
E. Library reading room
F. Museum

The free relationship of the diagrid museum structure to the foursquare library geometry is obvious, above, as skylights placed above essential exhibits seem to meander in like sheep grazing near an ancient temple. The edges of the triangular museum form glazed office walls behind which curators and interested scholars work to classify and study the treasures of the museum and to prepare new exhibits. Working with Herb Rosenthal, the Oakland Museum exhibits consultant, the architects devised the cruciform columns as a matrix into which displays can be placed. Three small theaters, each accommodating exactly one busload, present short films and students are able to walk into a full-size replica of a house of the Adena culture, a high point in Ohio's prehistoric Indian civilizations. Historical forms of transportation, bottom left, opposite page, form an exhibit in the history section. Two hundred Civil War battleflags dominate the Hall of Fame and its grand staircase.

HISTORICAL CENTER, Columbus, Ohio; Client: *The State Department of Public Works for the Ohio Historical Society.* Architects: *Ireland and Associates—W. Byron Ireland, partner in charge; George S. Bulford and Walter S. Withers, project architects;* structural engineers: *Korda and Associates;* mechanical engineers: *Kramer, Comer and Passe;* acoustical consultant: *Dr. Perry Borchers;* exhibit consultants: *Herb Rosenthal and Associates;* exhibit lighting consultant: *H. A. Williams and Associates.*

One of the five history teachers who serve as museum guides is briefing four or five groups of students who have just arrived at the museum, left. With her colleagues she will then take them through the exhibits, one of which, a giant mastodon, is shown below. The coffered roof of the auditorium forms the mound on which the doughboy statue stands. The reading room of the library, below left, is formed by four shear walls.

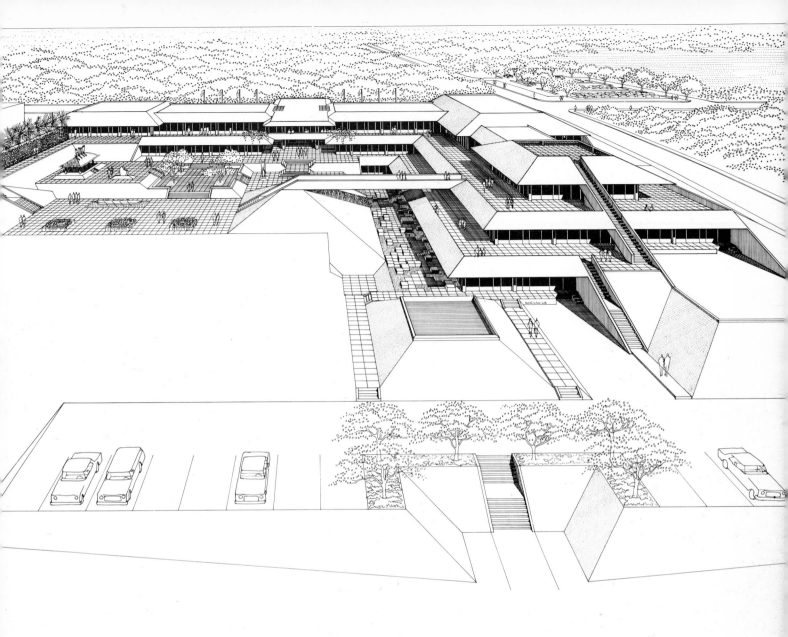

FLORIDA MUSEUM

Earth berms, concrete sun canopies and landscaped courts are the visual vocabulary that architect William Morgan has so effectively employed in designing the new Florida State Museum in Gainesville. The museum's fine natural history collection had previously been housed in a cramped office building downtown. The new site is a natural hillside on the northeast fringe of the University of Florida. Surrounding buildings, part of a biological research complex, defined the site but posed no problem of architectural etiquette. Morgan has treated the north and east elevations as simple but powerful earth forms crowned in concrete but giving little hint of what is within. The berm is sectioned only on the north side by a projecting entrance canopy (overleaf). On entering, visitors find themselves on the building's upper level overlooking an exciting sequence of interlocking sculpture courts and earth mounds.

The museum's functional relationships are clearly defined. The lowest two levels contain research and storage space for the department of

N 25

natural and social sciences. Offices line the wall facing the sculpture courts and generous precast overhangs protect the view windows. Small labs link the offices with storage ranges which are buried in the berm. By these simple juxtapositions, the three kinds of staff spaces can be concentrated for maximum convenience and flexibility. Loading docks at both levels lead to spaces where newly arrived materials can be cleaned, sorted, fumigated and catalogued before being put on display or into the research collections.

The upper level, in addition to a reception area, contains guides' offices and a large multi-media exhibition hall for the display of a collection that includes brightly-colored Indian potlatch and totems as well as the skeleton of a prehistoric mammoth recently recovered from under nearly forty feet of water in a swamp near Tallahassee. "Bertha," as the ancient fossil is called, was almost 85 per cent complete when recovered and is reported to be the best preserved lady of her kind ever found in the Southeastern United States.

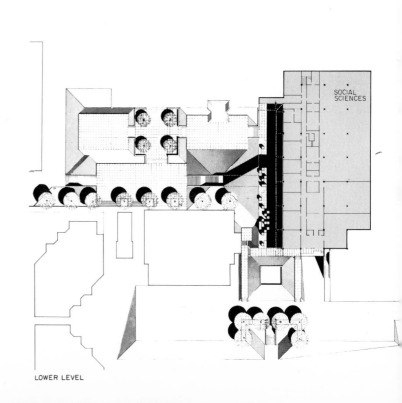

SOCIAL SCIENCES

LOWER LEVEL

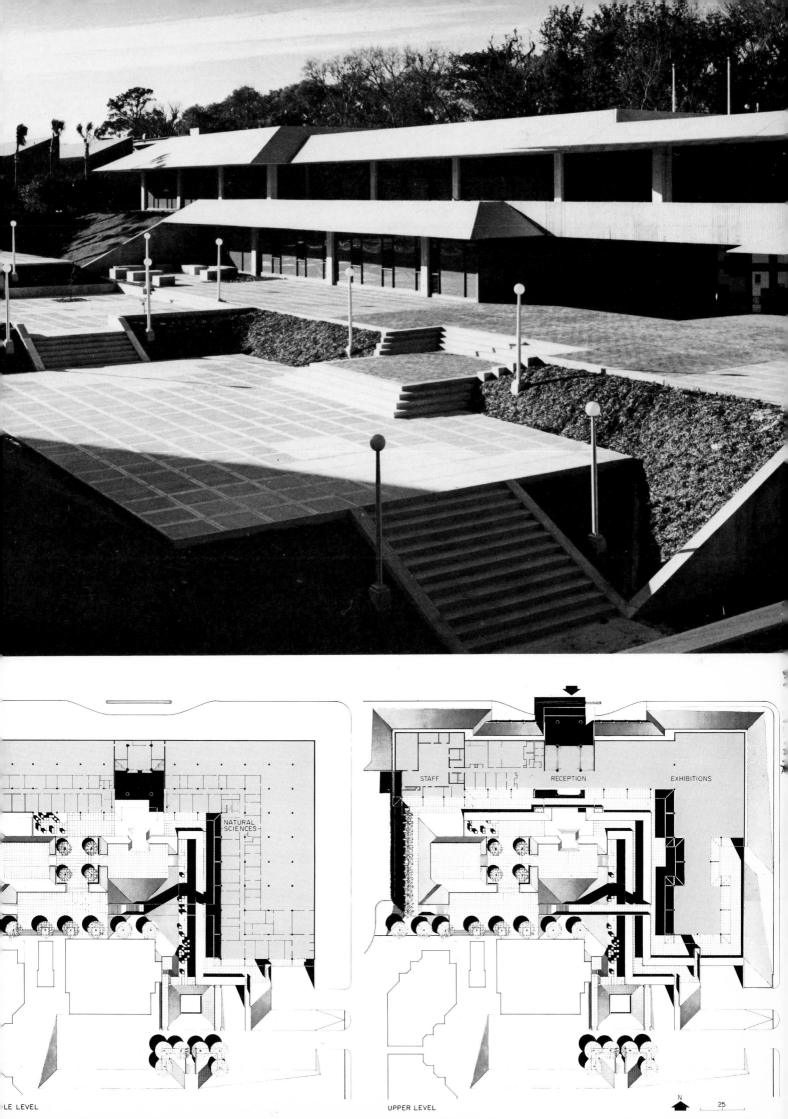

NATURAL SCIENCES

STAFF   RECEPTION   EXHIBITIONS

N   25

J. W. Hobbs

At the south end of the exhibition gallery, a bridge (opposite) leads to the top of an earth pyramid and down into the sculpture courts where the earth-form motif reaches its climax. This two-acre sequence of staged platforms provides more than a splendid and appropriate setting for archaeological display. It also serves as connective tissue between other adjoining but functionally disassociated portions of the campus. The museum's future expansion to the south will continue this process of unification.

Morgan has long been interested in earth-form architecture, and feels that contemporary architects have too long ignored its design potential. This exceptionally handsome museum, funded jointly by the Florida Board of Regents, private donors and the National Science Foundation, pleads the case for earth forms potently and persuasively.

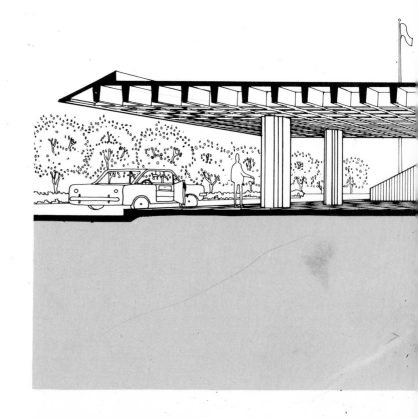

FLORIDA STATE MUSEUM, University of Florida, Gainesville, Florida. *Joshua C. Dickinson, Jr.,* Director. Architect: *William Morgan;* structural engineer: *Haley Keister;* mechanical and electrical engineers: *Evans & Hammond, Inc.;* general contractor: *The Auchter Company.*

William Morgan

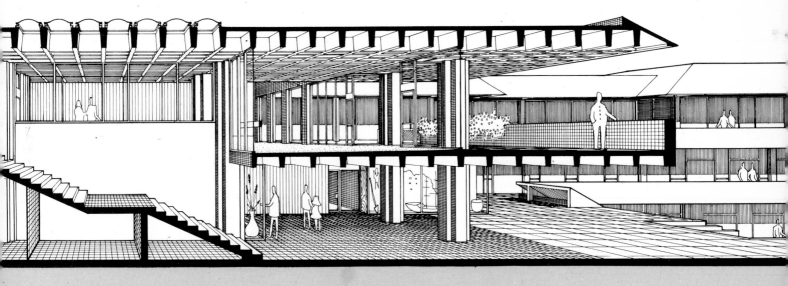

The museum's interiors are direct and appealing. In the reception area, photo above, concrete is left natural and carpeting is soft brown. Bright color accents are provided by graphics and posters advertising exhibits within. Waffle slabs are exposed in most of the spaces. In the 35,000 square foot exhibition area, the steel truss ceiling is painted black and equipped with flexible lighting.

Glass walls facing the court are protected by wide, canted overhangs that double as parapets for terraces above. Detailing has been kept simple both inside and out. All parking lots for staff and public are located at the site's perimeter where they are largely concealed by berms and planting.

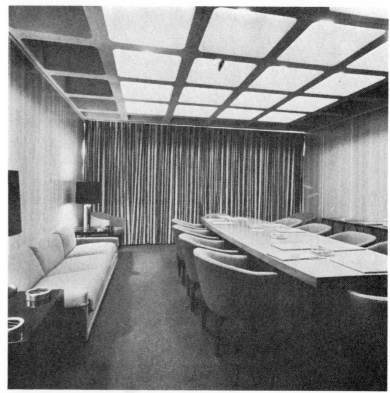

PEABODY MUSEUM

Architects Stahl/Bennett were originally retained simply to program a needed massive addition to Salem, Massachusetts' visually delicate Peabody Museum built in 1824. "The board of directors had been trying to face the reality for 10 years, and finally they were prepared to just see how big it would have to be." The program called for 46,000 square feet of new construction. To promote an acceptance of the reality, the architects kept at the Museum a block model of the old building, the newer additions to its rear, and the volumes of new construction that would result from the program; and they invited the board of directors to work on it, arranging the new volumes as the individuals saw fit. "Originally they thought it was just a problem of the elevation."

What the board finally got, was one level for internal functions below grade and two levels of exhibition space arranged to compete with the older building neither in fenestration nor in height. The original building became the counterpart to a new pavilion at the opposite end of the block, and is isolated from the addition by a glazed connector that reveals the original once-exterior wall to passers-by (a typical technique for Stahl/Bennett). The new concrete-framed building is like a high garden wall clad in a granite veneer, matching that of the still-important original building.

While the 28-foot bays are framed with a deep-coffered concrete slab at the roof to conceal lighting and air-handling ducts, the second and ground floors are flat slabs in recognition of the low floor-to-floor heights that had to be matched in the original building. The cost was $2.5 million. In the plan, the original building is to the upper left, and the new building is to its right. Others have been added on (bottom) in intermediate years and they represent a "catalog" of industrial architecture for the periods in which they were built.

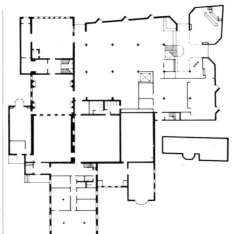

Steve Rosenthal photos

PEABODY MUSEUM OF SALEM, Salem, Massachusetts. Owner: *Trustees of Peabody Museum.* Architect of record: *Philip W. Bourne.* Program and design consultants: *Stahl/Bennett, Inc.—project architects: W. Eric Kluz, Martin S. Lehman.* Associate architect: *Bernard J. Harrison.* Engineers: *Souza & True, Inc.* (structural); *R. G. Vanderweil* (mechanical/electrical). Consultants: *William J. Cavanaugh* (acoustical); *William Lam Associates* (lighting); *Conmatan, Inc.* (specifications); *Leslie W. Buckingham* (cost). General contractor: *J. F. White Contracting Company.*

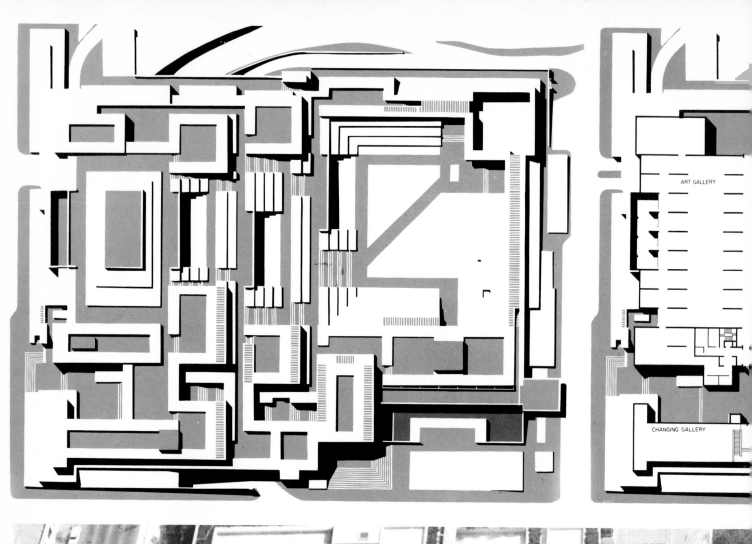

ART GALLERY

CHANGING GALLERY

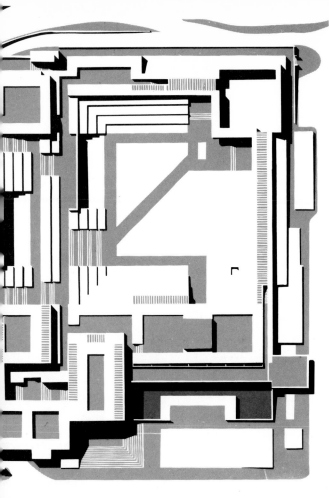

Oakland Museum

The city of Oakland, California now boasts a regional museum much of which has been constructed underground. Designed by Kevin Roche John Dinkeloo and Associates on a four-block site which slopes downward toward an inland tidal lake, it appears to be a terraced park rather than a building. Appearance to the contrary, the Oakland Museum is more than a handsome new public park. It is a huge $10-million complex consisting of three interrelated museums tucked under terraces and opening onto gardens, the latter designed by landscape architect Dan Kiley.

At the outset the city's program called for three separate structures to house the collections of Oakland's art, history and natural science museums. Architect Kevin Roche was convinced from the beginning that these three collections belonged together in one place. After careful analysis of Oakland's actual and potential urban design structure (page 153) Roche also decided that an urban park was urgently needed on the site as the first link in a chain of integrated work and leisure facilities designed to give order and coherence to the city. Since Roche believes that museums and parks belong together, the solution then became obvious to him—a three-part underground terraced structure with a park on top. The result as built has been widely acknowledged as an architectural triumph for Roche, but it also stands as strong evidence of his power of persuasion.

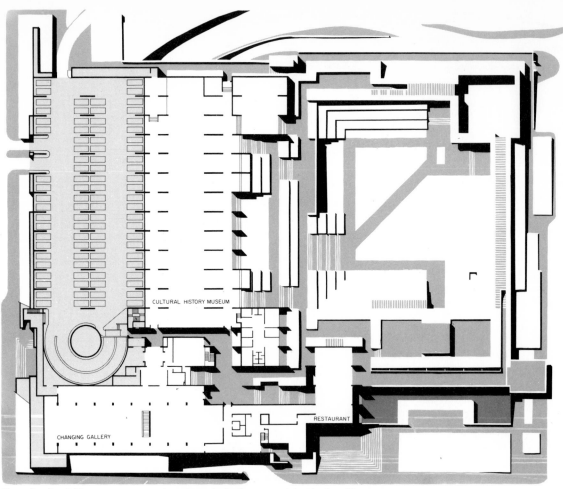

CULTURAL HISTORY MUSEUM

CHANGING GALLERY

RESTAURANT

Plan of cultural history museum and environs including second level of parking garage

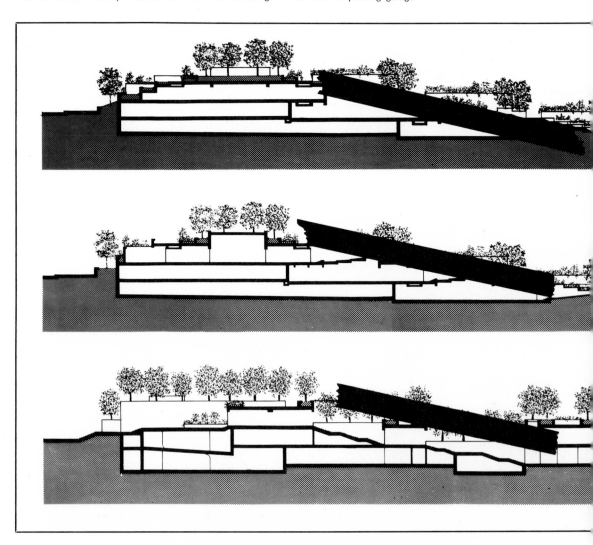

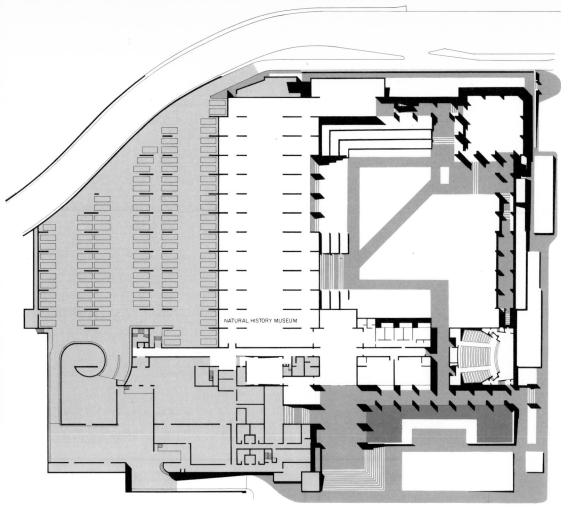

Plan of natural history museum and environs including first level of parking garage

NATURAL HISTORY MUSEUM

As the aerial photo (page 146) indicates, the Oakland Museum is a green oasis added to a city with only a fraction of the park area it should have by good U.S. standards. Unfortunately separated from Lake Merritt by the tangled expressway which blights the lake's southern shore (see top of photo) it is nonetheless a great urban amenity, already intensively used by the citizens.

The park functions not as a public square with easy access but more as a great landscaped courtyard. To get to it, one must first enter the building lobby since, for security reasons, there is no direct access to the park from the street. One needn't go through the museum to reach the gardens but there

are many points of access to them from the three galleries, which are placed on three separate levels to emphasize their distinctiveness, but which are spatially interrelated to establish their cohesion. The ease and delight with which the visitor can move from the study of art, cultural and natural history to the contemplation of nature itself, makes the Oakland Museum one of the rare places of the world.

As the sections (left) reveal, there are two stories of space below the art gallery, one story below the history gallery and none beneath the natural science wing. In addition to the 200-car parking garage, these spaces include loading docks, workshops, storage and employee facilities.

Chelmer Alexander photos

149

Light beige concrete, sandblasted for texture, is the principal building material both inside and out. The garden includes a pergola, a reflecting pool, small courts and shaded walks.

The planting consists of rich ground covers, colorful flowering shrubs and indigenous trees. Twelve cedars and seven redwood trees on the site were carefully protected during the construction period, and additional cedars and redwoods have been planted. Eventually the park will be a living "botanical museum" of ground covers, vines, espaliers, aquatics, shrubs, ferns, fern trees and dichondra. Almost all of the plants are watered and fertilized through an automatic irrigation-feeding system with four control stations. These controls permit automatic irrigation and fertilizing according to a pre-set program.

The exhibition facilities were planned to be independent of the structure and building finishes. They are the work of designer Gordon Ashby. In addition to working with the curators on the selection of materials to be exhibited in each museum, he designed exhibit cases, platforms, lighting and the displays themselves. An effort was made to achieve elegance in execution and detail. A minimum palette of materials was maintained—walnut, oak flooring, black and white laminated plastic surfaces, black anodized and white epoxy painted metal and chrome plated metal.

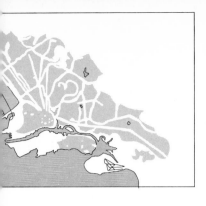

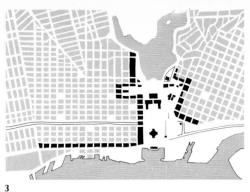

3

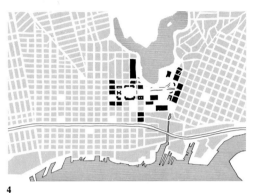

4

5

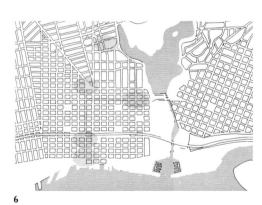

6

The local environment—as actually accomplished and hopefully envisioned—shaped Roche's plans for the Oakland Museum. "If the city is to have a sense of order," says Roche, "a building must be part of an over-all composition. It must dominate or be subservient to its local environment. Visual responsibility goes far beyond the limits of a site."

The architects made an extensive study of the Oakland area, not as a comprehensive report nor as a proposal for a city plan, but for their own use as part of a preliminary investigation in the orderly process of designing the Museum. The ultimate development (7) shows the Oakland Museum as constructed but includes a proposal for the entire area which Roche believes is deserving of serious consideration by the people of Oakland.

- -

THE OAKLAND MUSEUM, Oakland, California. Architects: *Kevin Roche John Dinkeloo and Associates—Philip Kinsella, associate on job;* engineers:

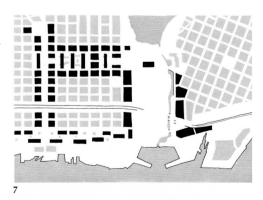

7

1. A park system for Oakland in a city plan report prepared in 1915 by Werner Hagemann, one of the great city planners of the time. It was based on recommendations made by Frederick Law Olmsted in 1868 and again by Charles Mulford Robinson in 1906. It proposed that a series of parks be developed along the natural creeks and canyons which would form green arteries into the heart of the city. On axis with the entry into the harbor, an island park was proposed—both to screen the industrial development in this area and also to provide a space for water sports and regattas. Unfortunately these plans were never carried out. The heart of the proposal for Oakland was the Lake Merritt Park and the Connection to the East Bay.

2. A closer look at the Lake Merritt Park and the East Bay connection. Hagemann proposed that the main north-south axis not be obstructed by buildings placed across, as the new civic auditorium (white rectangle) had unfortunately been, but rather that the axis should be emphasized by buildings placed parallel to it, thus preserving the free continuity of water and park.

3. Plan for a civic center developed in 1930 by the Alameda County Society of Architects, based on Hagemann's recommendations. It creates a formal park right down to the estuary to be bordered by public buildings. Two proposed buildings make a formal composition to the south of the civic auditorium. On the north side the plan follows Dr. Hagemann's suggestion for a plaza with fountains projecting into Lake Merritt. On the west side of this plaza the plan indicates a group of civic buildings around a mall. The first of these, the county court house, was built at this time. Roche believes this to have been an excellent plan. "While it may have been unrealistic about traffic," he acknowledges, "this was certainly excusable in 1930; had this plan been followed, Oakland would truly have one of the most magnificent centers in the country today." Unfortunately this scheme was forgotten during the war years through industrial development along the waterfront.

4. The 1947 master plan, an outgrowth of a civic center study begun in 1944, reflects a 1935 zoning ordinance which designated the waterfront for industrial use. The plan reflects the fact that the center of population had begun to move to the south and east and the belief that a civic center should not be located in a central business district because of land cost and the constrictions it places on expansion. The plan argues, therefore, that the civic center should spread across the park, tying the east and west together. It eliminates the rest of the proposed park and thereby destroys the estuary connection. The plan also indicates an elaborate intersection of roads, now built in a somewhat altered form. Roche criticizes this plan (fortunately never implemented) for closing the estuary connection, "an idea so logical that it has been re-occurring for over 50 years;" for isolating the cultural part of the civic center from pedestrian access and from the lake; for compounding the road network; for creating dead public space and for lacking visual unity and apparent connection to the city.

5. The Lake Merritt area in 1961 when Roche's studies for the Oakland Museum began. The 1947 plan had become obsolete, a site had been picked for the Museum which was inconsistent with that or any other earlier plan and the Nimitz Freeway had radically altered the traffic pattern of the area. It was apparent that at this stage Oakland had neither a civic center nor a plan for one which could be realized. So Roche began by taking a broader look at the whole city.

6. An analysis of the Lake Merritt area in the context of Oakland in 1961, which was still a city ringed by mountains revolving around a natural focal point—Lake Merritt—and facing an estuary and bay. Much of the land bordering the estuary, and now given over to junkyards, is publicly owned and can be reclaimed as park. Five distinct centers had developed by 1961. Bordering the northwest finger of Lake Merritt is a cluster of office buildings known as Kaiser Center. To the southeast is the courthouse area near the city auditorium, almost due west is the city hall and to the south near the harbor breakwall is Jack London Square, a highly successful development bordering the central business district.

7. Roche's proposal showing the elements which constitute the city tied together to *form* the city. His unifying means would be wide park-lined boulevards and avenues with a mix of commercial, cultural and private buildings. The excitement generated by shops, hotels, museums and theaters would give life to the green open spaces and to the public and private office buildings located within or under them. The Oakland Museum, which doubles as terraced green space, is really the first segment of Roche's grand plan based in part on the work of Hagemann. Roche believes that to have built a large building on the site would have been wrong for the city, architecturally and humanistically.

Ontario Museum

The Ontario Science Center, designed by Raymond Moriyama, is a museum of popular science and technology, with emphasis on the popular; a place where visitors may become involved in steering a spaceship, making electronic music, or creating the theatrical lighting for a scene from Macbeth. The function of the Center is like that of a museum in many ways— it houses identifiable exhibits of man's scientific world, it is meant to teach the visitor, the visitor moves from exhibit to exhibit—but it is not like a museum in its attempt to involve the visitors physically in each display, make them "operate" that display, and in its attempt at entertainment as well as teaching. To entertain and arouse curiosity in people, as well as educate them, was a major goal of the new museum from the time it was first conceived in 1964. In the next five years, there were several changes in the museum's proposed staff and some changes in program, but the goal of a participatory, innovative learning center remained. In notes made during design development, Moriyama wrote: "The center must be a place for everyone . . . It must arouse curiosity. It must be a place of wonder . . . It must fuse the visitor with ideas through active participation. It must be an emotional experience with intellectual satisfaction." This architectural goal has been translated into three buildings which do different things, as the Center itself is meant to do different things. The first structure is the Entrance Building (above) which introduces the visitors to the Center. The second structure—the Core Building—is the ceremonial and symbolic center of the complex. The third structure is the Exhibition Building, where the majority of the exhibits are displayed.

PLAN

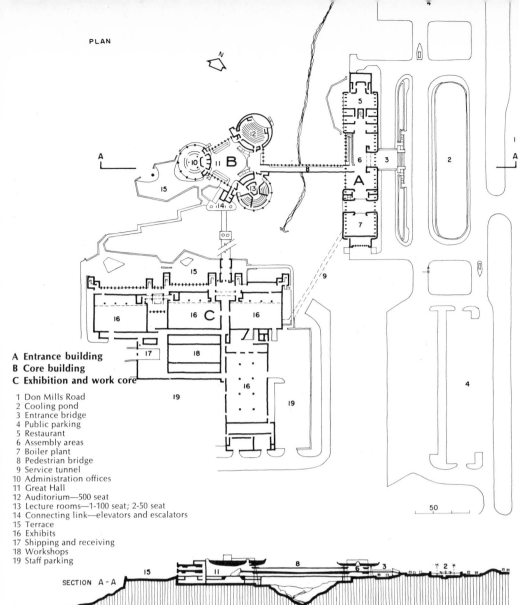

A **Entrance building**
B **Core building**
C **Exhibition and work core**

1 Don Mills Road
2 Cooling pond
3 Entrance bridge
4 Public parking
5 Restaurant
6 Assembly areas
7 Boiler plant
8 Pedestrian bridge
9 Service tunnel
10 Administration offices
11 Great Hall
12 Auditorium—500 seat
13 Lecture rooms—1-100 seat; 2-50 seat
14 Connecting link—elevators and escalators
15 Terrace
16 Exhibits
17 Shipping and receiving
18 Workshops
19 Staff parking

SECTION A-A

The Ontario Science Center had to accommodate two kinds of visitors; those in large organized groups, such as a class of school children, and single individuals or families touring without supervision. The long Entrance Building (overleaf) was therefore divided into two levels, one for each group. School buses or vehicles carrying organized classes drive into the main entrance, around the large fountain and reflecting pool, and unload at the lower ground level of the Entrance Building (overleaf) with its long sidewalk for parallel parking. The visiting group enters near the center of the long facade, into the flat-ceilinged space in the photo, overleaf. This is the student assembly area, with a series of large circular and sunken seating alcoves placed around the long, narrow space. Each seating alcove is a different color, and each class is assigned a color when they enter the Science Center. This device is important because an average of 60 groups, totaling about 1,800 students, visit the Center each day. The staff expects this number to increase to about 100 groups (maximum capacity of the present space) or about 3,000 students daily. And these 3,000 children will all be excited to be there, noisy and curious; it is a major organizational task to keep them together.

Individual and family visitors enter the upper level of the Entrance Building via a series of wide, low steps (photo below) and across the main pedestrian bridge spanning the bus driveway. Cars are parked in a large lot to the south of the reflecting pool and fountain; the lot is below the elevation of the road and other entrance features, so cars are hidden. Once into the building, individual visitors enter a space similar to the one for classes (one floor below), but with a gently lighted and undulat-

ing ceiling which reflects the entrance building roof. This is a coat checking and orientation space for the public, with a restaurant and cafeteria at one end and the boiler room and heating plant—glass enclosed, mechanized, and broadly displayed as part of the exhibition—at the other. The visitor stays briefly in the Entrance Building and then moves on through the Science Center. This whole entrance sequence just described is both logical—separating efficiently two kinds of visitors—and dramatic—preparing each visitor for the playful and curiously successful new architectural events to come.

From the Entrance Building visitors can see their next destination—the Core or "tower" building (two photos, left). They also discover for the first time the superb natural setting in which the Science Center is placed. The Core Building occupies the highest land of the site but is surrounded by trees and foliage, so it is difficult to see it from any single viewing point. It is the symbolic and ceremonial center of the complex, housing a great triangular hall for special exhibits and awards functions, a 500-seat auditorium, three smaller lecture theaters, the administrative offices and several special display areas. Lectures and seminars for the various student groups may be conducted here, as well as regularly scheduled and special classes for the general public. The Core Building is entered via a long, relatively constricted bridge (photo, below) which begins at the reception building and ends at the Great Hall. The craftsmanship and detailing are excellent in the Core Building, and one's attention becomes focused on these issues quickly. The interior walls, like the exterior, are concrete, with very rough and bold vertical ribbing. It is obviously a controlled texture, never haphazard; the brass fittings, such as the ones for fire hoses, are carefully joined with the rough wall, as are the other surface finishes such as sandblasted concrete, plaster, and terrazzo.

From the Core Building visitors proceed down, via the escalator and stair enclosure in the photo overleaf, to the Exhibition Building. This is the largest of the three buildings in floor area, and the real heart of the Science Center. The architecture here is understated and utilitarian; the exhibits are the thing. There is, again, very little of the usual "museum" atmosphere. The science arcade is filled with audience participation exhibitions that demand of

visitors that they touch, turn, squeeze, jump up and down, or talk. There is also elaborate laboratory apparatus for use by industry, institutions and supervised students for actual work; the equipment is on display in public areas and its use can be communicated immediately to the public. With genuine theatrical light control equipment visitors learn the rudiments of lighting on a model stage with scenes from Macbeth and Henry IV. There are 450 separate exhibits like this in the Center, most of them in the Exhibition Building.

Visitors sweep out into the landing at the top of the stairs of the Great Hall (above) having come through the pedestrian bridge from the Entrance Building. They proceed down the stairs and through any of the openings to the right in the photo, into the Exhibition Building. The Hall's main function is for occasions attracting large crowds, and as an antechamber to the several theaters around it. At left is a photo of one of the major spaces in the Exhibition Hall. The exhibits are brightly painted, usually mobile, and their graphics are always invigorating.

ONTARIO SCIENCE CENTER, Toronto, Canada. Architect: *Raymond Moriyama—David Vickers, project manager; John Snell, project construction manager; Thomas Motomochi, assistant construction manager; Donald Cooper, design co-ordinator; Bon W. Mueller, landscape; G. Ronning-Philip, interiors and furniture.* Structural engineer: *M. S. Yolles Assoc.;* mechanical engineer: *Nicholas Fodor and Assoc.;* electrical engineer: *Mulvey Engineering Ltd.;* soils engineer: *William A. Trow Assoc.;* acoustic and lighting: *Reevesound Co.;* contractor: *Pigott Construction Co.*

OREGON HISTORICAL SOCIETY

In planning a new central headquarters building to house its collections, the Oregon Historical Society wished not only to improve its service to the students, historians, and writers who have been its most faithful clientele but to provide facilities enabling it to reach out to a broader public.

The site is a full half-block (minus a 50 by 75-foot corner now occupied by a tavern) which lies between the so-called Park Blocks, Portland's institutional center, and the edge of the downtown area. The Society felt that the building should orient to both, openly relating to the public at ground level, and creating an exterior "special place" which would be identifiable to the public and tie into the fabric of the city. This set the parameters within which the architects met a program calling for museum, library, and office space, and "as much storage as could be accommodated."

The result is a three-story building, plus a full basement largely given over to storage. At street level, a special gallery, invitingly open on three sides, features changing displays designed to lure passersby. Above it is a second gallery which houses the Society's permanent exhibits and is fully enclosed to assure complete light control. The library occupies the building's third floor, with reading and seminar rooms, and staff offices ranged around the central core of open stacks.

The desired outdoor "special place" (or places, as it proved) were created with an assist from the sloping site and zoning requiring a sideyard—a combination that suggested placing administrative offices at basement level, opening to a landscaped court and public pedestrian way which links the Park Blocks with downtown. The administrative wing is roofed by a spacious garden court accessible from the main-floor gallery and lounge.

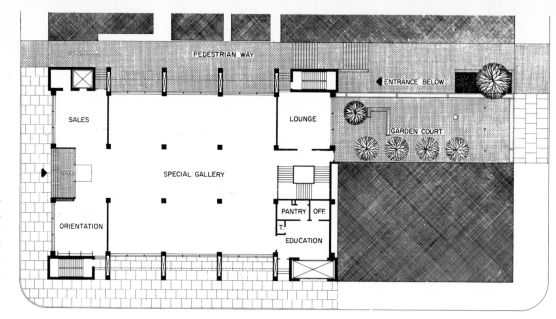

FIRST FLOOR PLAN

5

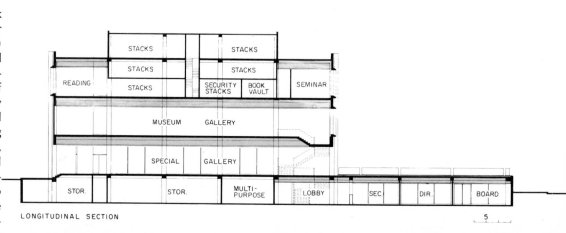

LONGITUDINAL SECTION

5

Art Huby photos

160

Building fenestration—or lack of it—(side elevation at left) reflects interior functions: open and enclosed galleries, and sunshielded library reading rooms and offices. To keep floor areas open and flexible, vertical penetration is confined to corner towers and main stair. Pedestrian way (below) gives through-block passage and provides access to basement-level executive offices topped by garden court. Spacious, uncluttered street-floor gallery for changing special exhibits (right and below) is glazed on three sides to lend a sense of openness and welcome, its paved floor and luminous ceiling providing a neutral background for displays. A portion of the library's comfortably furnished main reading room is shown below right.

HEADQUARTERS BUILDING, OREGON HISTORICAL SOCIETY, Portland Oregon. Architects: *Wolff-Zimmer-Gunsul-Frasca*; consultant: *Pietro Belluschi*; structural engineer: *Stanley V. Carlson*; mechanical engineer: *Thomas E. Taylor*; electrical engineers: *Grant Kelley & Associates*.

CHAPTER FOUR

CHAPTER FOUR

PERFORMING ARTS CENTERS

WESLEYAN

Middletown, Connecticut, where Wesleyan University was founded in 1829, is a small-scale town and, in keeping, so is Roche Dinkeloo's Center for the Fine Arts, completed a year and a half ago.

The elegant classical proportions of old houses, lining the street around the campus, suggested reticence, not assertion and, as a result, this concrete and limestone cluster of buildings, which cost about $12 million, muses quietly within view of the antebellum beauty of old-time architects like Ithiel Town and his partner A. J. Davis who, being rather far-out formalists for their day, constantly cribbing Persius and Schinkel, would probably find Roche Dinkeloo's work here needlessly deferential to the history around it.

The reason that the Center is deferential to the history around it is that the University, whose interests were represented by architect John Martin, a head of department here, insisted upon a style which

would be unfettered by style—meaning a style unfettered by aspects which would "date" its architecture in times to come. In this period, the mid-sixties, most clients, need it be said, were insisting on just the opposite—leaving indelible marks in the name of corporate clout or *kultur*. Wesleyan, with over 20 per cent of its enrollment of 2,400 in the arts programs, wanted simple surroundings—sounding boards of space and structure for the marks which *people* leave, or the sounds which they leave, or the sculptures and sonnets. In this six-acre grove of beeches and hemlocks and sycamores, Roche Dinkeloo gave the University a terse verse, written in cubic ciphers, about the virtues of stylistic subtlety.

Easily as sacred as its grove was a large playing field which, as any Old School Boy can tell you, is very sacred indeed. It is edged and set off by a graphics workshop on one side (see plan), by the

The Wesleyan Center for the Arts is a cluster of low-scale concrete and limestone structures ranged around an existing campus. The old playing field is framed by a graphics workshop, the 20,000-square-foot Art Gallery, a 414-foot Cinema Hall, the studios and faculty offices of the art and music departments. Undergraduate studios, bordering the northern edge of the playing field, are crisp double cubes with two-story north-facing windows and walled courtyards for outside classes in warm weather.

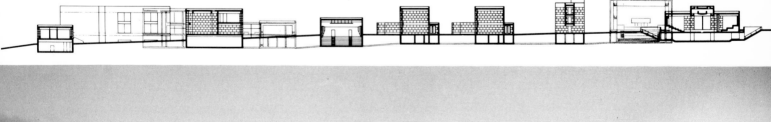

Recital Hall on the other and, connecting them, by a brace of two-story-high cubes, containing painting and sculpture studios. Walls of limestone—all the limestone here is unfinished, economical and rich with variations of color—enclose courtyards to the north of these studios, serving to underline that edge of the playing field.

The decision to go with separate small-looking structures, set along walks and paths, is not studied casualness. Thinking back to all the Middletowns one has been in, there is a significant aspect to all that Colonial or Revival charm. And that significant aspect has to do with how the walls meet the ground—straight down in pristine perpendicularity. Roche Dinkeloo's separate small-looking structures do the very same thing. A formal characteristic emerges from within a vernacular tradition.

The 414-seat Cinema Hall, the Recital Hall, the World Music Center, which contains an Indonesian array of instruments called a Gamelon, and the 548-seat Theater are all set partly underground,

around the grove, which made excavation easier, helped protect the trees and, of course, kept these major volumes in context with the Center's over-all scale.

It is interesting to note that, initially, these cubes were to be all concrete—formed up in a module measuring three feet eight inches by two feet six inches by 14 inches in thickness. But the concrete did not price out. The limestone, taken from the more gritty (and more interesting) strata, did. In the finished job, concrete reads, outside and in, as concrete is supposed to—as elements of span. The limestone, laid up in the module mentioned before, supports. The elements of span meet those of support as neatly as the elements of support meet the ground. This is not form-giving stuff, the gratuitous muscling in with preconceptions which so many architects have, quite rightly, rejected in recent years. Wesleyan is form-taking, creating from context, and for a client with the sensitivity to not settle for less.

In the Center's high-ceilinged and well-lit Art Gallery, which has

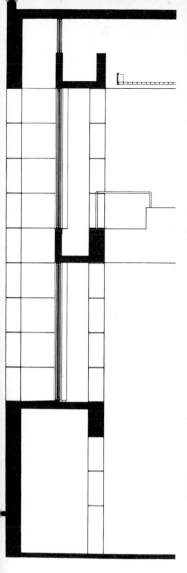

The continental-style, 548-seat theater, containing 23,700 square feet, combines theater and stage in a single room with a continuous metallic ceiling grid for lighting systems. Flexible panels permit a wide combination of stage style, from a thrust proscenium to a theater in the round. Large windows let in lovely views of the surrounding landscape while automatic blinds close out the light as the house lights dim. In addition to the theater, a 10,-000-square-foot World Music Center contains a rare Indonesian orchestra called a Gamelon, known for its sublte and homogenous tones derived from a varied set of gongs and percussion instruments. A concrete beam spans between two windows above a dance floor and is acoustically curved, a function which is reinforced by the angled windows which further act as acoustical resonators. The Art Gallery has a 4,100-square-foot main exhibition space, a seminar room above the entrance overlooks the Gallery. A second, smaller exhibition room, linked to the main space by a glazed colonnade, is lit only by an oculus in the roof, casting a ellipse of light on the richly textured limestone walls, itself a work of art.

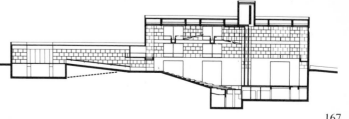

This ramp entrance to the Theater (above) points up the material and spatial texture of the Wesleyan interiors generally. A view of the double-level foyer inter-penetrates the ramp area, the experience enhanced by the planar composition of concrete, limestone, glass and carpet. The spacious side-aisles of the Theater itself, contrasting to the intimate foyer, provide a ceremonious, yet familial substitute for a lobby.

a 4,100-square-foot exhibition space, is a summation of what Roche Dinkeloo have achieved—an environment in which to find one's relationship to oneself. Past an assortment of the "latest" in electrified objects, past a shallow tank with fish noises coming from it, past sheets of glass set tactfully back from an outer edge of limestone folding around them, one enters a small dark room—only to discover, as if by accident, an ellipse of sunlight cast on the limestone through a circular plastic bubble in the roof.

"We worked for weeks, calculating that one," says Kevin Roche, saying as much as anything could about the over-all character and composition of this subtle, splendid group of buildings.

CENTER FOR THE ARTS, Wesleyan University, Middletown, Connecticut. Owner: *Wesleyan University*. Architects: *Roche Dinkeloo and Associates*. Engineers: *Pfisterer Tor and Associates* (structural); *John Altieri, P.E.* (mechanical/electrical). Consultants: *Bolt, Beranek and Newman* (acoustics). Contractors: *E & F Construction Company* (general); *Marino Plumbing and Heating Company* (mechanical); *S. Freedman Electric, Inc.* (electrical).

AMHERST

A recitation about the Fine Arts Center at the Amherst campus of the University of Massachusetts and the Center for the Fine Arts at Wesleyan University at Middletown, Connecticut, is implicitly a discourse about a decade called, with mixed regard, The Sixties. Architects Kevin Roche and John Dinkeloo, ensconced in a big brick hilltop house near New Haven, seemed remote from the flagellations of the American mainstream. But a decade later—ten years which took these two works from inception to completion—it is possible to wonder whether this designer and this engineer, this Sullivan and this Adler, were remote at all. Despite a chaos which saw the sentinels of social, cultural and political renewal vanquished, the search for new sentinels did not abate, especially in those outlying groves of academe where, sharing resources with nearby countryside communities, town and gown came together to learn how to paint, or how to look at paintings; to perform, or how to appreciate the theatrical and muscial message; to develop skills of expression, or how to respond to expression more fully. These buildings, conceived to instruct society's creative urge, are a reminder of the hold we must keep on our humanity.

Way back when, Ralph Waldo Emerson (who thought very highly of farming), published an essay canonizing agricultural values as the mainstay of society's strength. Education, art, science, philosophy, and ethics—all were to be found among the furrows, or so Emerson believed. But need it be said, such faith has been plowed under for over a century by the rampages of an urban, not rural, nation.

It is significant that during the fifties and sixties, America's educational explosion affected rural institutions as much as, if not more than, our city-slicker schools. Nowhere is this more evident than at the University of Massachusetts, located in the Berkshires near Amherst, where Emily Dickinson once sat in her room, day in and day out, writing sonnets and, in our own time, Robert Frost trudged through snow or fallen leaves saying things like, "I have miles to go before I sleep."

So does rural America, if the Amherst campus is any indication—most especially its recently completed Fine Arts Center, commissioned a decade ago during the culture boom, by Roche Dinkeloo Associates. The cozy 200-acre campus, which started out as an agricultural school, has now been put on the map as a regional resource of art, music, and drama. Roche and Dinkeloo were faced with creating, more than a cluster of interconnected buildings for a varied educational program, an increment of unity which could lend order to an architectural disorder that had piled up during the last 20 years—20 years which saw the University's enrollment climb from 4,000 to nearly 30,000 students.

In 1962, Sasaki, Dawson, DeMay Associates were brought in to do a master plan which, proposing a clear and strong planning structure for the campus, delineated a kind of ceremonial mall linking the

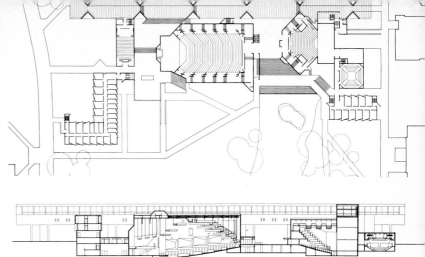

An interplay of assertive forms marks the relationship between the bridge-studio and the theater and auditorium beyond. Serving as a link between the sciences and humanities sides of the Amherst campus, the bridge and the colonnade running beneath it also serve as a transition between the contrasting classical and romantic qualities of the two sides of the Fine Arts Center. Faculty studios, the studio bridge, and the drama department frame the small 221-seat recital hall, the 2,200-seat auditorium, and the 668-seat theater. The great auditorium, one of the more enthralling and efficient houses in recent memory, has a dramatic reversal of tiers which is accomplished by hanging them from the exposed roof trusses. The concrete walls are faceted, providing superb acoustics without appliqued assistance. Three tiers of sound baffles and catwalks for lighting rise above the proscenium to create an octagonal lighting platform.

major access route, North Handley Road, to a big duck pond which has been the campus' central element of charm. The pond, with a little park edging around it, is framed by the University Library, a 25-story building by Edward Durell Stone, and a 10-story Continuing Education Center by Marcel Breuer. Assorted smaller structures, from the 1870's to the 1950's, complete this convivial chaos.

The new Fine Arts Center was designed, therefore, to relate to Sasaki's classy, grassy mall and to establish a tie between the flanking buildings, some devoted to the sciences, others to the humanities. What else, it might be asked, is art really for, unless it be to supply such a bridge?

Such a bridge is exactly what the architects came up with—long and low-lying, running about 650 feet, held up by widely spaced V-shaped pilotis which, in turn, hold up a well-lit studio space for undergraduate artists. This bridge is what one sees coming in on Handley Road and, then, the mall. Bearing out the ceremonial aspect envi-sioned by Sasaki, two reflecting pools have been placed to either side of this procession which, leading to the bridge, becomes an open-air colonnade that runs the length of the bridge, cadenced by the pilotis.

The bridge itself is a sequence of cantilevered elements balanced on and extending out from either side of the V-shaped verticals. The cantilevers are joined in mid-air with nary a notice—the result, as throughout this cluster of buildings, is of superbly formed and finished reinforced concrete. The bridge not only defines a convenient space at right angles to the mall—it also frames, as one walks straight-away under its span, a passage to the duck pond and to the heart of the campus. To the left of this transition is the 700-seat theater, and, to the right, a 2,200-seat auditorium for concerts and the like. Both of these houses, and the external massing—a melange of angles and facets—are cubistic in character. Beneath them is an art gallery.

The drama of this transition—from the more classical mall to the bridge and, beneath it, to the steps leading down to the pond—is

heightened by the juxtaposition of the emphatic linear quality, which the bridge presents, to the more romantic and random quality of the theater and auditorium masses. Looking to either side of the pass-through, as one proceeds toward the pond, a deep spatial gorge is chiseled out, textured by sun and sharp shadows against the clear-cut concrete surfaces. It is as one skips down, toward the pond, and trudges on around it toward the opposite side by Breuer's Continuing Education Center, that one is struck by the architectural sleight-of-hand which the architects have planned. For in contrast to the classical, ordered quality experienced earlier, a romantic array of interconnected structures spread out along the landscape—the theater, the auditorium, the wing of the drama department extending out on the right, the right-angle wing of faculty studios extending out to the left. Something Athenian gives way, gently, to something Emersonian.

One reason for this arresting contrast is that the $14-million Center was conceived to serve both the University and nearby com-munities of the Connecticut River Basin. So it was a requirement keep separate such facilities as classrooms, of which there are 17, an laboratory-studios, of which there are 75, and faculty offices, of whic there are 56—the requirement to keep them separate meaning serer for undisturbed practice. The studio bridge, with its sense of order an ceremony, is an element uniting the campus and inviting the publi Intimations of the more random scale beyond are seen through th colonnade beneath the bridge's formalist span.

There is nothing random about the interiors, nothing at all, eve as randomness serves a purpose outside. The 668-seat theater (righ adjacent to generous backstage teaching facilities and a nearby int mate studio theater, is both carpeted and its seats upholstered in dee orange. Continental-style and steeply banked, this arrangement brin audience and actors into a powerful proximity. The auditorium, sea ing 2,200 (pages 169 and 171), is simply one of the most magnifice rooms in recent memory. Tiers are hung from exposed roof trusse

held forward from the rear, and step upward toward the stage like the underside of a cyclopean stair. Faceted side walls assist sound.

Roche Dinkeloo Associates have fused the traditions of classical order and romanticism at Amherst. Visually, there is a constant give and take between both qualities of composition while they have created functional, ample spaces for students and faculty to slog away in. Inside, the auditorium and theaters derive from technical requirements and acoustical properties an engaging, unadorned esthetic. In fact, Amherst is derivation throughout, its drama a studied extension of program and place—the new virtuosity.

FINE ARTS CENTER, University of Massachusetts, Amherst, Mass. Owner: *Commonwealth of Massachusetts*. Architects: *Roche Dinkeloo and Associates*. Engineers: *LeMessurier Associates* (structural); *Greenleaf Engineers* (mechanical/electrical). Consultants: *Bolt, Beranek & Newman* (acoustics). Contractors: *Fontaine Brothers* (general); *HVH Mechanical Contractors* (mechanical); *Collins* (electrical).

CASA THOMAS JEFFERSON

It has been said that where there is no vision, there is a void. Brasilia conjures up both. A good place to go bananas over this pylon-studded polemic is on the upper tier of the rooftop amphitheater of Casa Thomas Jefferson, located in one of the city's more neighborly districts, and built by the USIA, always gung-ho for getting out good news, in collaboration with a local group called the Thomas Jefferson Cultural Council. Once not so hep about design, the USIA got out some good news here.

In contrast to the seething symbolism that one beholds from the rooftop, the Casa is a nice neat hit for humanism, with some of the spontaneity of a *favella* in Rio. A functional mix is contained within several two-level structures that are smartly scrunched together. Like iron filings, these fragments gravitate around a landscaped interior courtyard, a deliberately magnetic, unifying field of space with colorful flowers, exotic trees, and cooling pools of water.

At several points, the courtyard seeps out to the surrounding streets in the form of shoulder-squeezing, slit-like walks which, cut between the fragments at the far corners of the over-all composition, offer intriguing glimpses inside. Wider entranceways are positioned in the middle, but on either side of the courtyard, second level overhangs give a sense of intimacy as one comes upon the inner space, supplying a clear clue to the complex, yet cohesive nature of the architecture that edges it.

The functional fragments contain 20 classrooms and two language labs; offices for the school faculty, the USIS, and the Fulbright program; a 25,000-volume library, just inside from an angular terrace; and on the other end of the courtyard, just inside from a second terrace where receptions and performances are held, a two-story-high, skylit exhibition hall. Seen through the skylight, the rooftop tiers of the amphitheater edge upward, and beneath it is a 250-seat multi-use auditorium. Interpenetrating lines of sight pull the interior surfaces, done in white, bright plaster, into a spritely continuum. The reddish-pink stucco of the exterior, the hue of local clay, closes around this variegation—both a countenance of and a check upon the traits of complexity.

Embellished as the Casa is with sculpture, paintings, and crafts—part of a remarkable program of exhibits and lectures—its construction was deliberately kept simple: a reinforced concrete frame, with terra cotta infill walls, and poured floor slabs.

Local workmen felt at home from the start using local techniques, moving their families onto the site. The place is familial still.

CASA THOMAS JEFFERSON, Brasilia, Brazil. Owner: *Thomas Jefferson Bi-National Cultural Council.* Architect: *Mitchell/Giurgola Associates.* Associate Architects: *Alcides Rocha Miranda, Elvin MacKay Dubugras.* Engineers: *Robert Silman, Jose Parisi* (structural); *Flack & Kurtz, Andre Czajka* (mechanical/electrical). Contractor: *Coencisa, Brasilia.*

Dart Sageser

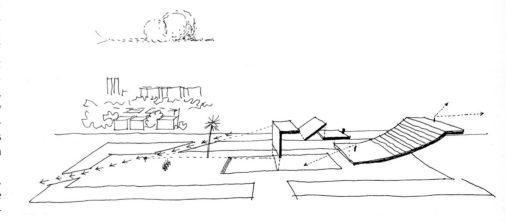

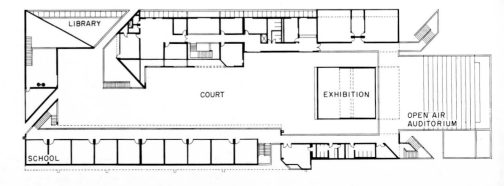

174

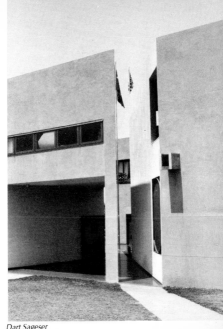

Unpretentious stucco walls set Casa Thomas Jefferson comfortably into its surrounding. Alternately low and narrow, entrances open into a lively, landscaped courtyard that discloses the functional fragments of the architectural composition. Entering one end of the courtyard, near the library (right) through slit-like walks, the exhibition hall is seen at the opposite end (bottom drawing, photo below right). Standing on the terrace in front of the hall (top photo, below), the plaster walls of the classroom and office wings ramble back toward the library. Inside the hall (top drawing), the rooftop amphitheater (bottom photo, below left) is glimpsed through a generous skylight.

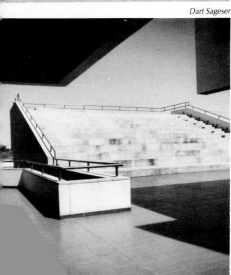

HAMILTON PLACE

The lack of construction funds to adequately house growing cultural activities is a common plight of governments in newer cities. A single multi-purpose theater has usually been the most that could be provided to house the diverse needs of a wide range of performing-arts. Such facilities have not always been artistic successes and—possibly as an outcome—have not received all of the public support that might be required.

A large part of the problem has involved acoustics. The requirements for symphonic music are usually incompatible with intelligible speech. They are achieved by a large room volume and hard sound-reflecting surfaces. The orchestra stage is ideally located within the audience chamber, without the separation provided by the traditional proscenium required by most plays. All the performing arts activities between the two extremes have their own special requirements, and complete acoustic satisfaction in multi-use theaters has been rare.

But new problem-solving techniques are appearing. The Edwin Performing Arts Hall at the University of Akron is capable of mechanical adjustment of the auditorium volume and shape. By contrast, Hamilton Place's 2,000 to 2,200-seat main hall relies on a few and relatively-simple means to solve acoustic adaptability problems. This Hamilton, Ontario, multi-use facility's success is due to the originality of planning in a fixed-room volume. There have been well-received performances of almost every kind: speeches, opera, musicals, rock shows, a full range of orchestras, plays and pop singers. The enthusiastic support of the city's citizens assures an on-going and lively program of varied presentations. A major part of this happy situation is due to the work of architect Trevor Garwood-Jones.

Hamilton has many heavy industries and—until recently—one of the more-visible diversions for residents has been the success of the local football team, the Tigercats. New dimensions are emerging. The theater building shown here, is part of Hamilton Civic Square, a development meant to give a new co-ordinated focus to the downtown area previously centered immediately to the east. Architect Ron Thom was advisor for the multi-block area, which is linked by raised walkways and plazas from the existing City Hall (and handsome older library) at the south end to a new "Jackson Square," a multi-use area at the north end (see plan, left). A new art gallery and trade center were designed—in the theater block—by Garwood-Jones. Planning of the theater included the considerations of butting directly against the future high-rise trade and convention center to the north (the two buildings share a service drive between them) and a second-floor-level plaza to the west. Parking for 800 cars has been provided under the plaza and art gallery.

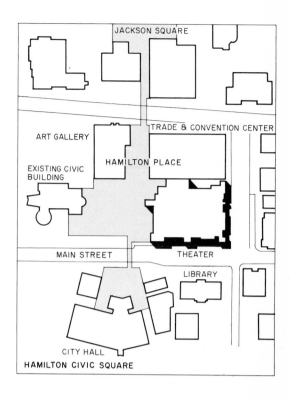

1 Main entrance
2 Lower lobby
3 Coats
4 Ancillary facility entrance
5 Studio theater
6 Upper lobby
7 Upper part studio theater
8 Meetings
9 Orchestra stage
10 Drama stage
11 Receiving
12 Office & entrance
13 Dressing rooms
14 Mechanical equipment
15 Dressing & chorus
16 Lifts
17 Workshop
18 Mechanical

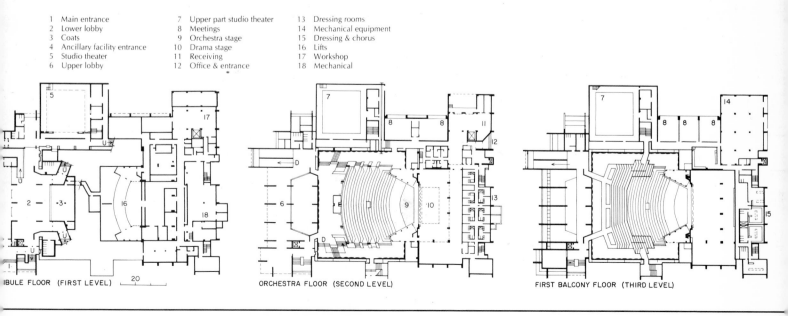

VESTIBULE FLOOR (FIRST LEVEL)   20

ORCHESTRA FLOOR (SECOND LEVEL)

FIRST BALCONY FLOOR (THIRD LEVEL)

Enthusiastic reactions by Hamilton Place's users and performing arts critics (including *The Times of London*) indicate success of the auditorium. Garwood-Jones had limited theater experience when he began this difficult commission, and he cites an open mind as a benefit. His one pre-conception was "not in any way to compromise acoustics." A two-continent study of theaters ensued. Acoustics consultant Russell Johnson began work early in the design process, and determined options available in shaping the auditorium. The approach has produced technological and visual dividends in a building utilizing concepts never previously tried at this scale.

The designers began by establishing the optimum acoustics for each of the performing arts to be displayed. Spatial characteristics were determined according to desired sound characteristics and the theater design recommendations of theater consultant Vincent Piacentini of Bolt, Beranek and Newman. For concerts, the main hall has a much bigger volume that required merely to enclose the area, because the plan (previous page) has been enlarged by incorporating parts of the lobby and the usually separate side corridors. The ceiling of the auditorium is the same height as that of the stage, and sound-reflecting brick walls are uninterrupted for their full height, since the balconies are suspended in the room. The optimum conditions for the long reverberation time generally required for symphonic music thus are achieved. To adjust the hall for speech, 18 velour banners can be lowered in front of the brick walls to provide acoustical absorption. (These are also raised in place of the dramatic effect of a stage curtain at the beginning of concerts.) The configuration of these walls is intended to break-up the echo-producing effect of the reflected sound waves of speech and to direct music to the listener. The relation of walls, balconies and banners can be seen in the top photo, right. The hall is square in order to reduce the distance between the farthest audience seats and the stage (less than 90 feet for concerts).

A major concern is the location of the sound source. Most drama continues to demand the comforts of a traditional stage: proscenium, fly loft, the marshalling areas of a curtain. Temporary concert enclosures in such locations either are cumbersome, or, if of flimsy construction, they dissipate sound into the stage area. Hamilton Place has two stages; one is forward and allows concerts to be played within the hall itself. The other allows drama to be performed behind a proscenium. The concert stage is surrounded by permanent (but adjustable)

Studio II

Dofasco

Studio II

cedar panels reflecting sound to the listeners. This is not a totally new solution, since Hammel, Green and Abrahamson produced a similar concept for a 1,000-seat auditorium in St. Joseph, Michigan but the application is new at this scale—and it works.

There is some apparent duplication of building volume to enclose the tandem stages, but a total $9.7 million construction cost here certainly beats that of two theaters of comparable sound qualities. The concert stage is a two lift arrangement on which—for a majority of performances—the hall's capacity can be increased by anywhere from 90 to 224 seats. These seats are not the usual make-shift variety; they are seemingly permanent, and they rise to audience level on motor-powered wagons, which are ordinarily stored under the main floor. When the concerts occur, the proscenium stage is completely sealed from the audience chamber by a fire curtain and an eight-ton cedar wall (seen in the center photo, right) which drops from the fly loft and provides acoustic reflection to the audience. The stage house is available for rehearsals and set construction; and the costs of setting up and striking some sets, and of erecting and dismantling a temporary orchestra enclosure, are minimized. The resulting flexibility was demonstrated in the first month of the new hall's daily use, when there were 13 different productions.

The systems for amplified sound are innovative here—although opera, chamber and symphony orchestras, choral groups and organs do not traditionally use electronic support. The control panel is in the box in the center of the audience (photo, p. 176). Every two seats are provided with a floor-mounted speaker and large speakers "bounce" sound from the brick walls surrounding the audience.

The complete facilities at Hamilton Place allow three performances, numerous meetings and one full-scale rehearsal to occur at the same time. A smaller Studio Theater takes the pressure off of the main hall for rehearsals and smaller productions, played to a maximum of 350 viewers, without the costs and complications of running the bigger facility. This room has inherent advantages over the main hall for unconventional presentations including theater-in-the-round. There is a flexible relationship between the movable stage and the audience. TV and cinema are filmed here. Two adjacent meeting rooms are each designed to alternate as a small recital hall or a green room. Public circulation to all of the functions outside of the main hall is routed through a separate entrance and corridor north of the main

lobby. The many simultaneous activities are provided with extensive backup facilities including dressing rooms, workshops mechanical spaces, storage and offices; these are contained in a four-story element of the building located behind the stage.

The main lobby is multi-level space rising to the full height of the main hall. The street-level entrance will eventually be supplemented by an orchestra entrance level connection to the planned plaza over the street to the west. The architect purposely avoided the large impersonal void that has come to characterize some lobbies in theaters of this size. Part of the lobby space is contained within the audience chambers. The outer portion is divided by the heavy concrete buttresses that give stability to the structure of the main hall. The resulting spaces have a more intimate character while maintaining functional and visual unification. The orchestra entrance level is conceived as a series of brightly furnished lounges which overlook the tile-floored lobby below, and are overlooked by the balcony crossovers. A stepped roof admits light by means of sloping clerestory windows, and the lobby's glass walls reveal the internal activity to the busy street outside. Public participation is thus encouraged.

Another part of Hamilton Place's acoustic success is the result of the building's structure. Despite the main hall's proximity to a major truck route on Main Street, there are no audible sounds within the room from passing trucks, other activities

within the building or the mechanical systems. There are really five separate structures that comprise the total building. Each has its own foundation and is independently enclosed and buffered by air-space separations. The main hall consists of two chambers—one within the other—separated by a three-and-one-half foot air space between walls and the depth of the trusses between roof and ceiling.

The separation of the five building elements allows the utilization of two types of structures. The original plans called for an all-concrete construction, but it was subsequently determined that the main hall could be built more quickly with steel framing, and that the cost savings would approach a half-million dollars. The remainder of the building was built of poured concrete, which is generally exposed on the interior and exterior. The resulting structural dichotomy has been expressed by brick-wall cladding inside and outside the main hall. Another economy was realized by the hanging of the upper balcony from the main-hall roof trusses. The result has been visually daring, and the cost of extensive separate foundations was saved (the lower balcony is doubly cantilevered over columns on realtively small foundations).

Construction was started with most of the planning in sketch form. The current tendency to emphasize speed of construction is making the "fast tracking" process more common, but—especially in a building of this intricacy—the perils are well known. It is a credit to the owners, architect and contractor that there is a high level of workmanship here, and that the September, 1974 opening was an event without "a hitch." The managers have yet to find what they would call "even a medium scale defect." The largest problem seems to be the parking of all of the patrons' buses; it was never anticipated that so many would arrive by the busload.

This performing arts theater is the first in Canada to realize a profit in its first year, and the reason is due primarily to an attendance average of 85 per cent of capacity at all performances. Concerts are sold out far in advance—especially those of the Hamilton Philharmonic which is currently conducting three concert series and uses meeting rooms for pre-performance lectures. Assistant manager Larry Russell, says that there was a wide range of performance types, in the first months, to determine those that would be the most popular, but "we don't know too much more today than when we started." Every type of performance has been a success. The management knows "a lot" about running a theater. Many shows are bought as a package to be presented by the theater management (other theater owners only rent their auditorium to entrepreneurs). Management offices are located on the top floor of the building element behind the stage house and they include the board of directors' meeting room shown below. A specially built table is covered with white plastic laminate. Windows of the offices can be seen on the rear of the building (photo right).

Income is also realized from rental—to local corporations, theatrical groups and TV stations—of the many meeting rooms and the two smaller theaters, during the times when these facilities would be normally idle. The main lobby is operated as a night club for theater goers after performances. The policy has produced revenue to the owners provides a highly visible active night life for the downtown's main street, and contributes to Hamilton Place's vitality.

HAMILTON PLACE, Hamilton, Ontario. Owner: *City of Hamilton.* Architects *Trevor P. Garwood-Jones—associate-in-charge, B. Harry Lennard.* Engineers *Omen Lee & Associates Ltd., SNC Filer Ltd., Canaly Otter Ltd.* (structural); *Quis & Associates Ltd., Keith Associates, Ltd.,* (mechanical/electrical). Consultants *Russell Johnson Associates* (acoustics); *Hanscomb Roy Associates* (cost); *Bolt Beranek & Newman, Inc.—*project manager; *Vincent Piacentini* (theater) General contractor: *Frid Construction Company.*

JUILLIARD SCHOOL

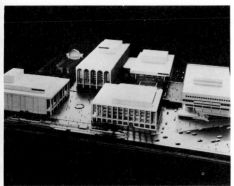

Model: Lincoln Center for the Performing Arts

Contained within the serene, well-ordered, simple and rather innocent facades of the Juilliard School (the world's first conservatory for all the performing arts) is an almost infinite variety of spaces fitted together with a sorcerer's skill in an arrangement as intricate as a Chinese puzzle. In the process of developing the kind of spatial organization required to satisfy the complex Juilliard program in a tight urban site with severe height limitations, Pietro Belluschi and his associate architects Eduardo Catalano and Helge Westermann have managed to tuck and fit the assorted instructional and performance facilities of a good-sized campus into one integrated structure.

Solving the structural, mechanical, acoustical and theater engineering problems posed by the organization of elements in this building called for all the skill and ingenuity at the command of the architects and their consultants. Rooms which on a larger site would normally be widely separated for acoustical reasons are stacked above each other, overlap or nestle side by side. The column-free larger halls which in most performing arts complexes are composed as separate elements under their own long-span roofs, are here framed to carry eccentric loads from the complicated spaces on the floors above. Minimum clearances due to the height restrictions made the coordination of structural elements, mechanical ductwork and stage equipment a challenging problem.

In the 12-year struggle to get Juilliard designed and built, the architects, with great patience and willingness to start over, produced about 70 different sets of preliminary drawings. The architects and engineers produced over 300 on-the-job sketches to coordinate structure and equipment during the construction process.

Because Juilliard remained in the design stage for so long and was begun last, its designers learned from the mistakes made in the other buildings at Lincoln Center. There was time, also, to sensitively adapt the school to its surroundings as it gradually became evident what its surroundings would be. Juilliard's travertine-sheathed exterior, a gift of the Italian government, is sympathetically related to the handsome facades of the Vivian Beaumont Theater by Saarinen with which it shares a small plaza to the north of the main square.

Juilliard's interiors are in some ways better than those of the other buildings. Its beautifully shaped wood panelled auditoriums, for example, prove that it is possible to create elegant halls in contemporary terms without resorting to skimpy evocations of the gilt, plaster and crystal decor of the great halls of the past.

The art with which the arts are housed affects them profoundly for the better. It is fortunate, therefore, that the incredible effort on the part of Belluschi and his team has produced such a fine building. Since Juilliard is a school for the musicians, actors and dancers of the future, it is appropriate that the best building at Lincoln Center should be theirs.

THE JUILLIARD SCHOOL, New York, N.Y. Owner: *Lincoln Center for the Performing Arts, Inc.;* constituent institution: *The Juilliard School.* Architect: *Pietro Belluschi—Eduardo Catalano and Helge Westermann,* associated architects; *Frederick Taylor, Robert Brannen and Joseph V. Morog,* project architects; *Austris J. Vitols, Robert P. Burns and William E. Pederson,* designers; *Joseph Zelazny,* resident architect and engineer. Structural engineer: *Paul Weidlinger;* mechanical and electrical engineers: *Jaros, Baum and Bolles;* stage design consultant: *Jean Rosenthal Associates, Inc.;* acoustical consultant: *Heinrich Keilholz;* special structures engineer: *Olaf Soöt;* organ consultant: *Walter Holtkamp;* interior furnishings: *Helge Westermann;* contractor: *Walsh Construction Company.*

© Ezra Stoller (ESTO) photos

Early in 1957 Juilliard voted to accept the invitation from Lincoln Center to move from Morningside Heights and relocate in a building to be constructed for the school by the Center. Great benefits were foreseen from having young artists in training at Lincoln Center.

The school's requirements kept changing and expanding, however, as the plans developed. In the early design period the size of the site had not finally been decided upon. (The land upon which Juilliard is built was not part of the original Lincoln Square Urban Renewal Project and was acquired separately without the urban renewal writedown.) During the design process the Drama Division was added to the school and George Balanchine's School of American Ballet was invited to function within Juilliard as an independent unit. At one time a multi-use complex was conceived which would have included shops and restaurants. The architects, further, had to adapt to changes in the administrative leadership of both Juilliard and Lincoln Center.

Juilliard is connected to the main plazas of Lincoln Center by a broad bridge across 65th Street. The principal access from Broadway is by means of a monumental stair and terrace. Extending for a distance of 350 feet along 65th and 66th Streets and 200 feet on Broadway, the building includes four stories below the street level and six (not including the mechancial equipment penthouse) above. The building contains approximately 500-thousand square feet and 8-million cubic feet of space. The cost, with furnishings, is $29.5 million.

Three of five entrances, one on 65th Street, another on 66th Street, and one at the Plaza level from the bridge all lead to a central lobby which serves the Juilliard Theater, Paul Recital Hall and the elevator corridor leading to the instructional and administrative facilities of the school. An entrance below the terrace serves Alice Tully Hall.

As the sections indicate, the Juilliard School has three general zones from the sub-basement to the penthouse. Beginning four storeis below the street, the lowest zone includes the performance areas of the Juilliard Theater and Alice Tully Hall, their supporting facilities, and a portion of the mechanical equipment. The uppermost zone, below the mechanical penthouse, consists of three instructional floors.

This intermediate zone contains the public areas, administrative services, lounges, Paul Recital Hall and the Drama Workshop.

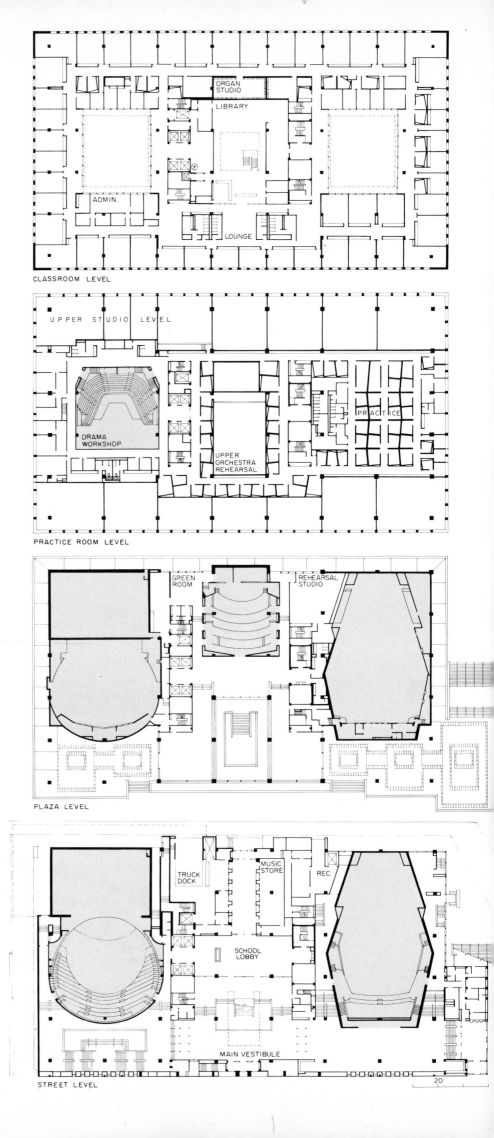

CLASSROOM LEVEL

PRACTICE ROOM LEVEL

PLAZA LEVEL

STREET LEVEL

A. Juilliard Theater
B. Drama Workshop
C. Lila Acheson Wallace Library
D. Orchestra rehearsal and recording studio
E. Paul Recital Hall
F. Alice Tully Hall

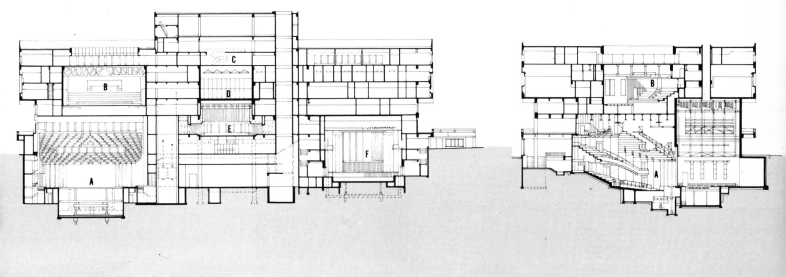

Although the facades are of travertine (a gift) and the floors are carpeted wall-to-wall (wherever appropriate to reduce noise levels) Juilliard is by no means luxurious. Because of rapidly rising costs, finish details were simplified wherever possible throughout the structure and more expensive materials abandoned. The wood paneling, for example, which had been designed for the principal lobbies, was eliminated and the concrete left exposed.

The photo (top left) shows the bridge across 65th Street connecting Juilliard to the north plaza of Lincoln Center. The top row of windows provides light and views for the large private studios and classrooms for group teaching located on the top floor. The large windows directly below illuminate the large double-story rehearsal studios on the north and south sides of the building which have two levels of single-story supporting facilities in the interiors. Underneath the overhang is another level of double-story rehearsal studios and below these, at bridge level, are the principal administration offices. All the outside windows of the studios and classrooms are triple-glazed to keep out street noise.

The photo (bottom left) was taken from the Broadway terrace over the entrance to Alice Tully Hall. A corner of Philharmonic Hall appears on the left. Both the Vivian Beaumont Theater and the Metropolitan Opera House can be seen in the background.

The lobby of Alice Tully Hall (opposite page, top left) has a purple carpet and gold accents. Miss Tully, the donor of the hall, took an active interest in its decor. The Juilliard Theater lobby (top right) is carpeted in crimson. The handsome globe-shaped lighting fixtures are of standard manufacture and are also used in Paul Recital Hall.

The principal lobby (opposite page, bottom) interconnects the Juilliard Theater and Alice Tully Hall. Stairs lead to the Paul Recital Hall directly above.

The most remarkable feature of the 960–1,026 seat Juilliard Theater is its movable ceiling which adjusts to three positions within a seven-foot range to change the angle of reflection of sound from the stage and pit and reduce the volume (and thereby the reverberation time) of the room for drama, or increase the volume and reverberation time for the performance of music. This ceiling, finished in basswood and cherry to match the sidewalls, forms a sound reflective shell, made of horizontal, overlapping curved and tapered tiers. It includes platforms and light bridges for stage lighting and provides access to all other overhead services. Since the entire structure is located over the audience, safety was of prime importance. The architects and the ceiling engineer Olaf Soöt chose a long-span one-piece structure over several smaller movable units. The selection of a long-span structure on heavier but simple machinery minimized the maintenance requirements, reduced the over-all cost, and provided a foolproof "fail-safe" system.

The basic structure consists of two main box trusses tied together by box-type secondary trusses. This box truss system forms the self-braced structural support for all the secondary framing, catwalks and ceiling panels. It is supported by four self-locking jackscrews and is held laterally by four guide columns, one near each jackscrew.

Each pair of jackscrews is driven by one main drive assembly. Because of the large distances between each pair of jackscrews, it was impractical to connect the main drives by mechanical means and, therefore, electrical synchronization with self-compensating leveling at predetermined stops was employed. Should any of the shafts or other drive train components become disconnected from the associated jackscrew drive, the ceiling will stop and cannot be operated unless the repairs are made. Additional interlock systems protect personnel and machinery. The ceiling is operated from a control station within the auditorium, but for the ceiling to move another button must be kept under constant pressure by an operator located in the catwalks with a full view of the service area.

The stage and lighting facilities of the Juilliard Theater and the three other halls were planned by Jean Rosenthal Associates, Inc. The associate engineer-in-charge was Clyde L. Nordheimer.

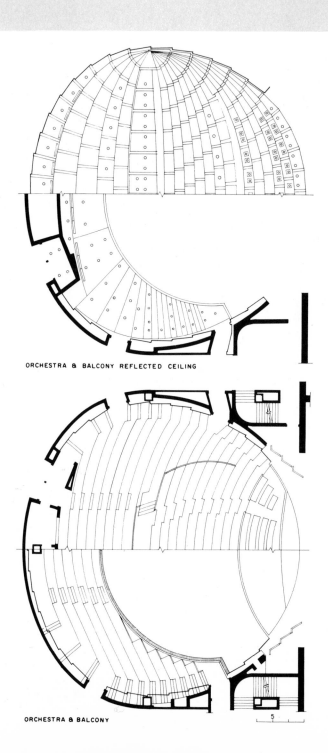

ORCHESTRA & BALCONY REFLECTED CEILING

ORCHESTRA & BALCONY

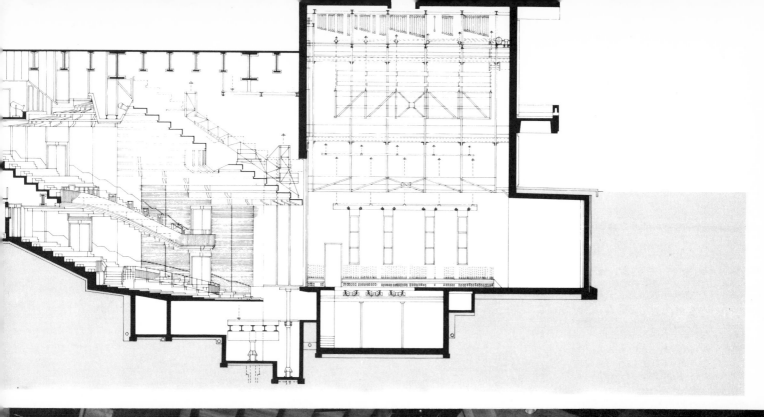

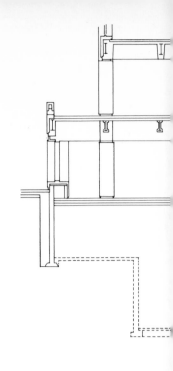

Tully Hall, unlike the Juilliard Theater, is not acoustically adjustable, and therefore cannot approach an ideal for each type of performance which will take place there. Lincoln Center, Juilliard, the architects, and their acoustician Heinrich Keilholz, considered of first importance that the hall meet recital and chamber music requirements. The 1,096-seat hall is not too large for this function and critical response to the acoustics for this type of performance has so far been good. Acoustician Keilholz points out that Tully Hall should not be used by large orchestras, and adds that if the acoustics prove good for other musical purposes than those for which the hall was designed "it will be a gift!" He attributes part of Tully Hall's acoustical success to the use of wood as a resonant material and points out that musicians like to have it around them. Dampening has been inserted where needed behind the wood battens.

The recital stage has a depth of 23 feet and an average width of 50 feet. An organ can be raised into position or lowered and concealed at the rear. For small orchestras an additional 14 feet of stage depth is obtained by stowing the first three rows of seats under the stage and raising a lift to stage level. This configuration will also accommodate modest theatrical performances. Draperies, lighting, pipes and other scenic devices are suspended from electric winch systems above the stage ceiling. The side walls pivot for access from back stage and a traveler curtain can be drawn across the stage.

In addition to the standard concert lighting, Tully Hall is equipped with a complete theatrical lighting system. If an orchestra pit is required, two additional rows of seats can be stored under the stage.

Facilities for film presentations have been designed into the space. A complete projection booth and sound system have been installed.

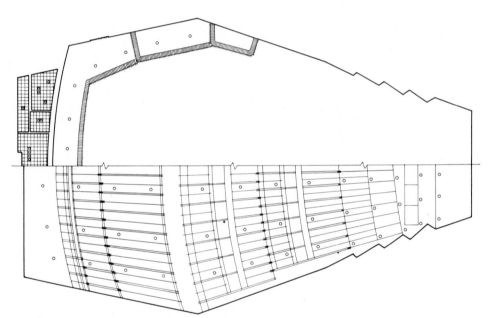

ORCHESTRA & BALCONY REFLECTED CEILING

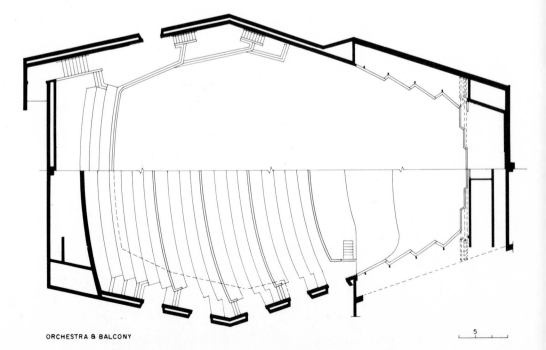

ORCHESTRA & BALCONY

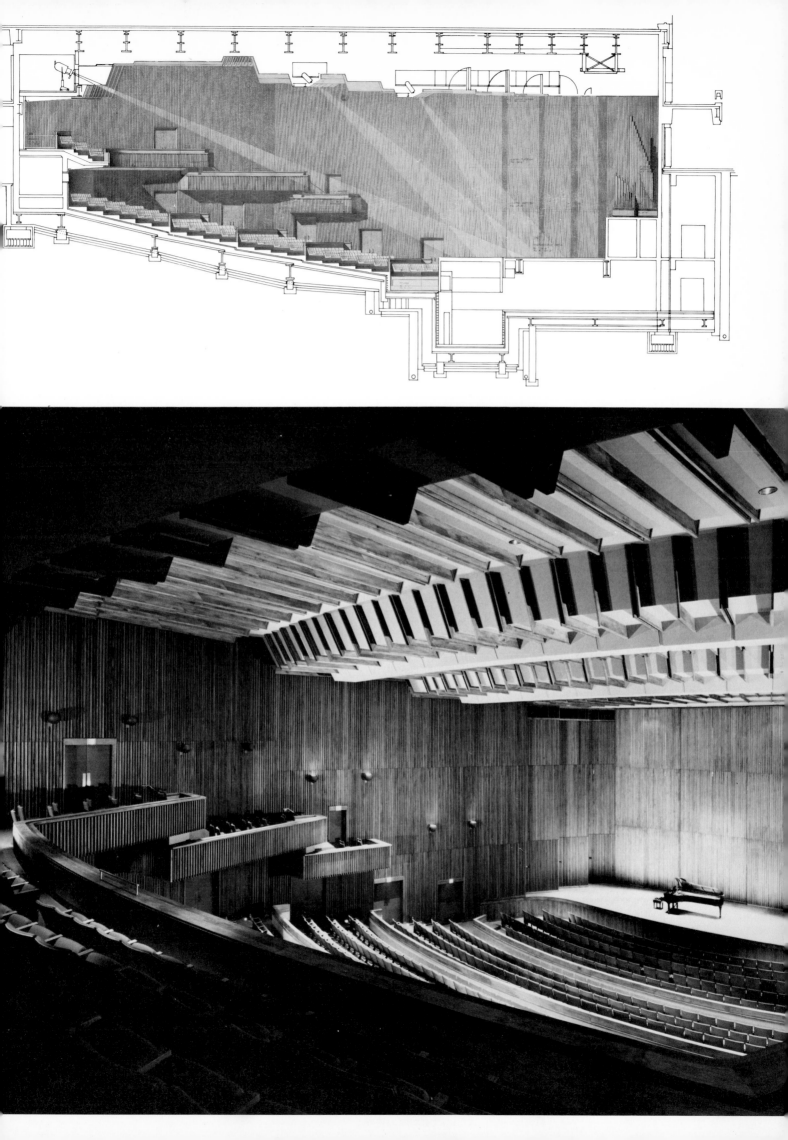

The Paul Recital Hall (top) seats 277 people. Its side walls and ceiling are paneled in cherry wood. Ceiling coffers are sloped to create optimum diffusion of sound. It is used for instruction on the Holtkamp organ, for recitals and as a lecture hall and has been volumetrically sized for these purposes. Private teaching studios (middle left) are carefully sound insulated, as are the practice rooms. These spaces had to be of minimum size to get as many as possible into the available space but large enough to provide proper sound diffusion and reflection. The organ practice rooms (middle right) required special wall and ceiling treatments to prevent the organ sound from becoming too "hard." The Lila Acheson Wallace Library (bottom) is located directly above the orchestra rehearsal and recording studio, which floats free of the structure to inhibit the transmission of sound.

All major sound-producing spaces are insulated from the structure. Each has a unique volume and special wall, floor and ceiling treatments. As a result, no two floors of Juilliard are alike, and floor slab elevations constantly vary. The building has cavity walls, solid walls, walls with insulation and walls without. Because of the intricacy of the plan, there is no direct transfer of loads to the foundation. Floor loads are huge and range from 250 to 280 pounds per square foot, including the concrete slabs, secondary slabs and floor finishes. The dance rehearsal floors, for example, are 18 to 20 inches thick and include steel springs 20 inches on centers. Because the biggest column-free spaces are near ground level, structural members are quite large to handle the long spans and the loads from above. There are steel composite girders which are 104 feet in length. Joseph Zelazny and Matthys Levy, associates of Paul Weidlinger, the structural engineer for Juilliard, point out that in spite of these complications there is a structural module of sorts. At the east and west ends of the building over the two major halls are 93 foot spans. Between them the columns are 46 feet on center. Spans are 35 feet the opposite way.

Of special interest is the fact that the northeast corner of Tully Hall is only 20 feet from the IRT subway. A special envelope was made for the hall. The engineers inserted a one-inch thick asbestos pad lined with cork between the foundation and its solid rock bearing. The perimeter wall of the theater was isolated from the structural columns so that the subway vibrations would not be transmitted.

Balthazar Korab

OPERA FACTORY

As in every other art form today, there are those involved in opera production who are searching for a new expression and others who seek to refine the classical approach. The new Musical Arts Center at Indiana University in Bloomington certainly represents the latter. As a performing environment it hews strictly to the pattern set by the Teatro alla Scala in Milan which opened in 1778. But wrapped around the opera house is a set of flexible lofts for teaching in which Woollen Associates of Indianapolis, the architects, have striven to maximize the process of teaching opera, thus its characterization by Evans Woollen as an "opera factory." The architects considered the possibility of an asymmetrical form for the building. They soon decided that since the side stages had to be equal, the enormous fly loft centered, and the house of traditional form, any major attempts at informal massing would not only be less economical than the built scheme but would seem unnecessarily contrived. Thus the off-center marquee and the reveals in the fascia above it are the only genuflections to the major approach which is from the left (above). The 39-foot-high Calder stabile is an effective foil to the main entrance and helps to give a sense of place

to the building. Although the concrete structure is beautifully detailed and executed, to some there is a disturbing sense of its being over-designed—too muscular and assertive—for its function. Students, ever alert to suspected pretense, have named it "Fort Bain" after the dean of the music school, Wilfred C. Bain, who was largely responsible for bringing the school both to its present eminence and the funds for its new teaching and performing facility.

The house of the new music center is much smaller than any commercial operation could afford to be, seating 1460 people. The main reason for that decision was that student voices, less mature than those of professionals, would be more comfortable in intimate surroundings. It is interesting to compare La Scala's horseshoe shape with the flatter, broader shape used by Woollen

Balthazar Korab

Associates (comparative plans, page 197). Not only are the back seats closer but the balconies and boxes (left) in the new house work far better than those in the European counterpart. The acoustics are excellent. Speaking of Bolt, Beranek and Newman's work, Harold Schoenberg wrote in the New York Times, "Whatever they did, it has turned out magnificently. As an acoustic installation, the Musical Arts Center ranks with any in the country. There is an even throw, the bass is full and resonant, everything has a natural quality. The reverberation period is, at a guess, rather short—say around 1.6 seconds. That is ideal for opera, and the Musical Arts Center was designed primarily for opera." The latter is of course what made it an acoustician's dream: not only is the audience much smaller than normal and the room unusually tall for its

depth, but it was designed for a single purpose—unlike most auditoriums which try to accommodate uses which have conflicting acoustical demands.

The continental seating arrangement—without aisles—is another way in which this opera house differs from La Scala. After taking into account the problem of late-comers who must pass everyone on their way to the seats in the middle, the architects note that for houses where the acoustical and visual sources and requirements are fixed, the system works well because it allows the audience to be closer to the stage (there are 19 rows of seats in the orchestra, the farthest row is 80 feet from the stage). It encourages a cohesiveness of response since audience reaction can spread unbroken by aisles which often serve as "firebreaks" to dampen the effect of the dramatic

ambience. Finally, not only does continuous seating promote greater safety in emptying the hall during emergencies, but because seats are farther apart than usual, it also promotes comfort for long-legged people. Where the seats in La Scala average 29 inches row-to-row, at the Musical Arts Center they are 40 inches on center.

Although the Musical Arts Center has fewer than 40 per cent of the Metropolitan Opera's 3800 seats, its backstage area is approximately 80 per cent of the New York building. And while the total distance at the Met across the stage including side stages is 40 feet greater, the actual playing stage is only 12 feet wider. Furthermore the Met proscenium width is fixed at 54 feet while that at the Musical Arts Center can vary from 48 feet to almost 70

feet. It is the hope of the designers that this feature will encourage future experiments in non-traditional opera staging. The orchestra pit has two levels, allowing the stage to be extended when a small orchestra is involved. The huge side and rear stages, as at the Met, each contain rolling platforms—stage wagons—on which scenery can be built and quickly moved into place. In addition, the rear stage wagon has a 48-foot diameter turntable which also can be used for set changes or other dramatic effects. The gridiron in the fly loft is 110 feet above the main stage and has 66 sets of counterweights as well as four light bridges that can be lowered to the stage floor for rigging and adjustment. The lighting controls are, naturally, very sophisticated and offer 200 preset combinations from the 288 circuits on the stage and in the house as well as automatic fading and other options.

Even though the building has the best theater technology available, Evans Woollen sees the challenge of the job not in organizing that, nor in designing the stage areas, but rather in providing the most flexible environment for training the 1600 future musicians and technicians doing their major work in the school. Thus the design of the ballet rehearsal rooms below the rear stage was as important to him as the performing spaces. Classroom and other instructional spaces occupy nearly two-thirds of the area of the building. The circulation between all these is clearly organized (right). It was the intention of the designers to mix the public and the students wherever possible throughout the building. The four semi-circular stairwells thus serve students as well as visitors about to see one of the 700 performances given each year.

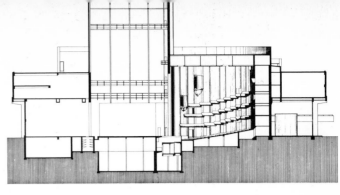

The backstage areas of the Musical Arts Center are spacious and extremely well equipped. The unusual proportion of stage to house is evident in the drawings and two panoramic photos (left) of the relationship of stage to house. The stage itself (top, far left) is 190 feet wide and 118 feet deep, about four-fifths the size of the Metropolitan Opera stage. The scenery production shop (middle, far left) and one of three ballet rehearsal rooms (bottom, far left) are typical of the generous loft-type teaching areas. The plan of La Scala (below), shown at the same scale as the other plans, is from "Music, Acoustics and Architecture" by Leo Beranek (Wiley). La Scala seats 2135, fifty per cent more than the Musical Arts Center in the same amount of space.

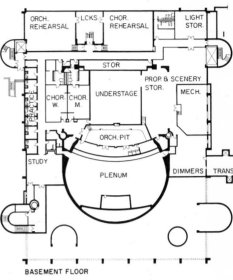

BASEMENT FLOOR

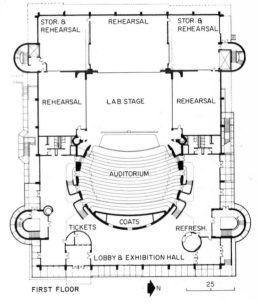

FIRST FLOOR N 25

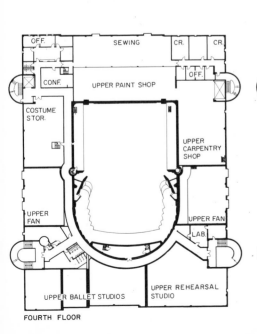

FOURTH FLOOR

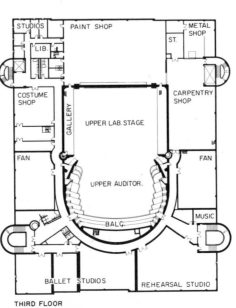

THIRD FLOOR

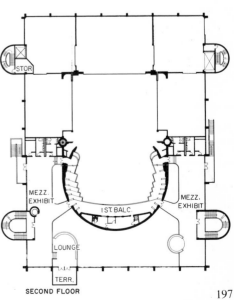

SECOND FLOOR

197

Circular forms appear in many guises in the Musical Arts Center. Applied silver graphics on the doors into the stairwells (left) echo the curve of the stair towers themselves, seen (below) through a round window in another stair tower.

INDIANA UNIVERSITY MUSI-CAL ARTS CENTER, Bloomington, Indiana. Architects: *Woollen Associates—Evans Woollen, principal; Lynn H. Molzan, project architect; Tom Weigel, Larry O'Connor and Peter Mayer;* engineers: *Fink, Roberts & Petrie* (structural); *J. M. Rotz Engineering Co., Inc.* (mechanical and electrical); acoustical consultants: *Bolt, Beranek and Newman;* lighting consultant: *William Lam;* landscape architect: *Frits Loonsten;* other technical consultants: *Ben Schlanger, Olaf Soot, Jean Rosenthal;* general contractor: *F. A. Wilhelm Construction Co., Inc.*

Milwaukee Krannert Center

This handsome structure, certainly one of the best performing arts centers built in the United States or Canada since the postwar building-for-culture boom began, is the result of a highly successful collaboration between theater consultant George C. Izenour, who programmed the center and engineered the stage mechanics, R. Lawrence Kirkegaard of Bolt Beranek and Newman, who was the acoustical consultant, and architect Harry Weese, who designed it. The architect's task was not easy. It is difficult to organize within three halls in a single building all the facilities which make it possible to effectively mount six different kinds of musical and dramatic performance. It is even harder, of course, to organize these elements into an esthetically satisfying result, as Weese has done.

Izenour praises Weese for having resisted a tendency which he considers detrimental to theater design—letting subjective criteria determine form. Weese, unlike other architects Izenour could name and did, put theater function first and allowed the physical imperatives of sound and sight to shape his spaces. These imperatives are met by particular volumes and dimensions usually recommended by the consultants. Unless the architect chooses to ignore the consultants his so-called form-giving is inhibited. "But Weese has so much talent," says Izenour, "it flows from his fingers—he made the building beautiful while accepting the constraints."

Built on an urban renewal site on the bank of the Milwaukee River—the $12 million center opened in September 1969. It is the home of the Milwaukee Symphony Orchestra, the Florentine Opera and the Milwaukee Repertory Theater. The new facility will host visiting opera, musical comedy and ballet companies, symphony orchestras and concert artists. As the site plan shows, the center is free-standing on an open site, adjacent to City Hall, appearing in the photo (left). It is highly visible from all sides, its Roman travertine-sheathed volumes are well articulated and exterior glass is used with restraint to allow for well-contained spaces within lit only by an atrium garden and skylights. The windowed cornice encloses office space. The balcony below adjoins a combination foyer and banquet room which overlooks the river to the west. Beneath the balcony is the entrance to Wehr drama theater and Vogel recital hall. The lower left-hand photo (overleaf) shows the principal entrance to Uihlein Hall, the major facility for concerts and opera.

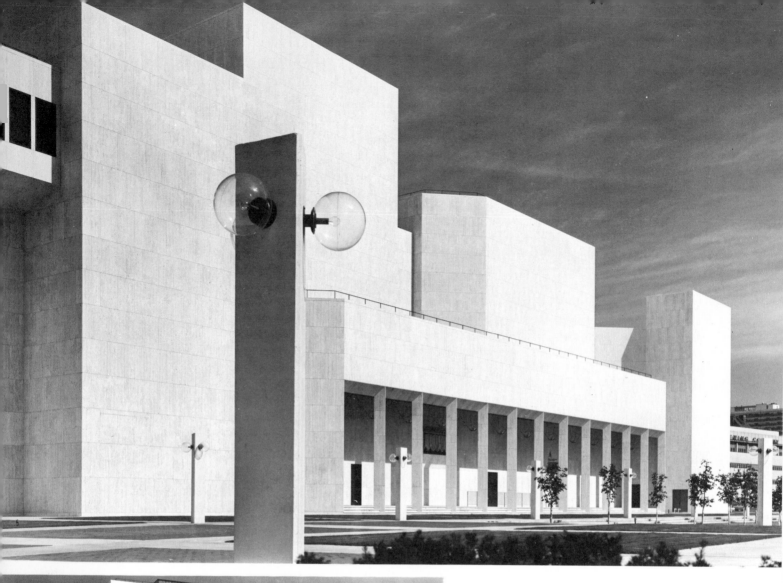

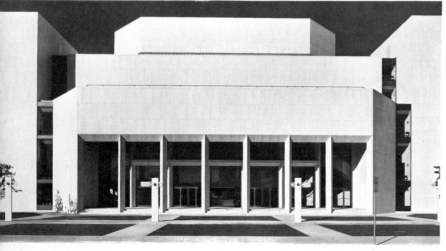

Balthazar Korab photo

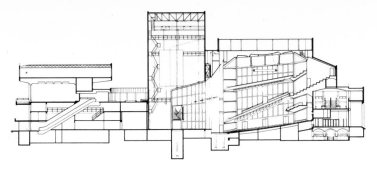

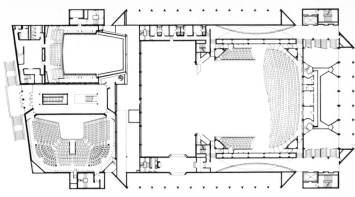

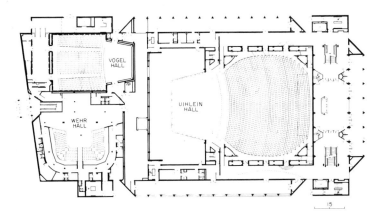

VOGEL
HALL

UIHLEIN
HALL

WEHR
HALL

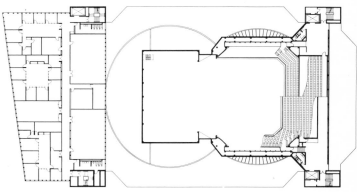

The organization of elements can be quickly understood if the section and plans are compared with the bird's-eye photo (p. 200). Wehr and Vogel, the two smaller halls, are on the river side to the west. Above them is Bradley Hall, which overlooks the river and is shown in the photo (bottom left and center). Above this hall and forming the cornice is the office floor. The stagehouse is the tallest element. The roof of Uihlein Hall slopes downward over the center loge. The entrance colonnade to the east, seven bays wide, is similar in elevation to the twelve-bay colonnade in the photo (opposite). The photo (bottom right) on page 200 is of Magin Hall, located just under the center loge and overlooking the entrance colonnade.

Weese brings daylight to the narrow lobby spaces on the north and south by means of crescent-shaped skylights. The curved passageways shown in the photos (bottom) are directly under the skylights. They break away from the straight walls, making crescent shapes of their own. Whether one looks up or down, the handling of vertical space is unorthodox and fascinating.

In these spaces carpeting and upholstered benches are a deep, rich red. Walls are a light ochre. The rims of the crescent shapes are lined with exposed light bulbs.

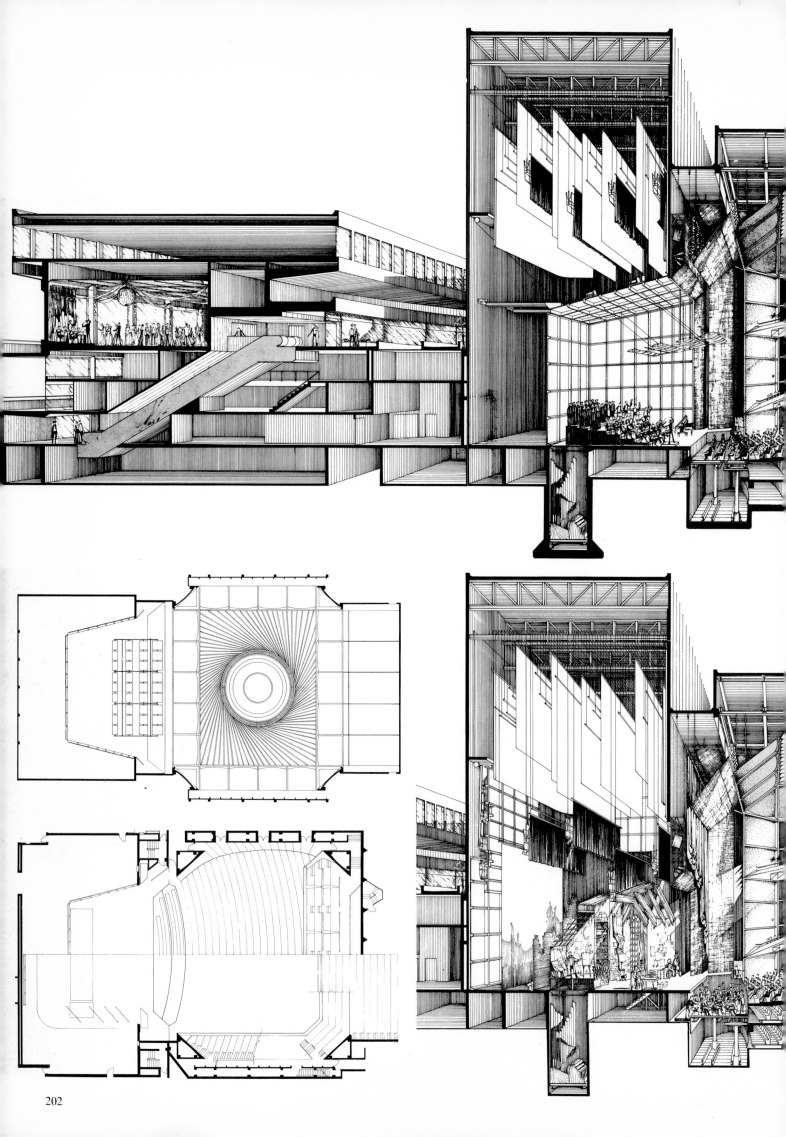

Orlando R. Cabanban photos

UIHLEIN HALL

The acoustical elements of Uihlein Hall, by Weese's wish, were to be architectonic—neither hidden nor applied. Where many architects of recent halls have chosen to conceal the essential acoustical modulation behind decorative screening, he elected to design it into the room. Because this reduced the range of acoustical adjustability, Bolt Beranek and Newman built and acoustically tested a 1/10 full-size model of the hall.

The acoustical design elements consist of the stage acoustical shell shown in place in Izenour's drawing for concert use (above) and for opera shown against the rear wall to permit full use of the 10-story fly space.

The plastic sound-reflective canopy has been designed to allow the musicians to hear one another better and to add intimacy and clarity to the mid-main floor sound from strings and woodwinds. The panels are adjustable at the touch of a button.

The movable teaser tormentor shown in the opera or musical comedy position (left) brings reflective surfaces close to performers, and the loudspeaker cluster into operating position.

The volume of the 2,327-seat hall provides the same length of reverberation as Boston Symphony Hall, long considered ideal.

Orlando R. Cabanban photos

The ceiling of Uihlein as well as the walls are ornamental plaster straw-colored with gold accents. These surfaces have been shaped and oriented to bring envelopmental sound to the listener at the right times, from appropriate directions, in the correct amounts. The chandelier is of glass and gold mirrors and is suspended by a beaded chain. The stage has an adjustable proscenium—45 feet by 64 feet for symphony as shown, and 16 feet by 36 feet for theater. The orchestra shell, demountable and flown like scenery when not in use, fills the full proscenium opening, extending the side wall paneling to unite the stage with the auditorium.

It is of unprecedented size for maximum coupling of sound from performer to listener. It is fabricated from 22 tons of dampened mild steel and has been modulated to keep brass and percussion from overpowering the strings and woodwinds. A pit in the stage floor adjacent to the shell's rear wall houses a pipe organ on a hydraulic lift.

WEHR THEATER

Wehr Theater has three quarters seating around a thrust stage. Designed in brick and exposed concrete with a steel lighting grid, it is the home of the Milwaukee Repertory Company. This 526-seat theater functions independently with its own scenery shops, costuming shops, rehearsal rooms and office space. Since a repertory house emphasizes acting and direction and minimizes physical production, stage facilities can be minimal.

There are two basic acoustical problems to be solved in a thrust stage theater such as Wehr. The first is to prevent noise interference from mechanical systems or adjacent spaces so that the full dynamic range of the actors' voices may be heard. The second is to make the space acoustically "dead" enough that the weak sound radiated from the back of the actor's head will not be garbled by late-arriving reflections from room surfaces. This must be achieved without making the space so dead that actors find it unresponsive to their voices. Bolt Beranek and Newman carefully shaped the hard surfaces to reinforce the actors' voices and "fuzzed" only those surfaces which could not contribute positively. Thus upholstered seating, carpeting and glass fiber above the lighting grid are the only sound absorptive materials required in the room.

thazar Korab

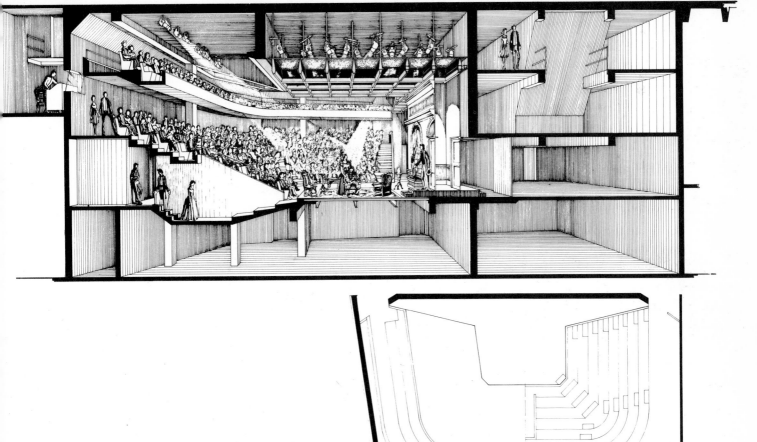

Vogel hall

Vogel Hall doubles as symphony rehearsal space and a recital hall. A small house, it measures 53 feet by 79 feet with a 28-foot by 36-foot stage. There are 482 orchestra and balcony seats. The exposed ceiling structure has been treated as a decorative coffering system. The side walls are covered with velour panels for dampening. Stage walls tilt forward to reflect sound back to the musicians and to prevent flutter. Oak parquet beneath the seats combines with the hard reflective surface of the plaster balcony soffit and ceiling to provide a short reverberation time for high articulation.

MILWAUKEE CENTER FOR THE PERFORMING ARTS, Milwaukee. Owner: *Milwaukee County War Memorial Development Committee.* Architects: *Harry Weese & Associates;* theater consultants: *George C. Izenour Associates;* acoustical consultants: *Bolt Beranek and Newman, Dr. Lothar Cremer;* structural engineers: *The Engineers Collaborative;* mechanical and electrical engineers: *S. R. Lewis & Associates;* landscape architect: *Office of Dan Kiley;* interiors consultants: *Dolores Miller & Associates;* contractors: *Klug & Smith Company.*

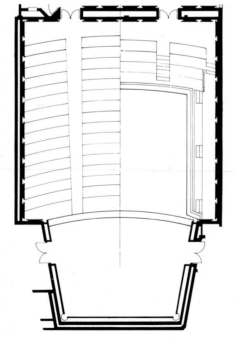

Balthazar Korab photos

Marx Theater

Since the performing arts are so much a part of the night, another important consideration is the use of artificial light as an element of architectural design. The bluish-white brilliance of the bare fluorescent tube makes a fine contrast with the warm glow of the incandescent bulb, and we have exploited this in the Playhouse lobby. Here the angular geometries are emphasized by vertical lines of fluorescent light applied to mirrors, horizontal lines of fluorescent light applied to the carpeted ceiling, and these in turn are contrasted with horizontal patterns of clear glass incandescent lights. At Simon's Rock bare tubes are used to outline the new additions against the existing trusswork, and incandescent spheres oppose these at random. This calligraphy of light can be used to reinforce the composition of a space or to transform it. In the Playhouse auditorium the audience first sees the room lit by incandescent warehouse floodlights which shine up at the overlapping patterns of the ceiling. Together with an arc of exposed incandescent bulbs, these lights emphasize the volume of the room. When these lights are dimmed and the stab of stage lighting appears, the room is transformed and only the stage has importance. Outside in the small plaza, blue airport lights are used to enliven the space and give orientation to the audience movement.

All of these designs are based upon the theater's basic confrontation between audience and performer and represent an attempt to heighten this event without imposing physical limits that are too strict, too uncompromising. Since the programed use for all contemporary structures, whether housing venerable institutions or new activities, is so quickly made obsolete by change, it seems wise to emphasize essentials.

Norman McGrath photos

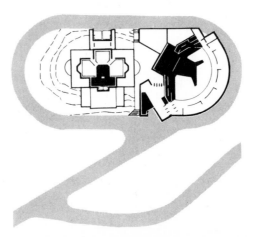

The site of the Robert S. Marx Theater is a grassy knoll located in Eden Park. The new 672-seat playhouse was the final phase of a five-year development plan. The three plans (opposite page, left) show the growth of the center since its beginnings in 1963: phase one—a thrust stage with 225 seats was built within a 94-year-old Victorian shelter house, and public facilities and an art gallery were added; phase two—administrative space and an outdoor terrace for chamber music were included; phase three—funds were raised entirely from the community and the $970,000 theater shown on these pages constructed. Costs were kept to $1,443 per seat (theaters with more luxurious public spaces but comparable production facilities are costing several times that.

The photograph at far left shows the main approach. Steps lead to a small plaza. The photographs on this page reveal the building's true size, which can be seen only from the downhill side. The walls are loadbearing.

Where it faces the plaza the new building appears small and in scale with its Victorian neighbor. The stainless steel roofs slope gently downward to reduce the height of walls which enclose the upper portion of lobby, backstage and shop areas. These walls, also of stainless steel, are a reflective surface presenting a shimmering, ever-changing image of the Victorian pavilion and the movement of people across the plaza. Airport taxiway lights of the standard beautiful blue, used in combination with incandescent bulbs in exposed porcelain sockets and wire cages, light the plaza at night. Architect Hardy has the pop artist's knack of taking familiar and prosaic objects and using them in fresh ways. For the first time these objects become beautiful or curious or funny—but as used by Hardy they are never wholly capricious. They serve their functional purpose as well, or better, than more standard, less inspired choices.

The five-level lobby is another diverting exercise in the transformation and exaltation of the mundane, and as such is an appropriately contemporary background for theatergoers. If in the future, as fashions change, this lobby is left as it is (as it should be), it will stand as an unrepentant period piece of the late sixties. Lowly ducts and air diffusers, hidden or screened until now, have become works of sculpture in stainless steel. Clusters of chrome-shielded fluorescent tubes, usually semi-concealed, are here exposed in all their nakedness in great vertical chandeliers. Even incandescent warehouse floodlights are used. Mirrors become a means to fracture space, to dissolve its edges and to create unexpected visual relationships and juxtapositions. And carpet is on the ceilings as well as the floors. Again this is no mere caprice. The carpet effectively lowers the noise level in this lobby during intermission.

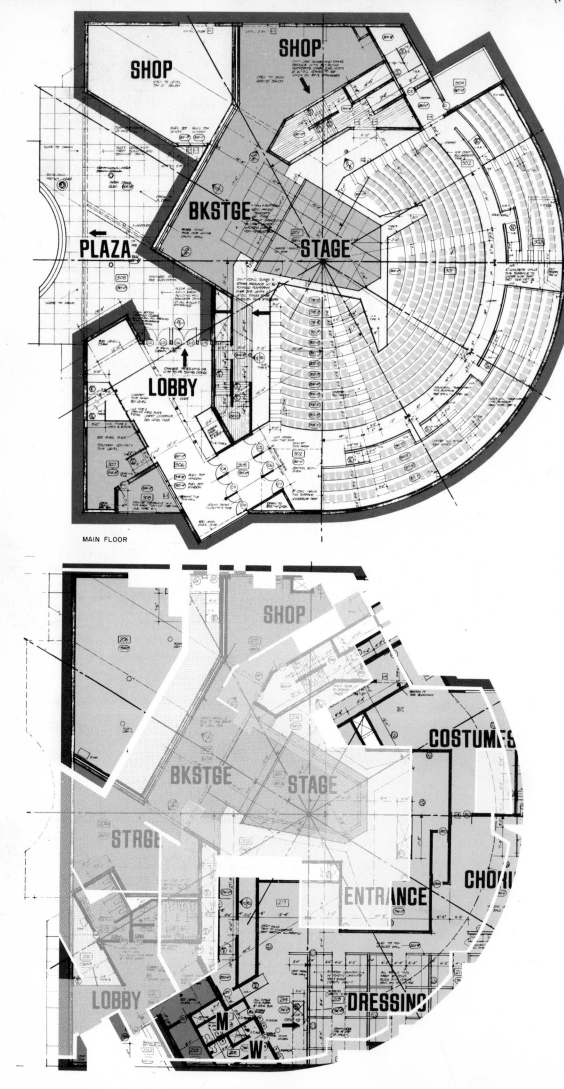

MAIN FLOOR

The asymmetrical thrust stage c
be entered by the actors from a
one of twenty-four points to acco
modate the style of producti
favored by theater director Broc
Jones. According to architect Harc
Jones had strong ideas from 1
beginning about what he wanted
do: "Brooks had thought throu
the style of production and the re
tionship of the audience to the p
formers and what the quality of 1
room was supposed to be and c
He wanted what we call the 'boc
end' concept, which to us mea
that when you are in a big amp
theater room you don't look at t
stage wall straight on, you lo
down at the floor and the back wa
What you see is the floor and t
wall together. Included within 1
audience's sightlines are the sic
walls, which we did not want
treat as decorative surfaces to attra
attention to themselves. We tried
make these walls work for the pi
formance to give as many ways
possible to get onto the stage. Eve
conceivable means of entry

212

that magic space was provided, and that's the reason why there are all those levels and holes and projections.

"In the beginning Brooks was opposed to an asymmetrical stage, but we as architects disagreed. Our point was that once you put a performance into a room with an audience, the performance becomes a three-dimensional thing which depends on movement as much as speech. There should be the opportunity to move in all sorts of ways which an asymmetrical stage provides. This led to the decision to surround the stage with a pit giving access at any point on its perimeter, not just from the vomitories. In Brooks' style of production actors and audience do not intermix—he thinks this demeans the actor. He wants actors to be larger-than-life-sized people. This was a further reason for cutting the stage off from the audience. The seating bowl doesn't touch the side walls either, except at the points where the audience enters and exits.

"Above all, we wanted to make sure that the auditorium had the quality of hard 'back-stageness'—that the only space to be soft and fuzzy would be where the audience sits."

To this end the architects not only exposed the building's structural and mechanical systems to full view within the auditorium, but also all the elements which are necessary to theater work. Lighting positions, catwalks, ladders—all are thoroughly revealed.

Upholstered seats with carpeted aisles and the audience itself provide the necessary sound dampening.

ROBERT S. MARX THEATER, Cincinnati. Owner: *Playhouse in the Park Corporation*. Architects: *Hardy Holzman Pfeiffer Associates;* supervising architect: *Robert Habel-Hubert M. Garriot Associates;* structural engineers: *Miller-Tallarico-McNinch & Hoeffel;* mechanical engineers: *Maxfield-Edwards-Backer & Associates;* acoustical engineers: *Robert A. Hansen Associates;* contractors: *Turner Construction Company.*

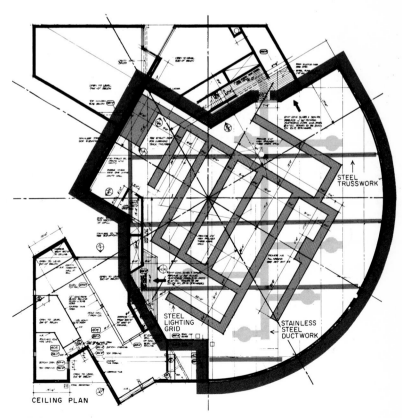

STEEL TRUSSWORK

STEEL LIGHTING GRID

STAINLESS STEEL DUCTWORK

CEILING PLAN

HEINZ HALL

When Loew's Penn theater closed its doors in 1964, after providing film and vaudeville entertainment for 37 years, demolition seemed inevitable. After all, on all sides of the Golden Triangle, old structures were being pulled down and replaced by shiny metal-skinned towers. But circumstances held a far different fate for the building.

On September 10, 1971, the Penn theater became the Heinz Hall for the Performing Arts. Plans to renovate the building for its new use began in 1968 after test concerts in the theater (see marquee, above) proved that not only did the room work well for symphonic music but that Pittsburghers were very willing to come downtown for concerts. Henry J. Heinz II, through the Howard Heinz Endowment, agreed to purchase the building and to substantially pay for the cost of rehabilitating it—approximately ten million dollars to date. The 2,730-seat hall will not only serve the renowned Pittsburgh Symphony but the Pittsburgh Opera, the Civic Light Opera, the Pittsburgh Ballet and the Youth Symphony as well.

Although the neo-Baroque opulence of the old movie palace remains, photo right (heightened if anything by the restraint and tact of the architects Stotz, Hess, MacLachlan and Fosner and their interior designer, Verner Purnell), the technical requirements necessary for revamping the building to its new use have been achieved economically and unobtrusively. In addition to restoring the Grand Foyer, the Grand Lobby and the hall itself to a tasteful reflection of the late twenties, the architects and their many consultants revised circulation patterns thoroughly with a new lobby (right center), intermission lounges and staircase, (right, bottom), provided three floors of offices for the various performing groups, added a wing behind the stage containing enlarged backstage space and other support facilities, and finally—under the direction of Dr. Heinrich Keilholz of Salzburg, Austria—added a large acoustical reflector above the proscenium and other refinements for optimal sound delivery in a multi-purpose hall.

Symphony, ballet, and especially opera performances, as opposed to moviegoing, require spacious and comfortable rooms in which to relax and greet friends during intermissions. The mezzanine plan shows two major additions for that purpose. A new horseshoe staircase from the main floor to the mezzanine brings the audience to a new lounge and to the Grand Foyer, formerly a space open to the main floor but now bridged at the mezzanine level to provide intermission space. Where once the marquee glittered, a four-story window reveals the Grand Lobby to evening passerby, (right). The newly-built ticket lobby is en-

tered by five doorways under copper-sheathed cupolas. The bulb-lined cupolas serve not only to shelter the entrances, but to screen the view of those in the lounge from flashing neon signs on the shops across the street, section above.

A six-story addition behind the existing building spans an important city utility right-of-way in order to permit a stage twice as deep as before. Two two-story rehearsal rooms, dressing rooms, practice rooms, instrument storage, a music library, performers' entrance and other circulation space is included in a compact new building.

The most intriguing technical aspect of concert hall design is, of course, the acoustical one. Here, Dr. Keilholz, who has an impressive list of accomplishments, including the final and successful work at New York's Philharmonic Hall, has used the classic technique of reflection from solid, hard surfaces to reinforce the energy transmitted to the listener by the orchestra or singer. A movable but heavily-built enclosure around the orchestra combined with the reflector, overpage, and panels flown above the players produces clear but lively sound images for a variety of performance requirements. In addition to these elements, Dr. Keilholz has specified an electro-acoustical system that permits sound reinforcement of certain productions, although not symphony or opera music.

HEINZ HALL OF THE PERFORMING ARTS, Pittsburgh, Pennsylvania. Architects: *Stotz, Hess, MacLachlan and Fosner*; acoustical and stage technique consultant: *Dr. Heinrich Keilholz*; engineers; *George Levinson, Inc. (structural), Meucci Engineering Inc. (mechanical), Hornfeck Engineering, Inc. (electrical)*; interior designer: *Verner S. Purnell*; general contractor: *Mellon-Stuart Co.*

Although the only changes in the audience portion of Heinz Hall (right) are new seats and a considerably restrained redecorating of walls and ceilings, the acoustical elements added to make it a first-rate symphony hall are quite evident. The large reflector above the proscenium (shown left) under construction with the circular frames for the twelve chandeliers hovering like space vehicles, is constructed of hard plaster on a steel frame. The orchestra enclosure is stressed seven-ply ¾-inch plywood sheets in movable steel frames that permit the enclosure depth to vary more than 15 feet. One of the two-story rehearsal rooms in the new wing (left bottom) has plywood baffles on walls and ceilings. The plans and sections (below) show that most of the changes in the renovation took place in the lobby and backstage areas of the building. Seating capacity was reduced by 700 seats because of increased seat spacing and removal of some seats in the uppermost balcony.

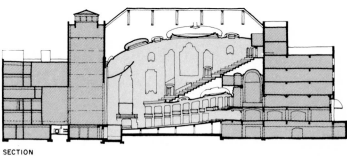

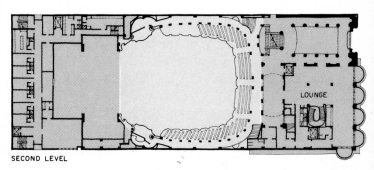

SECTION

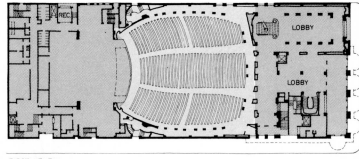

SECOND LEVEL

LOUNGE

REC.

LOBBY

LOBBY

FIRST LEVEL

PAUL MELLON CENTER

The Paul Mellon Center for the Arts has been conceived both symbolically and literally as a gateway between two Connecticut prep schools—Choate and its newly adopted sister Rosemary. The girls' school moved from Greenwich to become Choate's neighbor at Wallingford in September 1971. While sites for the new building were under consideration, architect Pei urged that the proposed structure become a principal means by which the about-to-be-built campus for girls would be linked to the older campus for boys.

Pei's solution can be quickly grasped by studying the axonometric projection (left) and the bird's-eye photo (above). The new arts complex is essentially two buildings, diagonally bisected by a broad curving pathway surfaced with tile and partially open to the sky, which culminates in a broad staircase. The juxtaposition of the curved and straight transparent walls, the portals and the stair produce an exciting spatial sequence. En route to Choate (top left) the interpenetrating assymetric design produces a quite different but still intriguing plastic effect.

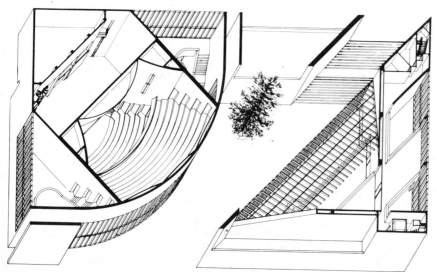

Joseph W. Molitor photos except as noted

As the top photo (left) partially indicates the arts center has been placed within and looks out upon broad surrounding meadows. These handsome open spaces were created at Pei's insistence from a site originally marred by inferior out buildings and too many nondescript trees.

The lounge (three photos at right) and the auditorium foyer (bottom photo at left) play an important plastic role in the diagonal spatial sequence linking Choate to Rosemary. Physically separated from the path by their transparent glass enclosures, these areas, nonetheless, are strongly connected to the center of things. Students in the lounge and visitors to the auditorium are never out of touch with what is going on along the path.

Originally the lounge was not in the program. Architect Pei, however, thought that the Choate and Rosemary students would need a special place to get together and that the projected arts center would be ideal for this purpose. If a lounge were made adjacent to the theater, art studios and practice rooms, a typical student's interest in art might grow from a first shy attempt to find common ground with the opposite sex. "The building is more than a gateway," says Pei. "It is also a trap, designed to lure the boys and girls to each other and to art." Painting, sculpture and weaving take place on the two cantilevered mezzanines within the lounge as the section (below) indicates. As can also be seen in the section, a portion of the auditorium is underground to bring the roof of the stagehouse in line with the well proportioned cornice height. The auditorium roof, although sheathed in concrete and originally intended to be framed by concrete Verendiel trusses, was finally constructed in steel because of time and budget.

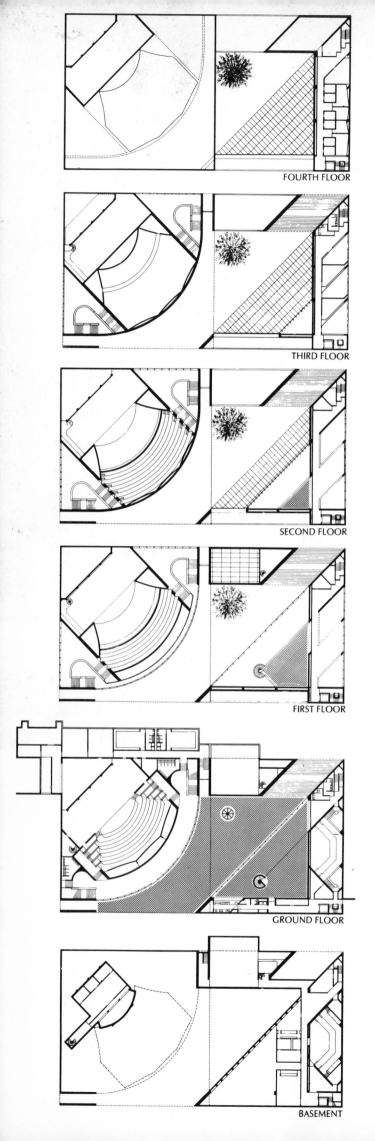

FOURTH FLOOR

THIRD FLOOR

SECOND FLOOR

FIRST FLOOR

GROUND FLOOR

BASEMENT

The arts center has six levels. In the basement of the theater wing are equipment and storage space, the trap room and the orchestra pit. In the teaching wing are the experimental theater and its storage, the recital room, a storage and mechanical room, miscellaneous office spaces and a small library. At the ground floor level are the court or pathway, the orchestra seating, stage and ancillary spaces in the auditorium, the upper level of the recital room in the teaching wing, and the main floor of the lounge. The first floor contains the balcony and its lobby, the first of two lounge mezzanines and the art studios. The second floor consists largely of the upper levels of the first floor spaces and includes the second lounge mezzanine. The third floor has class and seminar rooms in the teaching wing and a mechanical room behind the stage house. The latter room was improperly insulated from the stage because of unfortunate budget cuts, and presently is a source of objectionable noise during rehearsal and performance. On the fourth floor of the teaching wing are music practice rooms and the skylight.

Apart from the difficulties with the mechanical room, the auditorium acoustics work quite well. The room is flexible and expandable. For drama the auditorium seats 840, but the balcony can be closed off to create an intimate 400-seat theater. For music three configurations are available: an 800-seat theater with orchestra pit and full stage house for musicals, an expanded stage with retractable shell for orchestral performances, and a 400-seat intimate hall for recitals and chamber music using the retractable shell.

EXPANDABLE AUDITORIUM

840 seats

40   800

40   400

STAGE HOUSE

RETRACTABLE MUSIC SHELL

THREE LEVEL PIT LIFT

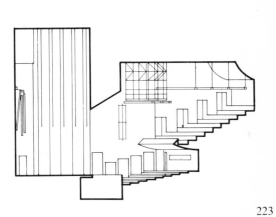

THE PAUL MELLON ARTS CENTER, Choate School and Rosemary Hall, Wallingford, Connecticut. Architects: *I.M. Pei & Partners—architect-in-charge—Ralph Heisel; project managers—John Scarlata and Paul Veeder; resident architect: Murray Kalender; interiors: Robert Lym;* engineers: *Olaf Soot* (structural); *Campbell and Friedland* (mechanical); theater consultants: *George Izenour Associates;* landscape architect: *Joseph R. Gangemi;* general contractor: *George B. H. Macomber Company.*

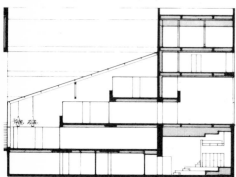

IOWA PRARIE AUDITORIUM

The new C. Y. Stevens Auditorium at Iowa State University is a free-standing piece of sculpture in a rolling gentle setting, full of grass and trees. It is refreshing to note that such architecture still is being commissioned, and that some architects get to occasionally practice architecture as it once was taught—when we believed there would always be grass and trees around buildings cities and people.

The theater sits on the eastern edge of the old campus in a new group of buildings called the Iowa State Center, and it was the first of the group to be completed; Crites and McConnell, Brooks, Borg and Skiles are the joint venture architects. The structure was designed to be successful

Julius Shulman photos

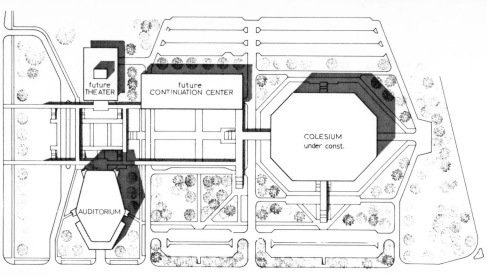

either as a theater for live stage productions or as an auditorium for speeches and symposiums. The problems of acoustics, and of site lines from seating to stage are crucial in both kinds of functions, and the building should be seen as a simple, direct powerful solution to both problems. The exterior follows directly from the spaces inside.

In section (page 228) the auditorium is shown to have about twice the rise in its seating from stage to rear as "normal" auditorium seating provides. The rise between rows is 4 inches near the stage increasing to 12 inches at the rear of the floor. The three balconies above, and their accompanying side balconies, are even more sharply sloped, as the section shows. The

clusion of three balconies, plus the strong [slo]pe of the seating has reversed what is [of]ten the high end of a theater: the stage [en]d with its space for flying sets. This space [is] accommodated in the Stevens Auditorium [wi]thin the general roof height itself.

The scalloped interior ceiling, and [rh]ythmic stepped pattern of the sidewalls [are] architectural responses to acoustical [ne]eds, determined by the architects, and by [th]e acoustical consultants, Paul E. Venek[lass]en & Associates. Sounds emanating from [th]e stage are properly resonated and mixed [th]rough these shapes, and through the [m]aterial of the surfaces themselves. The [pri]ncipal interior material is poured-in-place [co]ncrete, board-formed and left untreated after removal of the forms. Carpeting on the floor and fabric on the seats help baffle crowd sounds, and a system of drapes can be adjusted to provide greater or less sound absorption near the stage. The vertical aisle partitions between concrete piers are oak, and the scalloped auditorium ceiling is larchwood boards three inches thick. Larchwood was picked over cedar (which is the *exterior* soffit material of the roof) because of its greater density, and thus better acoustic characteristics in this application. The seating pattern is continental, as these photographs show, with no center aisle and with each row far enough apart for easy circulation between them.

On the exterior the major exposed material is again poured-in-place concrete, along with the exposed cedar over the roof soffits, and the dark glass between stair ramps. The easy stairs are simply expressed as nearly horizontal concrete bands on the exterior, with glass between them, and each ribbon terminates in the stair towers into which they empty. There are two entrance levels at the front of the auditorium/theater, one at ground level and one at the main floor level, which meets the exterior set of overhead walkways and plazas connecting all the buildings of the Center. Many of the walkways are in place now, so that the building seems to be reaching out with giant arms toward the land and the people around it.

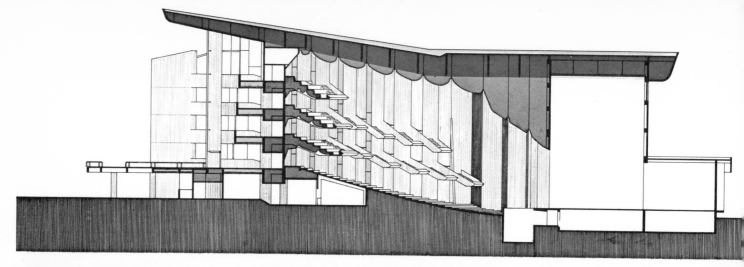

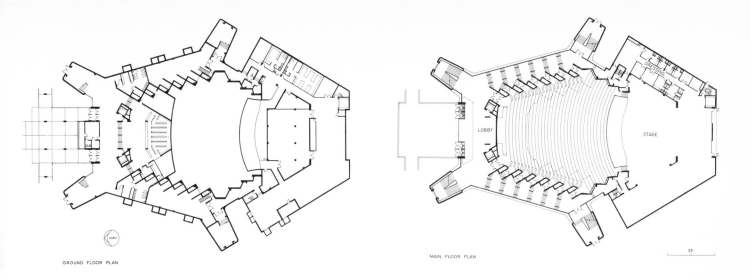

GROUND FLOOR PLAN

MAIN FLOOR PLAN

25

The roof is supported on the series of hollow concrete piers which surround the main space; these also carry hot and cold air. The roof is framed out in steel, with special girders spanning between piers, then standard bar joists, metal deck, and built-up roofing. Heating and cooling is provided from the university's central plant, eliminating the need for mechanical spaces, and possible sources of noise and vibration. The orchestra pit is equipped with a hydraulic lift; if needed the platform can be raised to stage level to provide additional working areas. There are four individual dressing rooms for stars, two large chorus rooms, and an actors' lounge backstage, along with ample room for scenery.

The whole theater, with its 2,637 normal seating capacity, cost under $5 million to build. That is a good price for a theater these days. With its careful proportioning and the direct, simple exterior expression of how it works and what it is, the Stephens Auditorium is very much in the first rank of modern architecture in the Midwest. There is still room to do buildings like this in some places, and it's rewarding to find them done well.

C. Y. STEPHENS AUDITORIUM, Iowa State University, Ames, Iowa. Architects: *Crites and McConnell; Brooks, Borg and Skiles;* joint venture. Acoustical consultant: *Paul E. Veneklasen & Associates;* general contractor: *Martin K. Eby Co.*

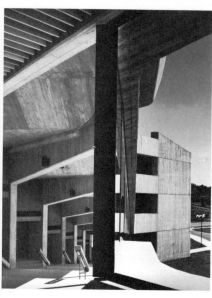

More dramatic in form and mass, but smaller by far in area than the Convention Center, Symphony Hall is a multi-angled, reinforced concrete building of elegant intention, decidedly a showplace with its rich-colored fabrics, crystal chandeliers and mirrored walls. It is set on a two-block site across the pedestrian concourse from the Convention Center and stands in a dominant position at one end of the main plaza. The same fluted beige concrete block used on the Convention Center covers with pleasing effect the exterior—and much of the interior—walls. Light and shadow play with varying effect during the day on its texture and on the angled soffits of the projecting fascia. The entrance to Symphony Hall, very different in design and scale from that of the Convention Center, reveals the grand lobby's 48-foot-high, 54-foot-wide mirrored wall and several of its 20-foot-long Italian glass chandeliers. The lobby carpet is traditional red, as is the upholstery for its 2,557 seats. The stage curtain is a spectacular creation of mylar embroidered in acrylic yarn in shades of pink, red, purple, orange and green, designed by the architects interior department and made by Jack Lenor Larsen. Where fluted block is not used on the interior, walls are faced with either white plaster or white oak panels. A number of works of art including sculpture and tapestries are placed in the building. Other sculptures and fountains are located on the plaza. The plaza on which both Symphony Hall and Convention Center stand is raised five feet above street level permitting a 1,125-car garage.

PHOENIX CIVIC PLAZA, Phoenix, Arizona. Architects: *Charles Luckman Associates—Edward R. Jones, director of Phoenix office; William L. Kourakos, director of design; John Schotanus, Jr., associate architect.* Engineers: *Magadini Associates* (structural), *Lowry and Sorensen Engineering Co.* (mechanical/electrical), *Sergent, Hauskins & Beckwith* (soils/foundation). Consultants: *Vern O. Knudsen* acoustics), *L. W. Sepmeyer* (sound system), *George A. Thomas* (theater consultant), *Charles Luckman Associates* (interiors, graphics, cost). Landscape architect: *F. J. MacDonald.* Contractor: *Del E. Webb Corp.*

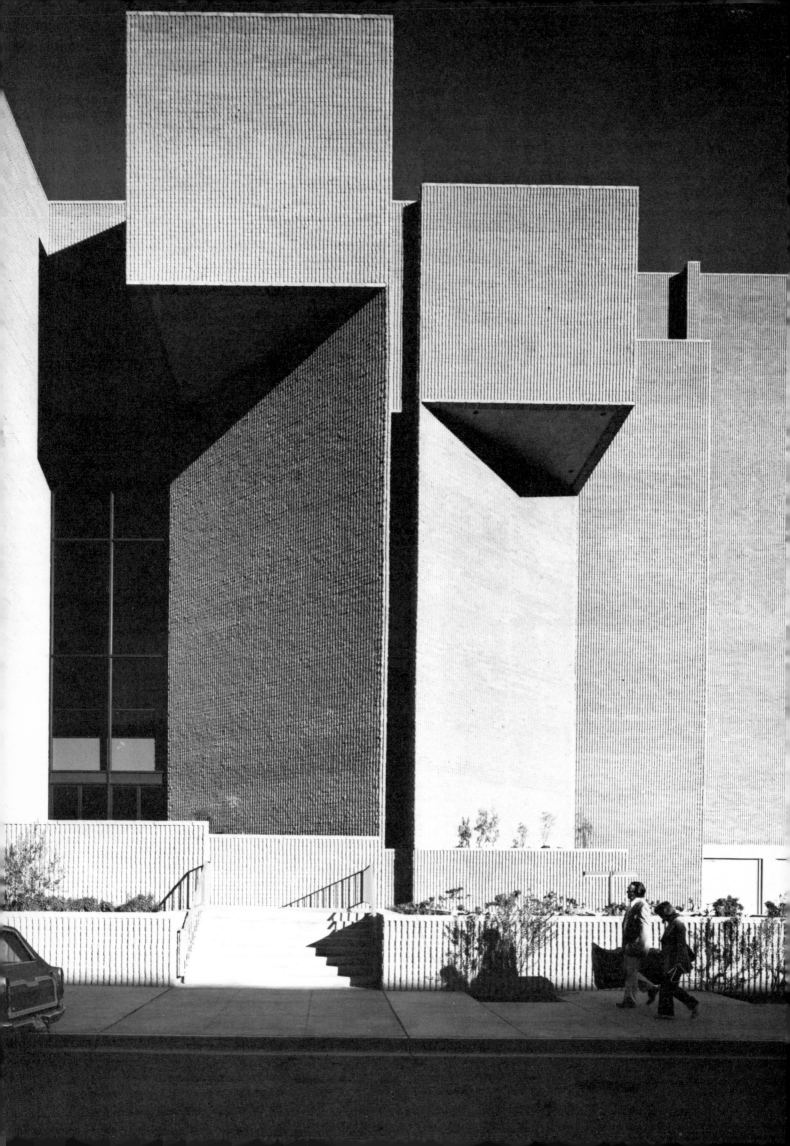

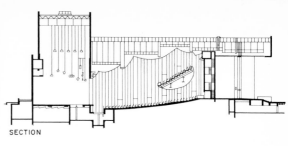

SECTION

An unusual feature of the hall is its 120-foot-wide, 643 seat "floating" balcony. Attached only to the side walls, the balcony "floats" free of the back wall, leaving an open space through which sound circulates. At the four corners of the main floor and at either end of the balcony are triangular refreshment areas. Also included in the building are the usual chorus and dressing rooms, a room and rehearsal hall.

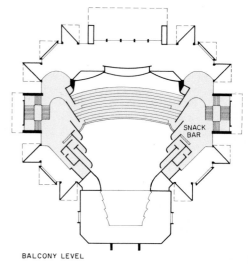

SNACK BAR

BALCONY LEVEL

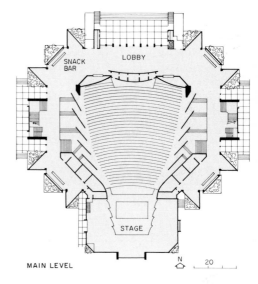

SNACK BAR

LOBBY

STAGE

MAIN LEVEL

N 20

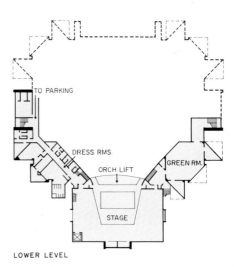

TO PARKING

DRESS. RMS.

ORCH. LIFT

GREEN RM.

STAGE

LOWER LEVEL

COMMUNITY CENTER, NEWARK, N.J.

The rehabilitation of carriage houses, in those communities lucky enough to have them, for residential use began as soon as the automobile replaced the horse-drawn carriage. As in most residential work, the architectural and legal problems are relatively simple. But when the carriage house is converted to public use, as was this one at the Newark Community Center of the Arts, the designer must deal with code requirements as stringent as those for new construction of the same type. Thus, a building of 2,000 square feet must accommodate two means of egress, provide adequate toilets, and meet the same codes as larger structures.

Hardy, Holzman and Pfeiffer Associates, architects for the renovation, have met those restrictions with their customary flair. With a limited budget and area in which to work, they have provided rehearsal and performance space for music and dance which works well and admirably captures the spirit of the school. Mrs. David Lass and Saunders Davis, music teachers in the Newark school system, established the Center in January, 1968. Enrollment grew so rapidly that new quarters were needed within six months. Grants from two foundations enabled the school to move into a large house in a once well-to-do Newark neighborhood. Soon afterwards the architects began the conversion of the carriage house behind.

Although the roof and some of the masonry of the existing building had to be replaced, the 20-foot-wide shell dictated the proportions of the revised design. The alley facade (top of the plan, below) remains as it was with all new construction toward the house (which now contains offices and music rehearsal rooms). Performance-goers pass through the house into a courtyard, which will be developed as an outdoor theater, across which they see the sprightly elevation (opposite). A split-level entrance leads down to toilets and mirrored rehearsal room with an elegant two-position barre and new hardwood floor. The stairs up bring audiences directly into a large room divided diagonally into stage and seating areas. Faced with a 2:5 plan proportion, the architects felt that the diagonal stage permitted the width necessary for dance movement, as a standard stage across one end would not, while not spreading the audience the entire length of the space. A new roof structure echoes and reinforces the stage angle while a clerestory over the audience increases the sense of enclosure about the stage. Performers can come onto the stage from a ramp leading to the lower floor or can enter from an alcove over the lobby. An adjustable stage lighting system adds a glamorous note.

NEWARK COMMUNITY CENTER OF THE ARTS, Newark, New Jersey. Architects: *Hardy, Holzman and Pfeiffer Associates*; general contractor: *Verfield Construction Company, Inc.*

Norman McGrath photos

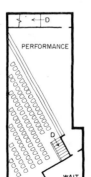

SECOND LEVEL   FIRST LEVEL

CHAPTER FIVE

ARCHITEC-
TURAL
ENGINEERING

BLOSSOM MUSIC CENTER

The soaring shape of the pavilion for Blossom Music Center, summer home of the Cleveland Symphony, grew almost entirely out of functional requirements for acoustics and sight lines; and its exterior texture and color were chosen to fit the natural, rustic environment. The structure was a logical response to the architecturally-conceived shape and consequent load-carrying requirements. The shell of the pavilion has a shape somewhat like a truncated cone. It follows the fan-shaped plan of the seating and tilts from a high point 94 ft above the stage floor to the perimeter opening, which varies from 25 ft at the center to 15 ft at the sides. The heights were determined by acoustical and sight-line requirements.

The roof is supported by single-plane pipe trusses, which in turn are supported at one end by a huge tipped steel arch-girder and at the other end by a column-supported girder located 25 ft from the perimeter. The tipped arch-girder bears on two large underground footings and is supported by 10 sloping, tapered columns located outside the pavilion's walls. The arch and these exterior columns are made of "weathering" steel, which, together with the russet-colored shingles of the shell, serves to complement the wooded landscape. The arch-girder was intended to be an architecturally-emphasized element as well as a major structural element, providing visual transition between wall and roof.

Many structural schemes were considered in the early design stages by the architect, Schafer, Flynn and vanDijk, and the structural engineer, R. M. Gensert Associates. These included: 1) a space frame spanning the entire area; 2) double-cable suspension systems with elevated supports over the stage; 3) a series of radially-oriented single-plane trusses supported over the stage; 4) a series of radially-oriented space trusses.

Hastings-Willinger

Jim Cross

Blossom Music Center, summer home of the Cleveland Symphony Orchestra, is designed to accommodate 15,000 people—4,500 in the pavilion and 10,500 on the sloping lawn around it. The orchestra pit seats 100 musicians, and the stage will take 200 performers. Behind the pavilion is a separate building for the Green Room, choral rehearsal room, and private rooms for conductor, soloist and others.

Final design is remarkably like the architect's original concept (below, center). Shape was derived from seating-plan, acoustical-volume, and sight-line requirements. The hundreds of tubular members of the roof trusses act as "micro-diffusers" of sound waves Clusters of speakers are concealed in the fascia at the edge of the roof to reinforce sound to the lawn area.

Frank Reed

Cable structures were ruled out because the structural engineer feared that temperature change might create a noise problem. The space frame offered the most elegant structure, but it required rather heavy articulation of members at its supports, creating a visual barrier. Thus the decision was made to work with space trusses as the initial approach, incorporating transverse framing for stability and for unification of the structural ceiling.

The fan shape of the pavilion and the height of the building above the stage set the pattern of radially-placed trusses. Each truss was to be framed with two top chords and one bottom chord to resemble a space frame in behavior and appearance. To resist wind forces against the high wall of the building, an inclined peripheral arch was placed where the

walls and roof meet. Wind forces from the opposite direction would be resisted by the inclined columns supporting the arch. Wind forces acting on either side of the building centerline would be resisted by the arch in lateral resistance, and transmitted by secondary bracing to the rear wall and to the columns at the open portion of the pavilion, where resisting moments would be set up between the roof and columns. Vertical loads and reactions from space trusses to arch would be transmitted by the arch as a beam to the inclined columns.

The supporting peripheral arch presented problems in itself. First, it was inclined and nearly parabolic. This meant that its top and bottom flanges were constantly warped with respect to the web section. Further, the inter-

section of arch and supporting inclined columns was different at all points except for the symmetry on either side of the building. At first the arch was interpreted as a single-layered skeletal system, but its lack of torsional resistance required it to be extended into a box-like skeletal system. The intersections of the three-dimensional skeletal arch and the space trusses were studied for two-, three- and four-joint connections. After building many models, the engineers concluded that it would be nearly impossible to detail, fabricate and erect nonsymmetrical three-dimensional systems coming together in a three-dimensional manner. Thus, the engineers decided to use a closed steel-plate box section.

Concurrently, studies were being made

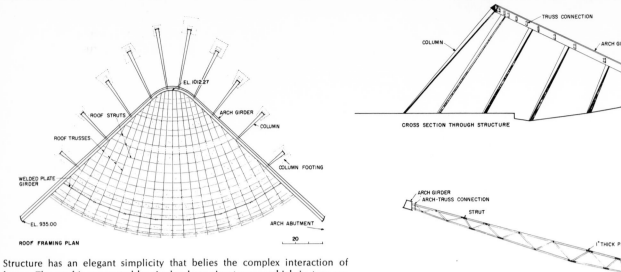

ROOF FRAMING PLAN

EL.1012.27

ROOF STRUTS

ROOF TRUSSES

ARCH GIRDER

COLUMN

WELDED PLATE GIRDER

COLUMN FOOTING

EL. 935.00

ARCH ABUTMENT

20

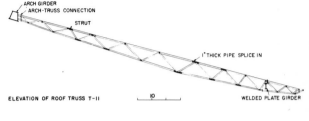

TRUSS CONNECTION

COLUMN

ARCH GIRDER

CROSS SECTION THROUGH STRUCTURE

10

ARCH GIRDER

ARCH-TRUSS CONNECTION

STRUT

1" THICK PIPE SPLICE IN

WELDED PLATE GIRDER

ELEVATION OF ROOF TRUSS T-11

10

Structure has an elegant simplicity that belies the complex interaction of forces. The roof is supported by single-plane pipe trusses, which in turn are supported by a huge arch-girder spanning 400 ft and a smaller plate girder at the other end. Holding up the arch are 10 tapered, inclined columns.

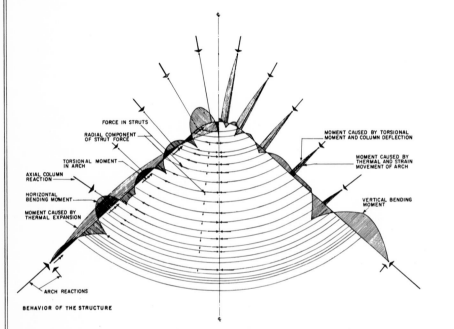

BEHAVIOR OF THE STRUCTURE

FORCE IN STRUTS

RADIAL COMPONENT OF STRUT FORCE

TORSIONAL MOMENT IN ARCH

AXIAL COLUMN REACTION

HORIZONTAL BENDING MOMENT

MOMENT CAUSED BY THERMAL EXPANSION

MOMENT CAUSED BY TORSIONAL MOMENT AND COLUMN DEFLECTION

MOMENT CAUSED BY THERMAL AND STRAIN MOVEMENT OF ARCH

VERTICAL BENDING MOMENT

ARCH REACTIONS

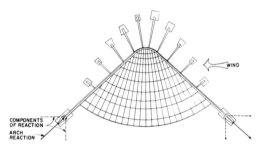

WIND

COMPONENTS OF REACTION

ARCH REACTION

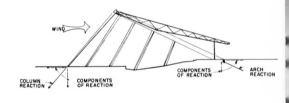

WIND

COLUMN REACTION

COMPONENTS OF REACTION

COMPONENTS OF REACTION

ARCH REACTION

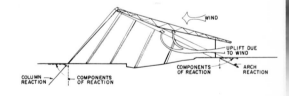

WIND

UPLIFT DUE TO WIND

COLUMN REACTION

COMPONENTS OF REACTION

COMPONENTS OF REACTION

ARCH REACTION

The arch and tapered columns not only transmit dead load of the roof to the ground, but work together to resolve wind forces. When the wind blows from the side, the "arch" provides a tensile component at one footing and a compressive component at the other. When wind blows from the back, the arch works in compression and the columns in tension; the opposite conditions pertain when the wind blows from the front, creating an uplift. Struts between the trusses transmit wind force from one side of the arch to the other. The various forces and reactions are shown above.

Columns are tapered in two opposite directions to take moment caused by torsion that occurs in the arch girder, and bending caused by static and temperature strain in the arch. Arch has stiffeners to prevent buckling. Further, webs and flanges are joined by full penetration welds, reducing the amounts of stiffening required.

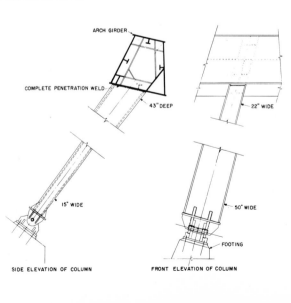

ARCH GIRDER

COMPLETE PENETRATION WELD

43" DEEP

22" WIDE

15" WIDE

SIDE ELEVATION OF COLUMN

50" WIDE

FOOTING

FRONT ELEVATION OF COLUMN

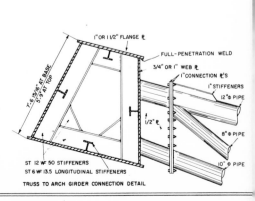

1" OR 1 1/2" FLANGE ℞

FULL-PENETRATION WELD

3/4" OR 1" WEB ℞

1" CONNECTION ℞'S

1" STIFFENERS

12" ⌀ PIPE

7'-6 15/16" AT BASE
5'-9" AT TOP

1/2" ℞

8" ⌀ PIPE

10" ⌀ PIPE

ST 12 WF 50 STIFFENERS
ST 6 WF 13.5 LONGITUDINAL STIFFENERS

TRUSS TO ARCH GIRDER CONNECTION DETAIL

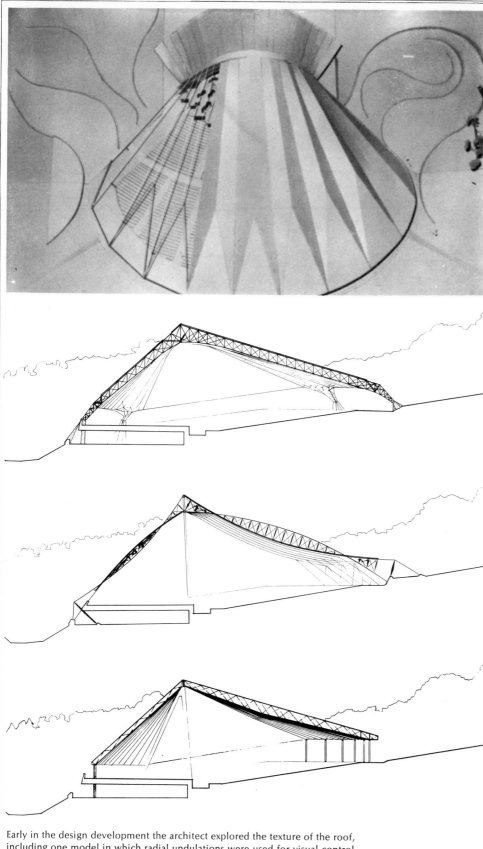

Early in the design development the architect explored the texture of the roof, including one model in which radial undulations were used for visual control of the surface. But since these were inconsistent with the acoustics and structurally inefficient, this approach was abandoned. Some early structural approaches are shown above. The space frame (top) provided an elegant structure, but required heavy articulation of members at the supports. The double-cable structure (middle) was thought to be possibly "noisy" when temperature change occurs. Space trusses (bottom) were seriously considered. This sketch shows a vertical arch rather than a tipped arched-girder.

BLOSSOM MUSIC CENTER, Peninsula, Ohio. Architects: *Schafer, Flynn and vanDijk—Ronald A. Straka, associate-in-charge of design;* consulting architect: *Pietro Belluschi;* structural engineer: *R. M. Gensert Associates—Miklos Peller, associate-in-charge of design;* mechanical and electrical engineer: *Byers, Urban, Klug & Pittenger;* general contractor: *Turner Construction Company;* steel fabricators: *The Kilroy Structural Steel Company, Tucker Steel Corporation;* acoustical consultants: *Heinrich Keilholz, Christopher Jaffee;* soils consultant: *David V. Lewin;* site consultant: *William A. Gould and Associates.*

for the columnar supports of the arch. At first they were made skeletal, like the arch. But the system appeared to be over-structured—i.e., the space truss supports were just as busy as the space trusses, even though they did less work. Next, the supports were tried as star-shaped struts with two pairs of cables for three-dimensional stability. But this solution had a redundancy because of the inherent lateral stability of the arch. So, cables were abandoned and stability was obtained by tapering the star-shaped struts so that they could resist wind moment.

The space-truss scheme had to be abandoned, however, because of the short construction time available (seven months), and the non-standard fabrication requirements. After many studies, it was determined that single-plane pipe trusses with variable depths should replace the space trusses, and tapered box columns should replace the star columns.

The great peripheral arch-girder (400-ft span by 200-ft rise) required engineering design considerations of combined longitudinal stresses for bending under vertical and lateral loads, in addition to tranverse stresses from eccentric connections of roof and wall trusses. Another major consideration was that of thermal stress. Lastly there was the problem of local buckling from load concentrations.

The inclined box columns (as long as 125 ft) supporting the arch were tapered in two opposing directions to provide end stability. Because these columns were inclined, they had to be designed to take secondary stresses resulting from an eccentricity of axial load.

The architect's concern for "correct" structure and the structural engineer's concern for esthetics are demonstrated by design decisions made concerning termination of the arch at the ground. A concrete abutment implied primary structural forces within the arch, whereas the arch was strictly secondary in behavior with respect to wind, and even less for vertical loads, because of its steep angle of inclination and intermittent supports. First, a triangular steel support was attempted. The relationship of roof slope, roof support and roof corner required a break in the thrust line of the arch between the two upper points of the triangle. This was contrary to arch action, so the end support was abandoned for a series of inclined V-shaped supports. This approach lacked sophistication, so it was finally decided to allow the base of the arch to disappear into the earth, thus minimizing the action of an arch required for secondary loads, and exemplifying the use of corrosion-resistant steel.

Deck of the structure is 4-in. tongue-and-groove wood plank, which, with lateral nailing of adjacent planes, provides a rigid diaphragm capable of transmitting horizontal and oblique loads. The 4-in. wood deck also acts as a thermal shock absorber, protecting the structural system against sudden changes in geometry.

Structural model (left) indicates geometry of space-truss scheme. Because of the complexity of fabrication, approach was changed to single-plane pipe trusses. Various column configurations (right) were evaluated. The triangulated columns seemed over-elaborated for the job; cable-guyed star columns contradicted the inherent lateral stability of the arch. The single-plane arch was changed to a box to give it torsional resistance.

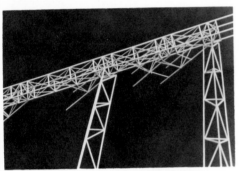

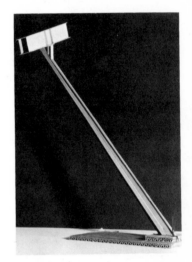

Intersections of three-dimensional skeletal systems were studied, but the engineer concluded that they would be nearly impossible to detail, fabricate and erect. For this reason, a closed steel box was selected for the peripheral arch. The intersection of inclined star supports and built-up arch was then studied. Merely setting the arch on these supports created a visual and structural tendency for them to twist away from each other. A short stub was introduced, but this posed architectural problems. Finally the doubly-tapered column was developed as the best solution.

Termination of the arch-girder posed problems for the engineer in terms of logical expression of its function. An exposed concrete abutment implied primarily arch action, but this was only a secondary function of the structural member. A triangular support at the end interrupted the thrust line, and so was contrary to arch action. Then inclined, V-shaped supports were considered, but the structure lost its sophisticated appearance. Finally, inasmuch as the arch-girder was to be fabricated of "weathering" steel, it was decided to continue the arch down into the ground, eliminating massive above-ground support.

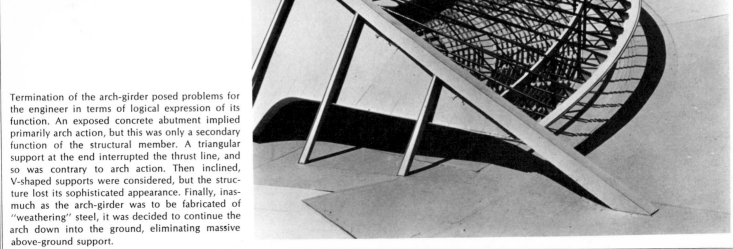

Field construction and shop photos give an idea of the scale and functioning of the roof truss system. The longest trusses span 175 ft and cantilever another 28 ft to provide a curved promenade. Pipe struts between trusses transfer wind forces from one side of the arch-girder to the other. Diagonal tie bars between trusses give them lateral stability. Pipe web members were contour cut by automatic machine to fit pipe chord members for neat welded connections. Pipe chords were fabricated with short sections of thicker pipe (1-in. wall) at panel points to take the large compressive loads of the struts. Further, design investigation showed that secondary stresses would be present around heavily-stressed web members, especially where the chord wall was thin.

One reason for using pipe for the trusses, it is said, was that a "closed" shape was desired for acoustical reasons. But this posed difficulties both for engineering analysis and for fabrication. The engineers had to design against collapse of the pipe chord members that could result from compressive forces transmitted by truss web members and wind struts. Because there is little literature on the subject, tests were made on actual joints, from which allowable design stresses were determined and minimum pipe shell thicknesses established. Since the required shell at some joints was more than that required for axial forces between joints, sections of chords at panel points having a thicker shell were butt welded to the remainder of the chord.

After several types of connections for the steel pipe truss members were investigated, it was decided to use a contour-cut welded connection. This would require the least amount of fabrication, as well as provide the most pleas-

ing connection. Because of the complicated shape of the contours, the web chord connections were welded manually. Fillet welds were used to avoid joint preparation and to speed fabrication. Where fillet welds were found to be ineffective, or difficult because of the small incident angle of the web member, small gusset plates were added.

All connections had to be unobtrusive. No connections were to be seen on the outside faces of the arch girder or on the columns. To stabilize the cross-section of the arch girder and to provide strength against buckling, internal stiffeners were used. Also, the connections of the stiffeners to the plates of the arch girder had to provide moment as well as shear resistance. Inasmuch as speed of detailing and fabrication were of paramount concern, fillet welding was selected as requiring the least amount of detailing, giving the neatest and strongest type of connection, and allowing use of the least material. Thickness of the arch

girder plates was kept as thin as possible because of the higher cost of "weathering" steel. Engineering studies indicated that an extra set of longitudinal stiffeners might have to be used on the web plates and on the bottom flange plates to prevent buckling. But it was found this could be avoided if the welds at the corners of the arch were complete-penetration. This was the fastest and least expensive operation, saving an appreciable amount of stiffener material and fabrication time, while providing a neat seam on the exposed surfaces.

The steel columns are stressed by axial load and bi-axial moment gradient, partly caused by the torsional moment in the arch girder, and partly by static and temperature strain movement in the arch. The full column section had to be developed at the joints, calling for complete-penetration welds at the splice points. Further, complete-penetration welds were required between column flanges and webs.

INDEX

A

Aalto, Alvar (architect), *59–63*
Adams, Frank (architect) of Stahl/Bennett, Inc., *10*
Albyn, Richard K. (architect) of Tarapata MacMahon Paulsen Corporation, *8–9*
Amitai, S. (associate architect), *48–49*
Architects Collaborative, The, Inc. (architects), *11–16, 21–25, 116–117*
Ashkenazi, Moshe (assistant architect), *103–106*

B

Barker, The James Madison Engineering Library, Massachusetts Institute of Technology, Cambridge, MA, *31–36*
Barnes, Edward Larrabee (architect), *94–99*
Bellini Lizero and Gozzi (associate architects), *86–87*
Belluschi, Pietro (architect), *183–192*
  (associate architect), *238–243*
Birkerts, Gunnar (architect), *42–43*
Birkerts, Gunnar and Associates (architects), *50–51*
Blossom Music Center, Peninsula, OH, *238–243*
Bolt, Beranek and Newman (acoustical consultants), *164–173, 176–182, 199–207*
Bourne, Philip W. (architect), *145–146*
Brighton Branch Library, Brighton, MA, *11–16*
Brooks, Borg and Skiles (architects), *225–230*
Brooks, The Memorial Art Gallery Addition, Memphis, TN, *107–113*
Brown Sciences Library, Brown University, Providence, RI, *5–7*
Brydges, Earl W. Public Library, Niagara Falls, NY, *26–30*

C

Cambridge Seven Associates, Inc., *91–93*
Catalano, Eduardo (associate architect), *183–192*
Center for the Arts, Wesleyan University, Middletown, CT, *164–168*
Centers
  Cultural
  Civic
    Chiba District Culture Center, Chiba District, Japan, *37*
    Hunter Museum of Art, Chattanooga, TN, *128–129*
    Jefferson, Casa Thomas, Brasilia, Brazil, *174–175*
    Scottsdale Civic Center, Scottsdale, AZ, *18–20*
  University
    Fine Arts Center, University of Massachusetts, Amherst, MA, *169–173*
    Florida State Museum, University of Florida, Gainesville, FL, *139–144*

Centers (*Cont.*):
Performing Arts
Civic
  Blossom Music Center, Peninsula, OH, *238–243*
  Hamilton Place, Hamilton, Ontario, Canada, *177–182*
  Heinz Hall of the Performing Arts, Pittsburgh, PA, *214–217*
  Loew's Penn Theater, Pittsburgh, PA, *214*
  Marx, Robert S. Theater, Cincinnati, OH, *208–213*
  Milwaukee Center for the Performing Arts, Milwaukee, WI, *199–207*
  Newark Community Center of the Arts, Newark, NJ, *234–235*
  Phoenix Civic Plaza, Phoenix, AZ, *231–233*
Academic
  Center for the Arts, Wesleyan University, Middletown, CT, *164–168*
  Juilliard School, The, New York, NY, *183–192*
  Mellon, The Paul Arts Center, Choate School and Rosemary Hall, Wallingford, CT, *218–224*
  Musical Arts Center, Indiana University, Bloomington, IN, *193–198*
  Paul Recital Hall, Juilliard School, New York, NY, *183–192*
  Stephens, C.Y. Auditorium, Iowa State University, Ames, IA, *225–230*
  Tully, Alice Hall, Juilliard School, New York, NY, *183–192*
Science
  Oakland Museum, Oakland, CA, *147–153*
  Ontario Science Center, Toronto, Ontario, Canada, *154–159*
Central Library, The, of Negev University, Beersheba, Israel, *48–49*
Central Library, Niagara Falls, NY, *64–65*
Chermayeff, Ivan (architect) of Cambridge Seven Associates, Inc., *91–93*
Chiba District Culture Center, Chiba District, Japan, *37–39*
Chiba Library, Chiba District, Japan, *37–39*
Ciampi, Mario J. (architect), *118–121*
Cloud, L.D. (architect) of Ford, Powell & Carson, *17*
Coram Library, Bates College, Lewiston, ME, *21–25*
Core & Research Laboratory Library, Northwestern University, Miller Campus, Evanston, IL, *52–58*
Crites and McConnell (architects), *225–230*
Cronenwett, Joal (architect) of James Sudler Associates, *77–82*

D

DeMars & Wells (executive architects), *59–63*
Denver Art Museum Building, Denver, CO, *77–82*
Derthwick & Henley (architects), *128–129*
Dietrich, Paul (architect) of Cambridge Seven Associates, Inc., *91–93*
Donat, Walter S. (associate architect), *116–117*
Dubugras, Elvin MacKay (architect), *174–175*
Duluth Library, Duluth, MN, *42–43*

E

Eitan, Dan (architect), *103–106*

F

Farmington Public Library, Farmington, MI, *8–9*
Fine Arts Center, University of Massachusetts, Amherst, MA, *169–173*
Fleckenstein, Charles (architect) of Gunnar Birkerts and Associates, *50–51*
Fletcher, Norman (architect) of The Architects Collaborative, Inc., *11–16*
Flint Ridge Museum, Licking County, OH, *124–127*
Florida State Museum, University of Florida, Gainesville, FL, *139–144*
Ford, Powell & Carson (architects), *17*
Fort Ancient Museum, Warren County, OH, *124–127*
Fort Hill Museum, Highland County, OH, *124–127*

G

Garvan, The Mabel Brady Galleries of the Yale University Gallery, New Haven, CT, *91–93*
Garwood-Jones, Trevor P. (architect), *176–182*
Glendining, E.A. (architect), *124–127*
Gonzales Associates (architects), *18–20*
Greenburgh Public Library, Greenburgh, NY, *66–67*
Gropius, Walter (architect) of The Architects Collaborative, Inc., *116–117*

H

Hamilton Place, Hamilton, Ontario, Canada, *176–182*
Hardy, Holzman and Pfeiffer Associates (architects), *234–235*
Harkness, John C. (architect) of The Architects Collaborative, Inc., *21–25*
Harkness, Sarah P. (architect) of The Architects Collaborative, Inc., *21–25*
Harrison, Bernard J. (associate architect), *145–146*
Heinz Hall of the Performing Arts, Pittsburgh, PA, *214–217*
Heisel, Ralph (architect) of I.M. Pei & Partners, *218–224*
Hisaka, Don M. & Associates (architects), *70–71*
Historical Center, Columbus, OH, *134–138*
Horne, John Gerald (associate architect), *40–41*
Hugh Newell Jacobsen & Associates (architects), *88–90*
Hunter Museum of Art, Chattanooga, TN, *128–129*
Huntington Gallery Addition, Huntington, WV, *116–117*

I

Ireland, Byron W. and Associates (architects), *134–138*
Izenour, George C. Associates (consultants), *199–207, 218–224*

J

Jaffee, Christopher (acoustical consultant), *238–243*
Jefferson, Casa Thomas, Brasilia, Brazil, *174–175*
Johnson, Philip (architect), *84–85*
Jones, Edward R. (architect) of Charles Luckman Associates, *231–233*
Jones, Walk & Francis Mah, Inc. (architects), *107–113*
Jorasch, Richard L. (architect), *118–121*
Juilliard School, The, New York, NY, *183–192*

K

Kaselowsky, Richard Museum, Bielefeld, Germany, *84–85*
Kawasi, Kiyoshi and Associates (architects), *100–102*
Keilholz, Heinrich (acoustical consultant), *190, 214–217, 238–243*
Kleinschmidt, Robert D. (architect) of Skidmore, Owings & Merrill, *52–58*

L

Lang, Robert (architect) of Stahl/Bennett, Inc., *10*
Leefe, James (architect) of Leefe & Ehrenkrantz, *83*
Libraries
  Ecclesiastic
    Mount Angel Abbey Library, Saint Benedict, OR, *59–63*
  Public
    Brighton Branch Library, Brighton, MA, *11–16*
    Brydges, Earl W. Public Library, Niagara Falls, NY, *26–30*
    Central Library, Niagara Falls, NY, *64–65*
    Chiba Library, Chiba District, Japan, *37–39*
    Duluth Library, Duluth, MN, *42–43*
    Farmington Public Library, Farmington, MI, *8–9*
    Greenburgh Public Library, Greenburgh, NY, *66–67*
    Portsmouth Public Library, Portsmouth, NH, *10*
    Scottsdale Civic Center Library, Scottsdale, AZ, *18–20*
    Sherborn Library, Sherborn, MA, *40–41*
  University
    Barker, The James Madison Engineering Library, Massachusetts Institute of Technology, Cambridge, MA, *31–36*
    Brown Sciences Library, Brown University, Providence, RI, *5–7*
    Central Library, The, of Negev University, Beersheba, Israel, *48–49*
    Coram Library, Bates College, Lewiston, ME, *21–25*
    Core & Research Laboratory Library, Northwestern University, Miller Campus, Evanston, IL, *52–58*
    Library-Research Center, Wright State University, Dayton, OH, *70–71*
    Robarts, John P. Research Library for the Humanities & Social Sciences, University of Toronto, Toronto, Ontario, Canada, *44–47*

Libraries, University (*Cont.*):
    Skidmore College Library, Saratoga Springs, NY, *17*
    Tougaloo College Library, Tougaloo, MS, *50–51*
    Trent University Library, Peterborough, Ontario, Canada, *68–69*
Library-Resource Center, Wright State University, Dayton, OH, *70–71*
Loew's Penn Theater, Pittsburgh, PA, *214*
Lorenz, Williams, Lively & Likens (architects), *70–71*
Luckman, Charles Associates (architects), *231–233*

M

Maeght, Marguerite and Aimé Foundation (addition to), Saint Paul de Vence, France, *86–87*
Mah, Francis (architect) of Walk Jones & Francis Mah, Inc., *107–113*
Marx, Robert S. Theater, Cincinnati, OH, *208–213*
Mathers and Haldenby (architects), *44–47*
Meier, Richard (architect), *74–76*
Mellon, The Paul Arts Center, Choate School and Rosemary Hall, Wallingford, CT, *218–224*
Milwaukee Center for the Performing Arts, Milwaukee, WI, *199–207*
Miranda, Alcides Rocha (associate architect), *174–175*
Mitchell/Giurgola Associates (architects), *174–175*
Morgan, William (architect), *139–144*
Moriyama, Raymond (architect), *154–159*
Mount Angel Abbey Library, Saint Benedict, OR, *59–63*
Museums
    Art
    Public
      Brooks, The Memorial Art Gallery Addition, Memphis, TN, *107–113*
      Denver Art Museum Building, Denver, CO, *77–82*
      Huntington Gallery Addition, Huntington, WV, *116–117*
      Kaselowsky, Richard Museum, Beilefeld, Germany, *84–85*
      Maeght, Marguerite and Aimé Foundation (addition to), Saint Paul de Vence, France, *86–87*
      Museum West, San Francisco, CA, *83*
      Norwich Cathedral Treasury, Norwich, East Anglia, England, *114–115*
      Oakland, Museum, Oakland, CA, *146–153*
      Renwick Gallery, Washington, DC, *88–89*
      Tel Aviv Museum, Tel Aviv, Israel, *103–106*
      Tochigi Museum of Art, Utsunomiya, Japan, *100–102*
      Villa Strozzi, Florence, Italy, *74–76*
      Winchester Cathedral Treasury, Winchester, Hampshire, England, *114–115*
    University
      Garvan, The Mabel Brady Galleries of the Yale University Art Gallery, New Haven, CT, *91–93*

Museums, University (*Cont.*):
    Scaife, Sarah Gallery, Carnegie Institute, Pittsburgh, PA, *94–99*
    University Art Museum, The, University of California, Berkeley, CA, *118–121*
    Historical
      Flint Ridge Museum, Licking County, OH, *124–127*
      Fort Ancient Museum, Warren County, OH, *124–127*
      Fort Hill Museum, Highland County, OH, *124–127*
      Historical Center, Columbus, OH, *134–138*
      National Museum of Anthropology, Mexico City, Mexico, *130–133*
      Oakland Museum, Oakland, CA, *147–153*
      Oregon Historical Society, Headquarters Building, Portland, OR, *160–161*
      Peabody Museum of Salem, Salem, MA, *145*
      (*see also* Centers, cultural)
Museum West, San Francisco, CA, *83*
Musical Arts Center, Indiana University, Bloomington, IN, *193–19*

N

Nadler Nadler Bixon Gil (architects), *48–49*
National Museum of Anthropology, Mexico City, Mexico, *130–133*
Netsch, Walter (architect) of Skidmore, Owings & Merrill, *31–36, 52–58*
Newark Community Center of the Arts, Newark, NJ, *234–235*
Norwich Cathedral Treasury, Norwich, East Anglia, England, *114–115*

O

Oakland Museum, Oakland, CA, *146–153*
Ontario Science Center, Toronto, Ontario, Canada, *154–159*
Otaka, Masato (architect), *37–39*
Oregon Historical Society, Headquarters Building, Portland, OR, *160–161*

P

Paul Recital Hall, Juilliard School, New York, NY, *183–192*
Peabody Museum of Salem, Salem, MA, *145*
Pei, I.M. & Partners (architects), *218–224*
Phoenix Civic Plaza, Phoenix, AZ, *231–233*
Pinnau, Casar F. (associate architect), *84–85*
Ponti, Gio (architect), *77–82*
Portsmouth Public Library, Portsmouth, NH, *10*
Prodanou, Michael (architect) of The Architects Collaborative, Inc., *11–16*

R

Raz, Dany (assistant architect), *103–106*
Reiter, Paul (architect), *118–121*

Renwick Gallery, Washington, D.C., *88–90*
Robarts, John P. Research Library for the Humanities & Social Sciences, University of Toronto, Toronto, Ontario, Canada, *44–47*
Roche Dinkeloo and Associates (architects), *146–153, 164–173*
Rudolph, Paul (architect), *26–30, 64–65*

S

Scaife, Sarah Gallery, Carnegie Institute, Pittsburgh, PA, *94-99*
Schafer, Flynn & vanDijk (architects), *238–243*
Scottsdale Civic Center, Scottsdale, AZ, *18–20*
Sert, Jackson and Associates (architects), *86–87*
Sherborn Library, Sherborn, MA, *40–41*
Skidmore College Library, Saratoga Springs, NY, *17*
Skidmore, Owings & Merrill (architects), *31–36, 52–58*
SOM
    (*see* Skidmore, Owings & Merrill)
Stahl/Bennett, Inc. (architects), *10, 145–146*
Stahl, E.A. (architect) of Stahl/Bennett, Inc., *10*
Stephens, C.Y. Auditorium, Iowa State University, Ames, IA, *225–230*
Stotz, Hess, MacLachlan and Fosner (architects), *214–217*
Straka, Ronald A. (architect) of Schafer, Flynn & vanDijk, *238–243*
Sudler, James Associates (architects), *77–82*

T

TAC
    (*see* Architects Collaborative, The, Inc.)
Tarapata MacMahon Paulsen Corporation (architects), *8–9*
Tel Aviv Museum, Tel Aviv, Israel, *103–106*
Thom, Ron (architect) of Thompson Berwick Pratt & Partners, *68–69, 177*
Thompson Berwick Pratt & Partners (architects), *68–69*
Ticknor, Malcolm (architect) of The Architects Collaborative, Inc., *116–117*

Toan, Danforth (architect) of Warner Burns Toan Lunde, *5-7*
Tochigi Museum of Art, Utsunomiya, Japan, *100–102*
Tougaloo College Library, Tougaloo, MS, *50–51*
Trent University Library, Peterborough, Ontario, Canada, *68–69*
Tully, Alice Hall, Juilliard School, New York, NY, *183–192*

U

University, buildings of
    (*see* Centers: cultural, performing arts; Libraries; Museums)
University Art Museum, The, University of California, Berkeley, CA, *118–121*
Urbahn, Max O. Associates, Inc. (architects), *66–67*

V

Vartiainen, Erik T. (architect for Alvar Aalto), *59–63*
Vasquez, Pedro Ramirez (architect), *130–133*
Veneklasen, Paul E. & Associates (acoustical consultants), *225–230*
Villa Strozzi, Florence, Italy, *74–76*

W

Wagner, Ronald E. (architect), *118–121*
Waldschmidt Systems of Hamburg, *51*
Walker, James A.S., *40–41*
Warnecke, John Carl and Universal Restoration, Inc., *88*
Warner Burns Toan Lunde (architects), *5–7, 44–47*
Weese, Harry and Associates (architects), *199–207*
Westermann, Helge (associate architect), *183–192*
Willis, Michael (architect) of Warner Burns Toan Lunde, *5-7*
Winchester Cathedral Treasury, Winchester, Hampshire, England, *114–115*
Wolff-Zimmer-Gunsul-Frasca (architects), *160–161*
Woollen Associates (architects), *193–198*

Y

Yoshar, Itzhak (architect), *103–106*